PERSPECTIVES
ON
TERRORISM

PERSPECTIVES
ON
TERRORISM

Edited by
Lawrence Zelic Freedman
and
Yonah Alexander

Scholarly Resources Inc.
Wilmington, Delaware

Burgess

HV
6431
.P47
1983

Scholarly Resources Inc.
104 Greenhill Avenue
Wilmington, Delaware 19805

Library of Congress Cataloging in Publication Data
Main entry under title:

Perspectives on Terrorism.

    Includes index.
    1. Terrorists—Addresses, essays, lectures.
    2. Terrorists—Psychology—Addresses, essays,
    lectures. 3. Hostages—Addresses, essays, lectures.
    4. Terrorism—Government policy—Addresses, essays,
    lectures. I. Freedman, Lawrence Zelic, 1919–
    II. Alexander, Yonah.
    HV 6431.P47   1983   303.6'25   83-3011
    ISBN 0-8420-2201-5

CONTENTS

I. PSYCHOLOGICAL DIMENSIONS OF THE TERRORIST

II. THE TERRORIST IN PROFILE

III. HOSTAGE TAKING AND ITS AFTERMATH

IV. RESPONDING TO TERRORISM

INTRODUCTION

Scientists at the Institute of Social and Behavioral Pathology at the University of Chicago began to study assassination and terrorism as special categories of political violence in the early 1960s. The institute's first conference on terrorism[1] was held in 1973 at the Center for Advanced Study in the Behavioral Sciences at Stanford University under the cochairmanship of Harold Dwight Lasswell and Lawrence Zelic Freedman, one of the editors of this volume. Many of the seminal ideas that since have become part of the common wisdom, or shared truisms, of the field were first expressed at that meeting.

Starting about a decade ago, there has been a dual flow of communications concerning modern terrorism. Headlines and televised terrorist happenings have raised social anxieties to a high level of worldwide concern. Political scientists and popular pundits, statisticians and intellectuals, and psychiatrists and psychologists have responded with data banks, opinion, and empirical and clinical observations on the perpetrators. Patterns of modes of terrorism have changed so rapidly that models and theories have had to yield to transient techniques and emergent information. Indeed, so limited have been the data that false analogies and marginal homologies have, by necessity, been invoked. For example, the Stockholm Syndrome, a term now widely used to describe the paradoxical or anomalous affection or even loyalty felt by the erstwhile hostage for his kidnappers, arises not from a political terrorist incident, but from a bank robbery in which a female hostage became enamored of one of her captors. But the novelty now has dissipated, the often ingenuous theories and expectations of the early writers have become more focused, and perspectives sharpened.

This collection of papers treats a diverse range of terrorist activities, from the skyjackings of the 1960s and 1970s, to hostage taking, to bombings and assaults, and to the implied and explicit dangers in the future of high-technology and nuclear weapons. The volume includes a number of papers prepared for a conference organized by the institute and held in November 1979 at the University of Chicago. Others were added in order to ensure a more complete presentation of the issues. The authors have been involved directly in the phenomenon of terrorism, ranging from

---

[1]Conference on "Terrorism and Terrorists," Institute for Social and Behavioral Pathology at the Center for Advanced Study in the Behavioral Sciences, Stanford University, H. D. Lasswell and L. Z. Freedman, eds. *Bulletin of the Institute of Social and Behavioral Pathology* (1973) 1, no. 1.

government policymaking, hostage negotiations, and studies of terrorists and released hostages to reviews of social responses. J. K. Zawodny, for example, participated in a partisan group during World War II. Anthony C. E. Quainton represented the State Department in its efforts to gather and coordinate information concerning terrorist activities throughout the world, to develop policy in response to terrorist action, and to evaluate the impact of the range of effective and ineffective, or even counterproductive, reactions to the intense and socially arousing stimuli of these political assaults.

This volume has been divided into four sections. In the first, "Psychological Dimensions of the Terrorist," Freedman discusses terrorism under the general construct of polistaraxia (upsetters of the community), together with the parameters of the psychology of the individual, the human ecology of their political context, and the future orientation of policy science. His approach is a convergence of his own experience synergistically focused with the philosophy of Abraham Kaplan and the policy science of Lasswell. Moshe Amon attempts to reify and rationalize the phenomenon of terrorism through the refraction of religious experience. Terror is a symptom of an attitude that is both gnostic and messianic, whose view is that this temporal and secular world has no right to exist. Both views are reflected symbolically in contemporary terrorism. Amon reaches this conclusion by a review of the sequential peeling away of man's protection against subjective vacuity and social nihilism. In the end, the terrorist believes that he dies as a sacrifice and as a redeemer, thus facilitating a new era.

Frederick J. Hacker contributes an analysis of the personal and political factors in terrorism. He plays with the notion of terrorism as theater. The psychological persona of the terrorist, as Hacker describes it, bears striking parallels with the narcissistic personality defined in contemporary psychology of the self. John W. Crayton presents an exposition of Heinz Kohut's psychology of the self. Kohut described narcissistic rage as springing from an early, profound, and crippling attack on the child's self-esteem by archaic, omnipotent figures. This rage, in its acute or chronic forms, is implemented through attacks motivated by revenge and reinforced by grandiosity. Crayton generalizes beyond the immediate terrorizing groups to the great terrorizing movements of the twentieth century. Ingenious and persuasive as these theories are, we must be cautious lest our preoccupation with the subjective aspects of the terrorist response appears to preclude the political realities and the tyrannical autocracies against which terrorists, whether rationally or irrationally, may be striking.

In the second section, "The Terrorist in Profile," Charles A. Russell and Bowman H. Miller have drawn a sketch of a model terrorist, integrating a wide range of data. These authors have compiled from material derived from comparatively few experiences with exclusively male terrorists. Dr. Zawodny, drawing on his experience as an urban guerrilla in World War II, gives a perspective on the functional inner structure of the terrorist organization. Centrifugal in nature, it relies on the one-to-one relationship between a leader and the individuals in a very small group.

Daniel E. Georges-Abeyie presents a theory on the reasons for female participation in terrorism. He contributes to our understanding of the traditional roles of men and women as well as their roles under circumstances of radical reorientation of the power structure and status quo. He surveys the rise of female criminality in general as an aspect of the changing role of women in contemporary cultural patterns; and, in parallel, he seeks to develop a theory of women as terrorists, distinct from nonpolitical criminals. Zeev Ivianski describes Andrey Zhelyabov, one of the architects of the late nineteenth-century *Narodnaya Volya* movement in czarist Russia. Unlike the middle- and upper middle-class terrorists of his group, Zhelyabov was born a serf. As a child, he witnessed the rape of his aunt by a bailiff. The larger political ambitions of this man may be seen as a desperate effort to kill the surrogate bailiffs responsible for the rape of the humanity he knew.

Central to any understanding of terrorism is the phenomenon of hostage taking. In the third section, "Hostage Taking and Its Aftermath," Clive C. Aston surveys political hostage taking in Western Europe. He provides a matrix against which to project the personal experiences of the hostage, the involvement of the negotiators, and the reaction of a fascinated and horrified public. Within this wider framework, Robert Hauben focuses on the Dutch experience. During the 1970s, the Netherlands suffered a number of terrorist hostage kidnappings. The sophisticated and integrated character of that small country, the accessibility to the freed hostages, negotiators, and the terrorists, and the time that has elapsed since the incidents all have made the Netherlands a unique *in vivo* arena in which both immediate and long-term effects have been studied and compared. Eric Shaw adumbrates the psychological aspects of being held hostage, of returning home, of the sanctions imposed or awarded by society, and describes the personal conflicts and the levels of resolution that these intrapsychic and social stimuli engender. Robert G. Hillman contributes a clinically sophisticated analysis of the subjective experiences of prison guards taken hostage during a riot.

In the final section, "Responding to Terrorism," Ambassador Quainton describes the dilemma of an official of a superpower attempting to implement a rational policy of action and reaction to this extraordinary dimension of political violence. M. Cherif Bassiouni expounds upon nonstate-sponsored terror-violence and the role of the media in terrorist episodes. Terrorism reflects the technology of the society in which it is active and is reflected by the media whose interest it arouses to a degree often disproportionate to the actual injury inflicted. In analyzing the functions performed by the media, Bassiouni contributes not only an illuminating view of the role played by the media, but a wide-ranging analysis of the entire phenomenon. Nehemia Friedland discusses policy considerations in the conduct of hostage negotiations. She emphasizes the effects of a "no-ransom" policy. Particularly intriguing is her analogy to Chicken, a confrontational game in which both players must participate, because the refusal to play is itself an admission of defeat. Martin Reiser and Martin Sloane develop principles for the use of suggestibility techniques from their pioneering work in hostage negotiations.

Yonah Alexander, the coeditor of this volume, sets forth the underlying terror that preoccupies governments and the peoples of the world at the prospect of the use of high-technology weapons, which are already available to individuals and small groups, and the possibility of nuclear weapons becoming accessible to terrorists. These are seen by some observers as plausible and by others as inevitable.

From this point of view, we are all hostages. And from this point of view, the distinction between the apocalyptic vision of general destruction brought on by governmental confrontation or suffered through small group access to methods of mass destruction, previously the prerogative only of nation-states, is obliterated.

The editors wish to thank the authors for their cooperation and valuable contributions. They both hope that this effort will stimulate further study and research in this important field of public concern.

Lawrence Zelic Freedman
Yonah Alexander

CONTRIBUTORS

YONAH ALEXANDER, Ph.D., is professor of international studies and director of the Institute for Studies in International Terrorism at the State University of New York. Dr. Alexander also is a senior staff associate at the Center for Strategic and International Studies at Georgetown University and a fellow of the Institute of Social and Behavioral Pathology at the University of Chicago. He has written extensively on political terrorism and is the editor-in-chief of two journals, *Terrorism: An International Journal* and *Political Communication and Persuasion.*

MOSHE AMON, Ph.D., received his B.A. from Hebrew University at Jerusalem and his doctorate in political science from Claremont Graduate School. He has taught history and philosophy in several American universities and currently is assistant professor in the Department of Religious Studies at the University of British Columbia, Vancouver, Canada.

CLIVE C. ASTON, Ph.D., a political consultant and analyst, earned his doctorate in international relations from the University of London. He has written widely on political hostage taking and related subjects and is the author of several papers for the United Nations.

M. CHERIF BASSIOUNI, J.D., is professor of law at DePaul University. He has taught and lectured at universities in this country and abroad and in 1970 was named an Outstanding Educator of America. The author of ten books and nearly eighty articles on criminal law, Dr. Bassiouni currently is secretary-general of the International Association of Penal Law and has served as a consultant to the United Nations. He is admitted to practice in Illinois and Washington, DC, and before several federal courts, including the U.S. Supreme Court.

JOHN W. CRAYTON, M.D., is associate professor of psychiatry at the University of Chicago. He has engaged in postdoctoral research at the National Institutes of Mental Health in Washington, DC. Dr. Crayton's current research includes studies of the interaction between somatic or metabolic factors and psychological ones in producing abnormal behaviors.

LAWRENCE ZELIC FREEDMAN, M.D., is chairman of the Institute of Social and Behavioral Pathology and Foundations' Fund Research

Professor of Psychiatry at the University of Chicago. He has served as a permanent delegate to the United Nations and as a consultant to its Economic and Social Council. Dr. Freedman also assisted in the drafting of the Model Penal Code for the American Law Institute. He has engaged in research and published numerous articles on aggression and political violence.

NEHEMIA FRIEDLAND, Ph.D., emigrated from Argentina to Israel in 1954. She is presently a senior research consultant in psychology to the Israeli Navy and an associate professor in the Department of Psychology at Tel-Aviv University, where she received her undergraduate degree. Dr. Friedland has engaged in research and published articles on interpersonal and intergroup relations, the social psychology of bargaining and conflict resolution, and processes of social influence.

DANIEL E. GEORGES-ABEYIE, Ph.D., is an associate professor in the Administration of Justice Department, Pennsylvania State University. A former faculty member at Southern Illinois University, Carbondale, and acting director of its Center for the Study of Crime, Delinquency, and Corrections, Dr. Georges-Abeyie has taught and lectured widely on urban geography, black studies, criminal justice, and terrorism. He served as technical adviser and expert witness for the defense in the 1977 murder trial of Fort Worth millionaire T. Cullen Davis.

FREDERICK J. HACKER, M.D., is professor of psychiatry at both the Medical School and the Law Center of the University of Southern California. Dr. Hacker also directs the certificate program in psychopolitics and conflict research at USC. In addition, he is chief of staff of the Hacker Clinic in Los Angeles, director of the Institute for Conflict Research in Vienna, and founder and president of the Sigmund Freud Society in Vienna.

ROBERT HAUBEN, M.D., has practised as a physician and psychiatrist in the United States and the Netherlands and has advised the governments of both countries on the effects of victimization and terrorism. He has served as the assistant medical director for mental health at the U.S. Department of State and as a member of the Interagency Team for the Reception of the U.S. Iranian Hostages. A founding member of the Committee on Victimology of the World Federation of Mental Health, Dr. Hauben is presently assistant medical director for clinical research at the CIBA-GEIGY Corp., Summit, New Jersey.

ROBERT G. HILLMAN, M.D., in full-time private practice in Santa Fe, has engaged in research on the Nancy-Salpêtrière controversy on hypnotism, the use of computers in teaching psychotherapy problems, and the effects of massive psychic trauma. While a student at the Medical School of the University of Chicago, he was awarded the Logan Clendening Fellowship for study in France. Dr. Hillman's residency was at Stanford University; he also earned a M.A. in the history of health sciences from the University of California, San Francisco. His memberships include the American Association of Clinical Psychiatrists.

ZEEV IVIANSKI, Ph.D., a resident of Kibbutz Ein-Harod in Israel, was a member of the Zionist underground in the Soviet Union from 1939 to 1941 and of the Fighters for the Freedom of Israel (FFI) in Palestine during the 1940s. Dr. Ivianski lectured from 1972 to 1980 in the Department of General History and Russian Studies at Hebrew University. He is the author of *Individual Terror, Theory and Practice* (1977) and numerous articles on terror and terrorism.

BOWMAN H. MILLER was chief of the Acquisitions and Analysis Division, Directorate of Counterintelligence, Headquarters Air Force Office of Special Investigations, at the time of the writing of his paper.

ANTHONY C. E. QUAINTON is U.S. ambassador to Nicaragua. After taking degrees at Princeton and Oxford universities, he entered the Foreign Service in 1959 and served in Sydney, Karachi, New Delhi, Paris, and Kathmandu until 1976, when he was appointed ambassador to the Central African Empire. From 1978 to 1982 he was director of the U.S. State Department's Office for Combatting Terrorism.

MARTIN REISER, Ph.D., directs the Behavior Science Services of the Los Angeles Police Department. He is a diplomate in clinical psychology of the American Board of Professional Psychology, a fellow of the American Psychological Association, and the director of the Law Enforcement Hypnosis Institute. Dr. Reiser has written four books and numerous articles on police psychology.

CHARLES A. RUSSELL, Ph.D., was a member of the U.S. Air Force, Office of Special Investigations, at the time of the writing of his paper.

ERIC SHAW is a fellow in psychology/psychiatry at the Paine-Whitney Clinic of the New York Hospital. He was formerly a staff member of the Working Group on High Technology of the Cabinet Committee To Combat Terrorism and a consultant to the U.S. Department of Defense on the crisis management of terrorist incidents.

MARTIN SLOANE was on the staff of the Behavioral Science Services of the Los Angeles Police Department at the time of the writing of his paper.

J. K. ZAWODNY, Ph.D., is professor emeritus of international relations at Claremont Graduate School and Pomona College. He has been a member of the Institute for Advanced Study, Princeton; a fellow of the Center for Behavioral Sciences, Stanford; and a research associate at the Harvard University Center for International Affairs. During World War II, Dr. Zawodny served in combat for five years with the Polish Underground Home Army (AK). He is the author of *Death in the Forest*, an account of the 1940 Katyn Forest massacre.

I.
PSYCHOLOGICAL DIMENSIONS OF THE TERRORIST

Terrorism: Problems of the Polistaraxic*

LAWRENCE ZELIC FREEDMAN

Terrorism is defined as the use of violence when its most important result is not the physical and mental damage of the direct victims but the psychological effect produced on someone else. Terrorism also involves, in addition to the act, the emotion and the motivation of the terrorist. Violence may result in death, injury or destruction of property, or deprivation of liberty. It becomes terror when the significant aim is not to attain these ends but, through these, to terrorize people other than those directly assaulted.

This distinction between terror and violence is not absolute. There may be violence linked with terror, in which the intention is to harm the direct victim, but the assault is linked to an act of terror which either preceded or followed it. There also is violence linked to terror in cases such as the freeing of a terrorist.

Whether a hijacking—skyjacking, for example—is an act of terror depends upon whether the intent of the hijacker is to escape from one country to another or to create terror as an ancillary effect by, for example, the holding of certain persons as hostages in order to secure the release either of the hijacker or of other terrorists.

Terrorism is a pattern found in seemingly non-terrorist political contexts and throughout the world. The trait which often characterizes this sort of terrorism is a sense of absolutism felt by the terrorist. His action is premised on an assumption of the existence of an absolute value. Terrorism in the service of an absolute value has a kind of psychologically reinforcing effect; that is, the extreme nature of the terrorist action results in reifying the absolutism of the value.

Why does the terrorist commit his act? We have postulated four hypotheses beyond, but not excluding, the sense of absolute value. They are presented in the order of increasing psychic depth, and in a sense, therefore, decreasing plausibility, because there is decreasing assurance of securing validation.

---

*A revised version of the article published in *The University of Chicago Magazine* 66, no. 6 (Summer 1974): 7–10. Reprinted by permission.

1) First, the reaffirmation of self-esteem. In the preterrorist situation there have been severe blows to self-image, the ego-ideal, self-respect, and the sense of oneself as an effectively functioning person deserving the respect and attention of others. So in the preexisting situation there is a painful awareness of a lack in this respect.

Within this there are two subcategories: It is one thing to have something taken away that you thought you had, and it is another thing to be aware that you never did have it. This may be a significant difference. The first subcategory may characterize the terrorism of the Middle East, where—after a long period of possessing a self-image of effective military prowess and cultural achievement, with religious reinforcement—people have been forced to contemplate deprivation.

The blacks in the United States, on the other hand, are recognizing that they have, in a racist society, been denied the affirmation of the virtues of ego-ideal, self-respect, sense of oneself as an effectively functioning person, deserving the respect and attention of others. This may be why violence, in a direct, immediate sense of striking out at known targets—even if displaced targets—has been one form of the response of American blacks. Invidious treatment came to be recognized for what it has been, and therefore it has been repudiated.

The terrorist act, as a device for either primary affirmation or for reaffirmation of self-esteem, may be related to activities characteristic of preliterate societies, such as scalp collecting or head hunting, where something is done to establish what a man is so that the common enemy may know how effective he is. Therefore, what we may see as a morally objectionable act may appear, given the subculture, essential to the society's functioning, because the aim is to produce an impression of strength in the ritual affirmations of prowess, and that is what we may find in terror. So, for example, it is more important to seize an airplane than to be given one.

2) The second factor is that of depersonalization. Depersonalization may be viewed as the key feature of the preterrorist situation and requires the perception of a group or of some transindividual entity. We may here use "group" loosely to refer to political entities. A nation or any organization may be defined and responded to as a group.

In these situations, not only the contrast between the individual and the group, but also a variety of other factors make the consciousness of existence as a person painful or ineffective or otherwise unacceptable. Individuality requires acceptance of a burden of responsibility. It can create a sense of impotence, a sense of impoverishment of the ego—a variety of factors. Depersonalized man is able, in a sense, to abandon his individuality and his status as a person and to act only as the instrument of a larger group.

3) The act of terror, like the other acts of violence, may be a method of establishing intimacy. Violence, or even the threat of violence, establishes a relationship that otherwise could exist only in fantasy. A person may feel that he is nothing, that he is incapable of arousing any interest or attention except when he is experienced by his human environment as threatening, or as creating in that environment a force of danger. By terrorizing he enforces recognition and, subjectively, feels a sense of intimacy with his victim.

The assassin, therefore, has this moment in the stage of history—and a moment with precisely those who have all the things which he believes he lacks. In the act of terror, therefore, there is the symbolic attainment of an end which is far more effective than what might be done by a direct act of violence only. The ultimate objective is not, through the use of violence, securing large sums of money or some arms or a plane or a ship. The terror creates such an impact on the consciousness of the significant others that the terrorist is recognized, is negotiated with, and is able to prove his power to bring the most powerful and admired figure of his group to his knees.

4) The fourth hypothesis is belief in magic, specifically, the belief in the magic of violence. Great indeterminance and, in a sense, superhuman powers or forces can be brought into play on the human scene through the spilling of blood. Violence is here seen as a kind of terrorist sacrament. In this sacrament there is not merely the dedication of human powers to the service of superhuman or godlike powers. As Kaplan has said, "An act of violence as a sacrament is involved, but it is a sacrament that is not merely the dedication of human powers to the service of the gods. . . . In spilling of blood there is not only a dedication to the service of the gods, but a device to compel the gods to my service. I have been a channel for them. I provide a way for them to enter my being and make themselves effective . . . In this transvaluation of values it is precisely the needlessness of the act and, from outsiders' viewpoints, the despicable features of the act, the killing, that are essential to it."

DISTINGUISHING TERRORIST FROM REVOLUTIONARY

We must also distinguish terrorists from revolutionaries. The revolutionary act may be terrorist or violent or both or, in some theories of historical process, neither. The distinction that is relevant here, as in other cases, is whether violence is significant because of its direct effect or because of its impression upon others. Historically, Marx and Engels were very much against terror. They saw it as a form of revolutionary suicide.

Their successors, the implementors at the governmental level, Lenin and Stalin, were exquisitely aware of, for example, the contribution of Nechaev, the nineteenth-century classical Russian terrorist. As they saw his acts as a vital precursor of the revolution, they saw the employment of terror by the government essential to the maintenance of the revolution.

As to the distinction between effect and political purpose, the effects of course include the unintended and the nonpurposeful in the ordinary irrational sense; but the effect anticipated at a deeper, unconscious level could be conducive, at this level of expectation or fantasy or hope, to making the individual or group bring about the desired effect. The effect, to emphasize this point, is on the spectator; and the spectator is the essential element. The person being terrorized is not the only victim—or even the most important victim.

It is the terrorism of the third party which distinguishes it from violence. A crucial distinction between terror and other forms of violence is in some cases that the link between the victim and the third party is direct. It is immediate. If the relation between the victim and the third party is symbolic, then we have an act on terror with implications of the demonic, the magic and the effect on the spectator as a purpose in itself.

For twenty years we have studied convicted violent offenders. Ten years ago, following the assassination of President John F. Kennedy, we embarked on an intensive study of presidential assassins. For five years we have been concerned with terrorists versus the violence against intimates and presidential assassins. When we studied the assassins of American presidents for evidence of conspiracy, we found none, nor has regicide been conspiratorial in parliamentary England.

The historical convention has been that the terrorist attacks of Eastern Europe and Russia of the late nineteenth and twentieth centuries were political conspiracies. This distinction can no longer be maintained. The comparatively few maladapted isolates in the United States who assaulted the president acted with no rational expectation that they would thereby effect significant political change. This has been contrasted with politically rational conspiratorial efforts of the terrorists in Russia in the 1880s and 1890s—politically sophisticated and rationally acting to effect political change. That terrorist movement involved a tiny group in Russia, proportionately no greater than the handful of individuals who have assaulted persons holding the highest political posts in the West. To an astonishing degree they resemble our presumably pathological isolates.

The assassin in the United States has been a young adult white man; physically he has been slight and small but not unattractive. (Surprisingly, with a small number of subjects studied mainly through clinical reports and historical sources, it was possible to predict the physical habitus, the developmental experience, and, within limits, the psychological set of the assassins before their murderous attacks on persons of major political importance.) He has experienced during his earlier development severe impediments to his achievement of an integrated, relatively homogeneous acceptance of himself as an adult male. These impediments included many social factors, some of them accidental. They were imposed on his family as a whole, suddenly and adventitiously, rather than on members of the family.

Such factors are important, but far more so is the invariable and psychically prepotent deprivation of an appropriate adult male, whether biological father or father substitute, who could provide the boy with a model whom he could imitate, whose habits and style he could absorb, and with whose values he could identify. This adult male must have been physically present, emotionally related, and, when available, he must have been a person whose values, style, habits, temperament, capacity for control, and level of rationality were consistent with reasonable adjustment to the social environment without, and a tolerable level of self-acceptance and self-esteem within.

As an adult the assassin suffered an intensity of self-loathing, a sense of humiliation and abasement, an absence of self-esteem, profound awareness that he received inadequate approbation by those who were significant to him in his environment. The intensity of such self-condemnatory, self-demeaning feelings and the reciprocal perception that the significant persons in his milieu would reject him and hold him in contempt is certainly, insofar as we may quantify subjective experience, as heavy a psychic burden as is borne by the more than 500,000 persons who have succumbed to so severe a form of incompetence and incapacity to perceive reality correctly, and to maintain themselves economically and socially, that they are labeled psychotic and are hospitalized.

Now, in combination, these characteristics distinguish the polistaraxic—that is a word derived from *polis*, community, and *taraxic*, upsetting, which unifies a variety of concepts: the upsetter of the community. It also enables us to distinguish homicidal presidential assassins from a vast number of psychotics, including paranoid schizophrenics, who have carried out personal homicide; soldiers who have, in millions, willingly slain or intended to slay strangers; foreigners in the service of their nation; mass murderers who have, in U.S. history, periodically murdered rather large numbers of persons who have been strangers to them; and threateners of the president by mail and by public and overt attempts.

One assumes that polistaraxic crime is in the service of a political goal. But one is mistaken. The goal is the destruction of the head of state. Says Nechaev: "Our task is terrible, total, universal and merciless destruction."

To quote from another figure: "Happiness is taking part in the struggle where there is no borderline between one's own personal world and the world in general. Happiness does not consist of oneself. ... I never believed I would find more material advantages at this stage of development in the Soviet Union than I might have had in the United States. In the event of war I would kill any American who put on a uniform in defense of the American government—any American. [This was written by Lee Harvey Oswald to his brother.] In my own mind I have no attachment of any kind in the United States. I want to and I shall live a normal, happy, and peaceful life here in the Soviet Union for the rest of my life. ... My mother and you are not objects of affection but only examples of workers in the United States." He became extremely disenchanted with Russia very shortly thereafter and returned to the United States—and murdered its president.

REHABILITATION, PREVENTION, RECONSTRUCTION

It is highly probable that the scientifically based stance of the world may very well cause the process we call alienation to go forward. Alienation may breed individuals, and particularly small groups, who are predisposed toward actions of defiance and destruction; alternative strategies available for action may involve the mobilization of large, concerted groups; and the expansion of modern technology is likely to be put in the hands of power elites of the globe, the basis of continuing surveillance of protest. Consequently any large-scale countermovement, through time, is likely to be perceived early by the Establishment and acted upon with tools regarded as appropriate. This, one suspects, increases the probability that more and more small groups and individuals will self-select themselves for performance of the kind of heroic role that is involved in terrorism. This is one of the constructs of the future that must be subjected to critical evaluation as our work proceeds.

Of course we are not only interested in causal, trend and projection questions; we are also interested in goals. Whatever the goals are, the development of normative policies or policy alternatives is profoundly affected by whatever set of goals we postulate, or when we act as an agent of some power group or other participant in the process, and undertake to execute its norms. So far as the political governmental process is concerned, one trusts that our deliberations will continue to produce contributions to the formulations and ultimate evaluation of policy alternatives for dealing with whatever dimensions of the terrorist process we decide to attempt to control.

Discussions of terrorism tend to become focused around one of the problems of sanction: the handling of positive or negative values in the flows in the society in such a way that conformity to the norms is elicited, or the norms are rearranged. All of us recognize that when we talk about deterrence we are concerned with the ways by which we diminish the probability that an act of an undesirable kind be completed. We discuss deterrence in terms of its relationship to motivational processes. But there are some other dimensions—other policy objectives—involved in a comprehensive sanction. For instance, it is useful not only to talk about diminishing the likelihood that the act be completed; there also is the problem which is involved when the act is started: what are the policies that one adopts, and when, to stop and bring about a withdrawal of such a process? How does one act at each stage?

There is the objective of rehabilitation—that is to say, undertaking to repair the damage which has been done by the series of acts involved. What we are trying to do in this situation is to take the relatives and children of those who have been killed and to figure out the sensible way to diminish that kind of damage for those who have been targets of these activities. Another objective might be labeled correction, only in the sense that it is concerned with the ways by which one changes the motivation of individuals who perform these acts. Acts of deterrence, for example, are addressed primarily to people who have some capacity for calculation of cost gains in terms of all that they value. We are concerned, in the development of alternatives in various contexts of policy making, with prevention, and the word here is simply intended to refer to the important ways of handling the existing institutions so that we diminish their provocative impact on others.

And now this last point, which, for the sake of formal convenience, we will refer to as reconstruction. This goes beyond prevention, raising the fundamental question of reconstruction of the institutional guesses by which values are shaped and shared in any given society. To what extent can we reconstruct the processes of society, from early socialization throughout later social development?

One can look at all of this in terms of the pre- and co- and post-, in relation to the strategy. To look at the actual administration of the instrument or procedure, the most obvious feature is the choice of a target. The terrorist's symbolic enhancement comes through picking that person who is significant to those from whom he desires response. Sometimes one enhances the target by a shocking location. The Borgias were very good at this, in selecting the church or a religious service as the location, in order to enhance certain effects. Clearly there sometimes is captivity, with a good many false starts—the victim is led out, ostensibly for execution, and then he comes back. There are the costumes, the masks, designed appropriately to enhance the symbolic potential—the sinister colors; the sinister sounds; taking, and having people worry about, hostages. There are the surprise hit-and-run killings, the tortures.

Kropotkin formulated the matter of terrorism as a strategy with some degree of precision. This is essentially the strategy which we have outlined. Kropotkin talked about symbolic enhancement of the particular act of violence as an element of terror. It is important to note the disproportionality between the immediate damage imposed upon the context and the potential damage generated by the act. To what extent is political support increased now? In a short period of time? Over a longer period of time? This is a peculiarly political question. How does one seize, consolidate, and maintain a power position?

The striking thing was that in the 1880s and 1890s there were several acts in the Mediterranean world indicating increased revolutionary demand on the part of radicalized elites and masses. However, in 1881 the killing of Czar Alexander II had little positive payoff for the movement and gave way, as a tactic, to other methods—alternatives which did pay off in terms of these movements. The notable thing was that terrorism often was bitterly criticized, by Communists and others, and the developing wisdom—true or false—was to drop terrorism as a strategy.

The assassin sees himself as the instrument of justice. He murders as an act of conscience. The political murderer who kills a stranger after careful, secretive planning does so for an ideal. Few personal murderers are convinced of their right to deprive another person of human life; most kill an intimate, one whom they have loved, propelled by a passion which extinguished, for that time, rational calculation. After the killing, the personal murderer often feels remorse, suffers from guilt. He frequently seeks punishment by turning himself in to the authorities. He attempts suicide. He blots out its memory. He forgets what he has done. He becomes converted to a religion.

The terrorist is not aware of love or hate toward his victim. After killing he feels neither remorse nor guilt. He rarely blots out memory of his act. Since the motive which preceded his decision was, so far as we know, an abstract ideal, it had the fanatical quality comparable to that experienced by a religious zealot. He does not turn to religion after his murder, but before it.

The Confederacy fulfilled for John Wilkes Booth his ideal society of a cultured aristocracy. Charles J. Guiteau [who killed Garfield] was driven by God to heal the conflict of party strife in a political organization. Anarchism, the claims of individual freedom against any formal government restrictions, drove Leon Czolgosz [assassin of McKinley]. Marxist economics, the rescuing of workers from capitalist exploitation, was Oswald's conscious "motive."

The terrorist has a political ideal. His murderous paroxysm fulfills it. When Sirhan Sirhan shouted, after shooting Senator Robert F. Kennedy, "Let me explain, I can explain," he almost certainly believed that his murder in the service of Jordanian nationalism would be persuasive.

Oswald "explained" in his historic diary. Czolgosz, when he said, "It is not right for one man [the president] to get so much attention and another to get so little," was explaining.

Unlike the personal murderer, the terrorist does not believe his victim has committed a private wrong against him. His sense of righteousness is unassailable. In each case, however, the terrorist murderer has struck the wrong target. The terrorist murderer, no less than the personal killer, strikes the mirror. He obliterates an intolerable image of himself which he himself has when he strikes out at his victim.

The assassin and the terrorist act politically, not only in the sense that they kill political figures, but also in the sense that they act and feel as though they were private soldiers in an opposing community, or perhaps that they themselves were an army. History has not fulfilled the fantasies of the nineteenth-century nihilist and terrorist assassins that overthrowing the dominant power would eliminate the violations of freedoms which provoked their assaults on the absolutist leaders. But the terror and assassinations continue.

The Phoenix Complex: Terrorism and the Death of Western Civilization*

MOSHE AMON

Is terrorism an unintelligible social, political, or cultural aberration, or a symptom signifying a certain stage in the development of Western civilization? If terrorism is a symptom, then in order to understand it we should consider exactly what it does signify and what is the nature of the civilization that has produced this symptom.

In terrorism are found the same elements of self-sacrifice, the attempt to burn and obliterate the present body, the rebirth of new life from the ashes of the old, and the promise of a messianic future that we associate with the legend of the phoenix. Terrorism is tolerated by large segments of our society, as if the social body itself declares a moratorium upon its own life in recognition that it cannot sustain itself any more. Destruction and death come then as a redemption from a way of life which has already reached a terminal stage. The rationale of a society for tolerating terrorism is much more significant than the rationale used by the terrorists themselves to justify their actions.

The terrorist's rationale has been identified with a gnostic mode of thought. The gnostic believes that this world has no right to exist; in the traditional form of gnosticism, he ascribes this knowledge to a source alien and external to this world. The denial of temporal culture is typical not only of the gnostic but of any messianic culture, especially in its acute stages, when redemption is imminent. At this point, during the conclusion of the pre-messianic stage, all existing forms are expected to terminate. In primitive religions, social order evolves eternally in an imitation of an eternal order. In a messianic society, the forms of the present are not worth preserving; they signify only that we have not yet reached our destination. When redemption is imminent, the old forms are expected to

---

*A revised version of the paper presented at the conference, "Psychopathology and Political Violence: Terrorism and Assassination," sponsored by the Institute of Social and Behavioral Pathology and the University of Chicago Department of Psychiatry, Chicago, Illinois, 16–17 November 1979.

disintegrate. Accordingly, the rule of Satan precedes the coming of the Messiah and represents the destruction which precedes and enables destruction. If we can assume that the upsurge of terrorism signifies such a stage in our own culture, then nihilism as well as communism, Moonism, Evangelicalism, and other messianic cults are symptoms of the same phenomenon. Let us first of all, therefore, examine the cultural climate which leads both to the justification of terrorism and the expectation of the destruction of our own civilization.

If we browse through the titles of books published in the last few years, terms recur such as "Decline," "Revolution," "Rebellion," "Mythology," "Mysticism," and "Symbolism." Mysticism and symbolism lead to the disintegration of language; they teach that what we think we hear and see is not really what we think, and that beyond is another content, another reality, the real one. The present rise of interest in mythology may represent a rebellion against the culture based on the teachings of Rome, Athens, and Jerusalem. In the last 150 years, these three cultures have had an opportunity to return to life, but none of the revivals resembles the originals. Their return as well as their present form only emphasizes the denial of the significance of the original forms. Instead, we find an evocation of early cultures from the periphery of Western civilization: primitive tribes, Indians, and blacks. We are beyond the ideal of the noble savage; now we worship the prehistoric non-noble savage. At the same time, the "back to nature" movements, which began in turn-of-the-century Germany, are striving to abolish the institutions, customs, and rituals of the past, which happens also to be our present. They all strive to untie the delicate knots which form the fabric of our culture. They all represent entropic trends which characterize acute stages in messianic ideologies. Those ideologies justify the dissolution of past forms and history, and therefore they precede the rise of terrorist movements.

To borrow from the wise words of old Polonius, when he spoke of Hamlet: "Though this be madness, yet there is method in 't." Terrorism is concomitant with the rise of messianic cults, and their rise in turn is concomitant with the rise of philosophies and religions from the periphery of Western culture, such as Yoga, Buddhism, and Hinduism. Terrorism has been heralded by a religious revolution which is only the last stage in a succession of revolutions which started in the sixteenth century.

In the Middle Ages, revolutionary movements were termed "renaissance"; they claimed to be a renewal of something already in existence. So also the Reformation claimed to be a reordering of something which had existed before, a return to the right formation. The medieval person faced an ideal past which set the norm for the future. Books propounding revolutionary philosophies were submitted as mere commentaries. But from the sixteenth century onwards, terms most commonly used in book titles were *novo*, new, modern. The sixteenth century itself was one of utopias, works expressing a rejection of the old coupled with a hope for a better future; these books explored the newly discovered principle of light, or enlightenment. The newly discovered America represented a foil to the Old World, which appeared distorted, corrupt, and hopeless. The concept of one single creation changed into a concept of continuous creation, while the leading principle was dubbed fire, or light. Among these books were Sir Thomas More's *Utopia*, Francis Bacon's *New Atlantis*, and Tommaso Campanella's *City of the Sun*.

All the sixteenth-century utopias drew from the principles of goodness and justice. Twentieth-century utopias, on the other hand, are antipodal to those of the sixteenth—Aldous Huxley's *Brave New World*, George Orwell's *1984*, B.F. Skinner's *Walden Two*. The leading theme in all of them is evil; they all express a feeling of desperation, a lack of belief that man can become better or shape a better world. Beethoven's hymn to the light turns into Georg Büchner's despair or Franz Kafka's helplessness: to the first's Wozzeck, madness is the only solution to the problem; the second's Josef K., in *The Trial*, does not know of what he is accused but is executed nonetheless. As we started this line of reasoning with Shakespeare, we may as well end it with William Butler Yeats:

> Things fall apart; the center cannot hold;
> Mere anarchy is loosed upon the world . . .
> The best lack all conviction, while the worst
> Are full of passionate intensity.

Both the sixteenth and twentieth centuries are high on messianic expectations which lead to the destruction of past forms. But the sixteenth century was suffused with the belief that the future will be better, while the twentieth century is rife with apocalyptic premonitions stemming from the recognition that evil cannot be arrested by human efforts alone. The sixteenth century represented, therefore, the beginning of the age of revolution, which strives to clear the way from everything inhibiting the disclosure of the perfect order at the end of the road, or the rainbow. The expulsion from the Garden of Eden started with man covering himself with a fig leaf; he later added layer after layer of clothing, more rituals, more customs, more mores. With the revolutions of the sixteenth century, this trend began to change. Western civilization started to undress, in the belief that once it began to rid itself of all those layers it would find itself back in Eden. The Fall and the need to dress are thought of as punishment, not privilege. It all started with the bite from the fruit of the Tree of Knowledge; therefore, at the last stage—that of removing the extra layers— we will have to do away with knowledge and intellect. Thus from the sixteenth century onward, we started removing kings and nobles, clans and families, social classes, and corsets, together with the social obligations and responsibilities associated with all those layers. And when Western man reached the stage of nakedness, there was no longer any need for the wisdom acquired from the Tree, so the image of God was discarded as well.

The more naked we become, the more we discover that the world which corresponds to this stage resembles Hell rather than Eden. Instead of the voice of God, we find the venom of the serpent. What is more, after Darwin, the creature residing in the Garden of Eden is a monkey, not a human being. We thus reach the end of the road. We try to erase history, but instead we erase ourselves. The conclusion of the enlightenment is self-elimination; the conclusion of the era of revolutions is terrorism. Revolutions commence with a hope that the future will be better than the past, but, as Nietzsche pointed out, that better future always turns into a worse past. When we remove the last layer with which history and knowledge have clothed us, nothing more remains for revolutions to remove. The next step inevitably is apocalyptic. The old phoenix reaches his predestined end; he is ready for self-destruction.

It is interesting to note that, since the seventeenth century, almost all social movements have been called revolutions, and each revolution claims to liberate us. Besides the "Glorious" in England, when James II was deposed, we have the American, French, Russian, and Chinese revolutions, together with the industrial, electronic, liberal, democratic, and others. Almost any major change in the last 400 years has been called a revolution, and each revolution is supposed to liberate us from some duty or obligation. Each revolution extends the privileges of the higher classes down to other classes, but without the same responsibilities. Climbing the social scale used to be coupled with an extension of duties and responsibilities, in line with the effort to become in God's image, as God is responsible for everything that happens in his kingdom. In the Garden of Eden, God charged man with the duty of keeping the garden. When Adam failed in this duty, he failed also to take responsibility for his failure; he blamed the woman, who in turn blamed the serpent. We may consider this the first bureaucratic act. As is the case with all bureau-cracies, the reward for evading responsibility is an extension of the sphere of responsibility, from Adam's garden to the whole earth. In the same fashion, each revolution covers a wider geographic area, and as we reach the stage of complete cultural nakedness, the whole world joins in the orgy.

In a strange way, there is a correlation between revolutions and the extension of cultural, as well as geographic, boundaries. Martin Luther referred to the Old Testament and the image of the fighting prophet. While climbing the steps to the guillotine, the leaders of the French Revolution compared themselves to characters in Plutarch's *Lives*. Napoleon intro-duced the West to the Middle East, and after him the ancient cultures of Egypt, Babylonia, Assyria, and Akkadia were brought to light. And as these ancient cultures arose from their graves, the influence of the religions and cultures of the East grew stronger and stronger. We can find too a correlation between the rhythm of the dissolution of Western institutions and the creeping influence of ancient cultures and religions. The more we approach the stage where societies disintegrate into individuals, the greater becomes the influence of cultures and religions directed toward erasing and subjugating the ego and self. We revert to the stage when Adam said, "not I": no *I* is yet in existence. Man becomes more and more afraid of being called by name and having to take responsibility; therefore he hides under the cover of anonymity or membership in the working class, a party, the Third World, or the black world. And with the disintegration of mankind, we witness also the disintegration of language—the unique human quality—into a jabbering of slogans and labels.

Since Plato's day we have been aware that a world of shadows exists beside the real world; most people believe the shadow to be the real one. When an individual relinquishes his personal responsibilities and devolves them upon the social body, be it a party, union, or state, he turns into a shadow; he becomes a pseudo-human being. Without personal responsibility, no personality can exist; man becomes a nonentity. He may get a feeling of power and may even believe that the act of joining a party is an act of responsibility, but there is mere pseudo-responsibility and pseudo-power. A person who joins a group that takes over the responsibility for his actions does not exist any more; therefore, the group can send him to perform suicidal missions. The group is responsible only for his destruction, not for his existence; by joining it, he has already ceased to exist as an individual. It is significant that the spread of personal reliance on the state is concomitant with the growing influence of mythologies and the rise of romantic schools of thought, which propose to abolish all forms, and of modern art, which actually does abolish all forms. At the same time, philosophers do not speak any more of willpower, only of roles and interests.

Terrorism is just the last stage in the age of revolutions, the last step in a trend toward social and cultural disintegration. The direction is toward self-negation. The externalization of self-negation leads to the negation of everything else. The nucleus of Western civilization has always been the individual. With the rise of the masses to politics, of mass production and of mass culture, the undivided self is fragmented into roles and interests. When a person says, "I will," he takes upon himself a certain responsibility, and the whole world no longer is indifferent: responsibility signifies the relationship between all the parts of the world; responsibility is the universal energy which keeps the world alive and responsive. Without taking personal responsibility, man does not exist; the world can exist without him. The terrorist is the product, and the most perfect representative, of this trend to evade responsibility. He is not responsible for the existence of anything; he turns over the responsibility for all his actions to a group which likewise is not responsible for the existence of anything. As such, the terrorist forms the ideal match to strike the fire to burn the old phoenix: he dies with it as a sacrifice and as a redeemer, thus facilitating the birth of a new aeon and of a new era.

BIBLIOGRAPHY

Cohn, Norman. *The Pursuit of the Millennium.* London, 1957.
Dostoyevsky, Fyodor. *The Devils (The Possessed).*
Elias, Norbert. *The Civilizing Process.* New York, 1978. English translation of the 1939 German publication.
Hayek, Friedrich A. *Road to Serfdom.* Chicago, 1944.
Huizinga, Johan. *Homo Ludens.* Boston, 1950.
Lewy, Guenter. *Religion and Revolution.* New York, 1974.
Nietzsche, Friedrich. *The Will to Power.* New York, 1968.
Ortega y Gasset, José. *The Revolt of the Masses.* New York, 1950.
Rosenstock-Huessey, Eugen. *Out of Revolution.* Norwich, VT, 1969. The writer finds this to be the most intriguing and thought-provoking book published in this century. Many of the ideas dealt with in this paper came to him while reading this book.
Solzhenitsyn, Alexander. *Speaks to the West.* London, 1978.

Dialectic Interrelationships of Personal and Political Factors in Terrorism*

Acts of terrorism are incomprehensible if we look at only their political motivations and effects and ignore their psychological bases. On the other hand, to attempt to explain terrorism by considering only the personality structure or psychodynamics of the terrorists is to fall prey to a reductionism that conceals or distorts the impact of terrorist acts on the victims, the audience, the terrorists, and the world at large.

The medical model in and of itself is simply not sufficient to evaluate, let alone "treat," terrorism or terrorists, even if mental health values are smuggled subtly into the model to replace the outright moral and frequently moralistic evaluation of good and bad. Is terrorism never legitimate? Is every society, no matter what its structure, entitled to protection from terrorism from below, regardless of the terrorists' methods and aims? The very legitimate, even crucial, inquiry into such questions is obscured by pressing these problems into the Procrustean bed of medical alternatives and coming up with such paradoxical formulations as healthy terrorism and pathological societies.

The bulk of this paper will deal with terrorists as justice collectors, seeking remedy for injustice by unrestrained legitimation of all means used in the service of their cause. The dynamics of identity will be discussed with special emphasis on the cause-effect reversal between group egotism and personal self-sacrifice. The terrorists seem to serve a cause, but in fact the cause serves them and their own wishes; they often die in its service, victims of self-deception and puppets of their own illusions and delusions. Also, the use of ostensible political goals for purposes of rationalizing violent acts will be pointed out, stressing the "benefits" of the action high for action addicts and fanatics of simplicity. The fanatic representatives of

---

*A revised version of the paper presented at the conference, "Psychopathology and Political Violence: Terrorism and Assassination," sponsored by the Institute of Social and Behavioral Pathology and the University of Chicago Department of Psychiatry, Chicago, Illinois, 16–17 November 1979.

the cause will be described in terms of "as characters," who act and feel
and think not individually, but only as representatives, as parts of a larger
whole, carrying out their assigned missions to serve a higher design. After
discussing the syndrome of "ego in the service of regression," a closing
attempt will be made to find the beginnings of a future reality principle,
which encompasses not only the satisfaction of individual, but also of
group, identity needs.

TERRORIST TITILLATION

Body counts are vulgar, and one innocent life taken as a result of
terrorist activity is one life too many. Yet the fact remains that our
indignation against terrorism seems out of proportion to the number of
victims that, in the last twenty years, has not amounted to more than the
casualties of one ordinary day of combat in World War II. A hundred
thousand or millions died in Cambodia and other places recently without
exciting us too much, while terrorism not only preempts the headline but
also involves us all in strong, empathic participation. This tremendous
discrepancy between the public and scientific interest terrorism arouses on
the one hand, and the relatively small number of victims involved on the
other hand, is the measure of terrorism's dramatic impact.

Why do such comparatively minor events have such a major effect
upon us? Terrorism is great theater. It is great fun for the perpetrator and
for the audience. In fact, it is carried out for audience entertainment. It is
show business. The Iranian students who kept the American diplomatic
personnel hostage in Tehran may not have been very good at studying, but
they were experts in managing to attract world attention. It is the dramatic
appeal that makes terrorism the glamorous growth industry that it is and
will remain as long as the mass media, under the guise of information,
entertain their public at prime time with stories of terrorism and titillate
the imagination of an increasingly more passive public.

The intrinsic dependency of terrorism and mass media on each other
certainly is an important factor in making terrorism a fast-spreading
growth industry, since without the probability of notoriety, and hence
contagion, terrorism could not flourish. However, it is not sufficient to
point out repeatedly that terrorist actions have a seductive appeal for
predisposed individuals with a character structure and personality organization similar to that of the terrorists, or to complain that as long as
terrorism is rewarded by the virtual certainty of widespread publicity, the
expectation of such terrorist success will remain an important motivation
for future terrorist acts. Making media the sole scapegoats confuses the
dangerous transmission and reinforcement of a psychosocial evil with the

sources and the significance of the phenomenon itself. Society will continue to pay a high price in violence for its insistence on being entertained by violence.

Mass media certainly have become the main agents of our mythological instruction. Due to the necessity to entertain and titillate at the lowest level for maximum audience pseudoparticipation, mass media tend toward the glorification of violence and are in favor of what this writer has called cinematogenic solutions. The erstwhile relationship between reality and its reporting and picturing in the mass media has been reversed; now it is the mass media reproduction that produces reality and strongly suggests the presumably viable, popular options. More and more do we want solutions to big social, national, and other problems according to the fashion in which Errol Flynn and John Wayne solved these problems. We are sure the cavalry (the good guys) will arrive at the last moment, and all will be right with the world and in balance again as before. Didn't it work at Entebbe with the *Mayaguez*? Why not try the same thing in Tehran? We did, with the well-known disastrous results which, however, for a large part of the population and the scientific community, did not seem to be an opportunity for learning from our mistakes, but an occasion to assert that we should have acted long before and we will certainly do it again. Cinematogenic reality has to triumph ultimately over all real difficulties; doesn't that happen all the time in the movies and on television?

MENTAL ILLNESS AND POLITICS

A large part of the psychiatric population in this or any other country at any time in history is beset by mental symptoms called delusions or hallucinations that appear to have a political or religious content. There are hundreds of thousands of medically sick people who hold extremely strong religious and political beliefs, by which they tend to rationalize and legitimate their delusional or hallucinatory thoughts. These thoughts originate in personal, physical, or psychological factors. Hence, the use of political or religious creeds as justification for idiosyncratic behavior does not at all exclude a diagnosis of mental illness. This is not a reversible statement. It does not mean that strongly held political or religious beliefs indicate mental illness; it only means to express the popular observation that mental illness is compatible with religious or political creeds strongly held and vigorously expressed. Politicization of mental and emotional disturbances is extremely common.

Political and religious convictions demand certain personality structures that are either preformed to meet the requirements of a creed or are formed, or at least reinforced, by that creed. Political and religious thinking and acting are psychologically motivated and have a psychological dimension, although this dimension sometimes is denied by the "Marxist type" interpretation that claims the exclusivity of economic motivation and also by non-Marxists who believe that conventional, easily understood motivations make psychological explanations unnecessary. Even the courts do not call in a psychiatrist when a criminal act, let's say, is motivated by money gain or by jealousy. This situation is treated as though it were not psychologically motivated, although hardly anyone would seriously deny that jealousy or greed have psychological motivations; in these common "afflictions," they can be discovered just as easily as in any kind of political or religious behavior.

Hence, it is not surprising that analyses of any political or religious leader or follower will unearth psychological factors conducive to that type of behavior. In other words, political and religious beliefs and actions are interwoven, intermingled, interrelated, and intertwined with personality factors created or reinforced in part by just that kind of collective or individual political behavior. On the other hand, any actual or imagined political or religious figure is capable of rationalizing and propagandizing his actions as political or religious, no matter how peculiar, idiosyncratic, deranged or "crazy" they may be. Consciously or unconsciously used, legitimation by politics is a dignifying mechanism that often conceals personal bias or personal pathology.

Some time ago, the writer suggested a division of types of terrorists according to their psychological motivations. Terrorists can be roughly divided into three groups: the crazy, the criminal, and the crusading. The emotionally disturbed are driven by reasons of their own that often do not make sense to anyone else. That is why they are called crazy, a colloquial designation the writer uses with reluctance because of its judgmental connotation. The motives of those criminal terrorists who use illegitimate means to obtain personal gain are well understood; they want what most other people want, but they resort to socially disapproved methods in order to achieve their goals. Crusading terrorists, the most typical, are idealistically inspired. They seek, not personal gain, but prestige and power for a collective goal; they believe that they act in the service of a higher cause.

The pure ideal type is rarely encountered; each may have traits of the others. Many criminals are severely disturbed or try to exploit various causes for personal gain. Some mentally ill individuals are attracted irresistibly to crusades or engage in personally motivated antisocial acts. Crusading terrorists often have emotional problems; some have criminal backgrounds. Some crusaders become more violent and criminal and splinter into smaller, more radical freelancing units, while some criminals adopt, in prison and out, the justifying and comforting identity of a cause. Convicts often believe themselves to be victims of racial, sexist, and political persecution; they think the evil forces in society are responsible for their plight, not any fault within themselves. Yet, within limits, the differentiation among crazy, criminal, and crusading terrorists remains useful and valid, sometimes even vital, because the distinction determines the widely varying courses of action for meeting or treating the terrorist challenge.

The terms "criminal" and "crazy" are labels that pretend to be descriptive but often merely express disapproval. The criminal is loathed; the crazy is pitied; both are feared. Punishment is legitimate only when the offender can be blamed. The criminal can and must be blamed, because he willed his evil deed; he is bad and should be punished. The mad person cannot be blamed, because he did not have free will, but that does not make him any less dangerous.

Crazy is used to describe unusual, unforeseen, and incomprehensible conduct. In societies that by repression or ignorance are intolerant of any deviation, persons may earn the derogatory label just by being different; the community then takes protective and therapeutic measures against the "guilty" person.

The typical crusading terrorist appears normal, no matter how crazy his cause and how criminal the means he uses in the service of this cause. He gains his strength not only from his comparatively intact ego but also from his enthusiastic membership in a group onto which he has projected and externalized his conscience. He is neither a dummy nor a fool, a coward nor a weakling, but a professional—well-trained, well-prepared, and well-disciplined in the habit of blind obedience.

These categories, so neatly described, overlap. Subsequent experience has shown that the writer's divisions are more significant to the evaluator than to the evaluatee. As a rule of thumb, we tend to call criminal or crazy or both the terrorist we disapprove of, but if we sympathize with the terrorist or his cause, we will be inclined to place him in the category of crusader. The distinction has little merit in nosologically classifying the perpetrators, but it serves its purpose by demonstrating the observer's bias. How does that work? By considering the Russian revolution, National Socialism, the Cuban uprising, and the Iranian upheaval purely as the psychological problems of Stalin, Hitler, Castro, and Khomeini, we obtain the scientifically doubtful yet emotionally gratifying conviction that all these people are crazy or criminal or both. We then are permitted to treat them as crazies and criminals and to lock them up or worse. Yet in serious scientific discourse, it can be shown that this psychologizing of the problem produces an immunization strategy. By making the accusation of mental illness stick, everyone else is acquitted of guilt or participation. The social, legal, economic, and other bases of all these movements need no longer be considered. Everyone except the leader, who has been psychologically examined *ad nauseam*, is let off the hook. It can be stated in the same breath that while the politicization of emotional disturbance is often a conscious or unconscious mechanism to dignify, enhance, and justify this disturbance, the description of political phenomena as purely psychological tends to confine, minimize, and immunize them; this makes them a topic of psychopathology that need not be dealt with by remedial social measures or anything else of that sort.

JUSTICE COLLECTORS

Many years ago, the psychoanalyst Edmund Bergler coined the term "injustice collectors" to describe patients who constantly believe themselves wronged and eternally find evidence for their inner feelings of rejection and suspiciousness by confirming external evidence. Adding a new facet to the psychology of terrorists, let us call them "justice collectors." Terrorists act in response to a grievance. They respond actively to what they perceive to be an intolerable injustice by taking matters into their own hands; they are insatiable in collecting justice in retaliation.

Four successive stages can be stipulated to account for the general genesis of the terrorist act. First, an individual, or a small or large group, becomes aware of either real or imaginary oppression, thus ending the state of "happy slavery" in which submission by the "victim" is accepted as a way of life. Second, oppression no longer is regarded as natural, biological, and unavoidable. For instance, as long as women believed that they were an inferior breed, confined in their activities to the kitchen, the church, and the children, their awareness of oppression did not matter because they accepted the fact that their peculiar status was the result of immutable biology. Hence, they took little action until they found that the difference between women and men in biological structure did not of itself justify the purely social evaluation of women as inferior. The next step then is characterized by the realization that alleged inferiority is not biologically ordained but socially prescribed, which means that this status socially may be changed. Third, after people recognize that they are oppressed and that this oppression is social and therefore somewhat arbitrary, dependent on historical circumstances, they begin to believe that action should be taken simply because action can be taken. At that time, the oppressed individual or group appeals to the world and eventually to its own group for help and remedy. Yet if this remedy is not forthcoming, some people, the so-called terrorists, then advance to the next stage. Fourth, self-help by violence occurs, because presumably nothing else will help.

This belief that nothing except violence helps may be totally mistaken or delusional, but it also may be realistic. In any case, these four stages that often overlap each other are necessary for bringing about terrorist activity.

Remediable injustice, the basic motivation for terrorism from below, has multiplied in modern times because both the awareness of injustice and a belief in the availability of remedies have increased enormously. The successive waves of terror and terrorism, advertised and imitated like fashions, are neither isolated events nor parts of a deliberate, conspirational master plan; rather, they are the symptomatic, logical, and psychological expressions of a novel situation prevailing all over the world. The root causes of terrorism are not deprivation or oppression as such, but the perception and experience of injustice and the belief that such injustice is not natural or inevitable, but arbitrary, unnecessary, and remediable. In an inflation of rising expectations, the unfulfilled promises of abundance, equality, independence, and sovereignty provoke bitter frustration and a spreading feeling of needlessly suffered injustice that can and should be terminated by violence. Highly advertised and eagerly copied, spectacular violence has had its most impressive success after violence itself had been officially declared futile, unrealistic, and obsolete as a coping device.

Modern terrorism, which combines utter ruthlessness and self-sacrificial dedication with a fanatic belief in the justification of destructive acts, has raised the ultramodern question of whether any option but violence and counterviolence is appropriate, effective, and realistic in the contemporary world. The terrorist's motto is, "Destroy in order to save." Should it be countered with the equally simplistic and terrorist response, "In order to save, destroy the destroyers"?

THE ACTION HIGH

Many intelligent and well-informed terrorists acknowledge that their deeds, no matter how desperate and spectacular, probably will not effect much change either now or in the long run. However, some terrorists are quite reconciled, though by no means resigned, to the role of martyrs who, unlike heroes, do not succeed but fail honorably. At least they know that they tried: the unshakable belief that they work, fight, and die for purposes transcending their own narrow interests gives them that fanatic self-righteousness which makes their often self-destructive acts so destructive, dangerous, and contagious. The deed performed for apparently nonegotistical reasons, for an ulterior purpose, becomes violent without restraint when the display of individual courage is but slavish obedience to orders from above, a manifestation of relief from the curse of individuation.

In this identification with a cause and its representatives, the terrorist, by giving up his individual will, individual responsibility, and individual interest, experiences the high of liberation from his own problems, guilts, and anxiety. The cruel act, considered morally superior to mere thinking or talking, mystically and realistically confirms membership in the identity group; the self-sacrificial super-macho act radically removes all doubt, distracts from all personal problems, and permits full aggressive gratification without self-punitive guilt, shame, doubt or anxiety, in the name and for the sake of the higher cause.

ACTION ADDICTS AND FANATICS OF SIMPLICITY

In the illusion of certainty (of doing more than one's own thing, namely, the right thing), the certainty of the illusion that nothing less than spectacular violence will influence reality becomes a firm conviction which transforms ordinarily self-protective individuals into fanatics, indifferent to personal danger, ready and even eager to sacrifice their own lives. The cause, usually represented by an organization of terror from above, gives the promise of unity, wholeness, cohesion, and unanimity. The National Socialists expressed it in the slogan, "One People, One Empire, One Leader."

By insisting on a fully united and intact "in" group that gives all its adherents the feelings of family, shelter, and security, the enemy image also is simplified and unified. One definite enemy is provided in whom all the evil in the world is condensed and manifested. This one enemy appears in many different guises and manifestations in many different places, but he is always the same, the principal and sole manifestation of all evil. If this one enemy can be eradicated, the principle of the good, the healthy, and the valuable represented by one's own identity group will have been triumphant; by instant salvation, all problems will disappear.

The unity of the identity group also provides the projective screen and images with the prefabricated content of such projections for selective use, thus facilitating the fantasy of a radical, sudden, and total resolution of all conflicts and difficulties, if only conventional, legal, and humane inhibitions against unrestrained violence can be overcome. To soldiers, heroes, and martyrs (or instruments, puppets, and marionettes) of the cause, every gratification that can be rationalized to serve one's own cause and to destroy the enemy is permissible and even required. The fanatic representatives of the cause are indeed "as characters" who act and feel and think not individually but as representatives, as parts of a larger whole, carrying out their assigned missions to serve a higher design. The lofty morality of the group, indifferent to all human suffering, transcends the narrow boundaries of individual narcissism, in order to confirm and strengthen the more powerful group egotism that satisfies the hunger for an unlimited exercise of power and fills the thirst for dependent submission.

The unifying identity conferring worth, belonging, and meaning to the individual is the group, under the cover of which the terrorist can gratify his most elementary, infantile, and grandiose desires for omnipotence, omniscience, narcissistic satisfaction, and aggressive release. This all-deciding and all-justifying group is often only the concrete product of the member's need to belong; the group ideal to which he is sworn to obedience reflects only his own hopes and fears. He seems to serve a cause, but in fact the cause serves him and his own wishes. He often dies in its service, the victim of self-deception and a puppet of his own illusions and delusions. Barbarization performed and condoned in the name of a higher purpose constitutes regression to infantile states of automatic obedience and ecstatic emotionalism. Brutalized children of all ages thus invest their "direct actions" and the propaganda of the deed with historic significance. As Ralph Waldo Emerson wrote, "Terrorism feels and never reasons and therefore is always right."

BELONGING

The degree of functional rationality is no measure of substantive rationality; that is to say, the choice of an appropriate means to bring about certain ends is not a choice of "reasonable" ends. Desirable ends may never be reached due to the deficient means chosen or used, and, conversely, excellent functioning means may promote an unworthy (irrational, infantile, destructive, regressive) goal. Ernst Kris described in psychoanalytic terms the process of controlled regression, or regression in the service of the ego, observable in artistic activity, psychoanalysis, creative efforts, love, and the like. In many case studies of terrorism, we can observe a phenomenon or mechanism that could be called "ego in the service of regression." We see repeatedly that highly developed, well-functioning, capable, goal-directed ego activity is put in the service of regressive purposes. Under certain conditions, archaic primitivism of terrorists' aims and organizations may employ the sophistication of technology as justification for crude simplistic ends and engage the seemingly voluntary services of committed, well-functioning, intelligent, and therefore particularly dangerous individuals.

In terrorist strategy, the disturbing complexity of inner and outer conflicts is crudely simplified and moralistically reduced to one: the conflict between good and evil, between us and them. Terrorism, and also war or warlike escalated confrontation situations, is attractive to the impatient, the disturbed, the searcher and seeker, the mistreated and the injured, because of its radical simplification, reduction of complexity, and moralistic polarization with the built-in certainty of being on the right side. The implicit promise of instant liberation and salvation after the enemy's destruction irresistibly lures the bored and the desperate, not just by providing ready-made projective images of inner conflict resolution and political rationalization for personal conflicts, but also by supplying subculturally approved and internalized defense systems which can serve as introjected superego and behavioral guides in all conceivable situations. The appeal of action fascinates and hypnotizes the terrorist. The fanatic of "either/or" simplicity becomes an action addict, who needs the kicks and highs of the spiritual deed to experience his own identity which, in fact, he has surrendered to the drug-like need to belong.

The terrorist deed is intended to alarm and to illuminate; in the glaring searchlight of explosive action, an imperfect society is shown to be evil, perverted, and hopeless. The bare face of oppression is relieved by terrorism's shortcut to "real reality," which rips off every hypocritical disguise; hence, the need can be experienced as the moment of truth, an extraordinary, memorable, unique event which elevates everyday, profane, and trivial routines from the depth of dreary repetitiveness to the height of a sacred game with rich, symbolic significance. Participation in such a hallowed ritual means, for the terrorist, the acquisition of his own lasting importance and the establishment and reaffirmation of a mystical bond to his community. By acquiring eternal life within the community, he has overcome the dread and transcended the reality of his own death.

PSYCHIATRIC TASKS

The psychiatrist is accustomed to inquiring how the problem originated before he can tell what should be done about it. Research into terrorism so far has been hampered by the limitations created by fear of excessive "sympathy" with terrorists; this fear has prevented the formulation and comparative study of remedial steps. It is as though a psychiatrist were given only a few symptoms of the disturbed patient but would not be permitted to ask or to listen to how it all happened, when the symptoms originated, and what the patient was thinking and feeling. Every experienced psychiatrist has heard a thousand times the complaint of the patient, or a relative of a patient, that he cannot talk to that man or that woman or that child or that group. Presumably he cannot negotiate with them. That is precisely where the work of the psychiatrist starts: to negotiate with those who by ordinary means, or by "rational means," are unapproachable. This is where the work of the psychiatrist, or the diplomat, the troubleshooter, the politician, or the humanitarian, begins.

An attempt to understand does not mean condoning or advocating the type of conduct the psychiatrist tries to analyze and possibly influence. The attempt to understand the conditions under which violence happens is not to be confused with an advocacy of violence. The well-worn statement, "The freedom fighters of the one side are the terrorists of the other side," is trite and at times demonstrably wrong, but ignoring the subjectivity and arbitrariness of the moral judgment separating terrorists from anti-terrorists, the good guys from the bad guys, reduces all further inquiry to mere condemnation and the expression of indignation. It does not matter whether doctors call illness what other people call badness. Nothing has been added cognitively if we consider the terrorists bums or bastards rather than possessed by some peculiar sickness, even if it is not quite clear what that sickness may be. The only definitional characteristic of the peculiar insanity which allegedly infects them is that we all disapprove of it. However, if we should suggest that this so-called badness virus is only some form of poverty, either of economics, resources, education, or of choice or options, then we, or any society, will be accused of being infected ourselves by a kind of collective death wish which paralyzes all healthy resistance, unless we do not recognize terrorist rebelliousness as a symptom. The insistence on the consensus of total disapproval stipulates that if terrorism is not called a symptom, this failure in itself must be a symptom. Circular reasoning always returns to the point of origin, confirming to its own satisfaction what it sets out, not to prove, but to assert for its own approval.

After advocating that the psychiatric approach, which is essential and necessary though in and of itself not sufficient, be permitted in the study of terrorism, little more need be said; what follows has been stated repeatedly by many observers and by this writer. The terrorist situation needs to be defused and deglamorized, after we get away from our ethnocentric arrogance in the belief that only our frame of reference is rational, reasonable, and acceptable. We, the good guys, should try not to copy the terrorists, either by using similarly brutal means of antiterrorism or by imitating their symbolic actions; for example, by burning the Iranian flag in response to Iranians burning the American flag.

Modern terrorism is a novel challenge that must be met with new ideas and new approaches. Law enforcement officials have difficulty in accepting this fact of modern life. Accustomed to dealing quickly and decisively with lawbreakers, they are inclined to meet force or threats of force with superior counterforce and to make use of delay only in order to muster strength sufficient to overwhelm the offenders. Prestige and a strong sense of righteousness, legitimacy, and power are important compensations for the danger and criticism inherent in the security officers' immensely difficult job. They do not fear the criminals, but they fear any appearance of impotence or inefficiency in dealing with criminals. Like all those whose main business is violence, they are afraid not of danger, but of mockery and ridicule. What frightens them is not loss of limb or life, but loss of face. They regard alternatives to violence or hesitation in the use of force as despicable weaknesses. Because they have been trained to act tough, they are inclined to regard toughness as a virtue in and of itself.

Modern terrorism is an international problem, an import-export growth industry that is exchanging trade secrets and personnel. This fact needs emphasis repeatedly in order to make more palatable the necessary diplomatization and legalization of strategies of negotiation and compromise. Modern-day terrorists move around quickly; they use psychological and technological weapons of considerable sophistication and danger to extort and blackmail highly valued property and lives. Terrorists cannot be prevented from attacking almost any place in the world, but measures should be taken to minimize the damage that cannot be avoided.

Terrorist enterprise consists of conflict polarization and the escalation of dramatized and glamorized violence; therefore, antiterrorist tactics should depolarize, deescalate, deglamorize, and defuse. The moralistic luxury of name-calling and blame-calling will have to be sacrificed to the need to save human lives; this is not only a humanitarian consideration, but also the best chance to prevent copycat and follow-up terrorism. Dramatic, spectacular violence is imitated or avenged by more spectacular violence. Nonviolent solutions to conflict have an educational impact that reaches far beyond the specific instances of their successful employment.

The alternative to, and the remedy for, violent direct action is innovative social action. All progress would stop if there were no new inventions and practical improvements. But no industrial firm would put a product on the market without having first conducted extensive experiments to find out whether it works. Why not engage in systematic and intuitive social experimentations? In an era of rising expectation and identity claims, people cannot play forever by game rules designed to make them lose. A change of social game rules is preferable to the perpetuation of injustice, hallowed by habit and tradition.

Many claims of injustice certainly are exaggerated, and clearly not every injustice can be corrected. But this should not be an excuse to avoid relieving those causes of injustice that can be relieved. The best antiterrorist strategy is not a countercrusade, in which we become terrorists in different guise, but the remedy of such grievances and conditions that can and should be remedied. The active search for social and national justice gives us the moral stance to firmly stand our ground to do whatever we can in order to protect our future and preserve our liberty. The time to act nonterroristically is now.

BIBLIOGRAPHY

Cooper, H. H. A. "Whither Now? Terrorism on the Brink." In *Contemporary Terrorism*, edited by J. D. Elliott and L. K. Gibson. Gaithersburg, MD: International Association of Chiefs of Police, 1978.

Hacker, F. J. *Crusaders, Criminals, and Crazies: Terror and Terrorism in Our Time.* New York: Norton, 1977.

———. "Terror and Terrorism: Modern Growth Industry and Mass Entertainment." In *Terrorism: An International Journal* 4 (1980).

Jackson, G. *Surviving the Long Night.* New York: Vanguard Press, 1973.

Kupperman, R., and Trent, D. *Terrorism, Threat, Reality and Response.* Stanford: Hoover Institution Press, 1979.

Laqueur, W. "The Futility of Terrorism." In *Contemporary Terrorism*, edited by J. D. Elliott and L. K. Gibson. Gaithersburg, MD: International Association of Chiefs of Police, 1978.

Ochberg, F. M. "Victims of Terrorism." In *Journal of Clinical Psychiatry* 41 (1980).

Parry, A. *Terrorism: From Robespierre to Arafat.* New York: Vanguard Press, 1976.

Pierre, A. J. "The Politics of International Terrorism." In *Contemporary Terrorism*, edited by J. D. Elliott and L. K. Gibson. Gaithersburg, MD: International Association of Chiefs of Police, 1978.

Segre, D. V., and Adler, J. H. "The Ecology of Terrorism." In *Encounter* 40, no. 2 (February 1973).

Trotsky, L. *Terrorism and Communism: A Reply to Karl Kautsky.* 2d Eng. ed. Ann Arbor: University of Michigan Press (Ann Arbor Paperbacks), 1961.

U.S., House of Representatives. Committee on Internal Security, *Hearings on Terrorism*, pts. 1–4. Washington, DC: Government Printing Office, 1974.

Terrorism and the Psychology of the Self*

JOHN W. CRAYTON

Some aspects of the psychology of narcissism relevant to the question of terrorism will be outlined here. Whether or not terrorist acts are symptoms of individual pathology, their description, categorization, causation, and possible modification are legitimate topics of scientific study. Also, each terrorist act, regardless of its origin in or impact on economic or political institutions, arises out of an individual psyche.

Two considerations need to be addressed prior to embarking on any psychological inquiry into terrorism. First, psychological descriptions of behavior have a way of sounding like justifications for the behavior, making it seem morally right or absolving the terrorist of responsibility. The moral and legal aspects of terrorism, although not entirely separable from psychological descriptions, are thorny issues in themselves. Psychology may contribute to those fields, but it cannot be the basis for settling moral and legal problems. Second, let us accept as axiomatic that behavior is determined by multiple factors. Although the focus will be on the particular psychological factors, we must recognize the possible crucial nature of individual biological, intrapsychic, group, social, or cultural factors in particular cases.

CHARACTERISTICS OF TERRORIST BEHAVIOR

Terrorism is an attempt to acquire or maintain power or control by intimidation, by instilling a fear of destruction or helplessness in the objects of the terrorism. Terrorists usually operate in groups or under the banner of a cause. The group or its cause usually is highly idealized, and

---

*A revised version of the paper presented at the conference, "Psychopathology and Political Violence: Terrorism and Assassination," sponsored by the Institute of Social and Behavioral Pathology and the University of Chicago Department of Psychiatry, Chicago, Illinois, 16–17 November 1979.

an air of absolute conviction is held about the truth or rightness of the group's aims. The terrorist unit tends to develop out of a situation of deprivation, be it poverty, minority status, disenfranchisement, or prejudice. All of these characteristics are typical of exaggerated group narcissism. Furthermore, terrorists have the impression, rightfully or not, that they cannot achieve their goals by legal means; in other words, they feel that they lack access to a responsive social system.

Terrorist groups usually are led by a charismatic figure who personifies the plight of the group and its unswerving certainty that it is right. This leader frequently appears to outsiders to be "crazy" and to behave in a bizarre manner, but to members of the group he can do no wrong.

Terrorists crave publicity through exposure in the press and television. Highly visible sites such as the Munich Olympic Games are attractive arenas for terrorist acts. Similarly, terrorists favor distinctive uniforms, catchy slogans, and various other conspicuous paraphernalia. This publicity tends to enhance the self-image of the group and the self-esteem of the individual members.

Finally, a puzzling aspect of terrorism is the reaction of a particular class of victims of terrorism—hostages—to their captors. Hostages frequently adopt the views of their captors, befriend them, and, as in the case of Patty Hearst, assist in carrying out terrorist activities. This Stockholm Syndrome has been attributed to the unconscious guilt of the hostages over their captors' demands.

THE PSYCHOLOGY OF THE SELF

The psychology of the self, as developed in the recent works of Kohut, Kernberg, and in the earlier writings of Freud, Hartmann, and others, is particularly concerned with factors that contribute to the development and maintenance of healthy self-esteem. It is necessary to consider some basic concepts of normal and abnormal narcissistic development. Kohut suggests that there are two basic lines of psychological development which begin at birth and extend into adulthood. First, the individual grows and develops his repertory of interactions with objects outside of himself, his parents, his friends, and his environment. He has instinctual aims toward others, such as the wish to love, to be loved by another, to be competent, and to succeed. The study of the development of the individual's relationship to objects and people other than his own self has been the subject of most of Freud's writings, as well as many psychologists since Freud.

Alongside this "object-instinctual" line of development, according to Kohut, is a second narcissistic line of development which is concerned with the individual's relationship to himself—how he views himself.[1] The first phase of this development process, the phase of primary narcissism, is characterized by the infant's all-encompassing involvement with himself, with no clearly differentiated sense of an "I" and a "you." This phase gives way as the developing infant interprets more of what transpires in his environment and confronts the painful realities of an imperfect world. Primary narcissism is replaced by two alternative psychological forms: the "grandiose self," and the "idealized parental imago." The child may attempt to maintain his perfect grandiose self by rejecting as "not me" all painful or bad aspects of his self and situation. Alternatively, the child may give up this attempt at preserving his grandiose self and instead seek narcissistic balance by contact with an idealized extension of himself, an idealized parental imago. In short, the child declares, "If I am not perfect, I will at least be in a relationship with something perfect."

These two narcissistic reactions have both positive and negative aspects and can be both useful and deleterious to the individual, depending on individual circumstances. The grandiose view of the self, when adequately attenuated by reality testing, is an essential ingredient of healthy ambition, self-confidence, and the development of mutual, loving human relationships. Unneutralized, the grandiose self produces individuals, such as sociopaths and insufferably arrogant people, who lack regard for others. Similarly, the idealized parental imago contributes to a healthy regard for others and to the maintenance of societal ideals and customs. However, when the reaction is excessive, it can produce a state of helpless defeatism, overly high expectations of an idealized other, and a vulnerability to disappointment when expected responses are not forthcoming.

It is important to emphasize that the lines of development outlined by Kohut are normal. Each of us goes through these successive stages, which lead optimally to a well-balanced, modulated, comfortable sense of one's self in relation to the outside world. Each of us, having gone through these successive stages in our development, is vulnerable to a return to one or the other of those phases, when placed in situations that rearouse the threatened sense of self. In other words, an empathic or narcissistic insult to an individual can reawaken infantile grandiosity or an infantile dependence on an idealized parental imago.

---

[1]The concept of the self has been the subject of much debate in psychiatric literature. Some authors have posited a self as a mental representation of one's being made up of one's concept of who he is—his appearance, attributes, talents, and shortcomings. For others, the self also may include a more active, dynamic aspect, since it becomes a matrix through which all ideas, actions, and feelings are experienced. While the precise nature of the self has not been satisfactorily resolved, the self as an idea we have about ourselves has been a useful concept.

NARCISSISTIC RAGE

When an individual is frustrated in his attempts to maintain healthy self-esteem and cohesion, he may react with a variety of responses, which may be more or less useful. Shame and anger, if not overwhelming, can be the basis for constructive efforts to reestablish self-respect and healthy regard for and by others. However, narcissistic defeat frequently leads to a reaction of rage and a wish to destroy the source of the narcissistic injury.

> Human aggression is most dangerous when it is attached to the two great absolutarian psychological constellations, the grandiose self and the archaic omnipotent object. The most gruesome human destructiveness is encountered, not in the form of wild, regressive and primitive behavior, but in the form of orderly and organized activities in which the perpetrators' destructiveness is alloyed to absolute conviction about their greatness and with their devotion to archaic omnipotent figures.[2]

Kohut believes that there is a biological basis for this response of rage. Narcissistically vulnerable individuals respond "to actual or anticipated narcissistic injury either with shamefaced withdrawal or with narcissistic rage,"[3] analogous to the fight-flight pattern delineated by Cannon and others. Narcissistic rage comes "from the need for revenge, for righting a wrong, for undoing a hurt by whatever means, and deeply anchored, unrelenting compulsion in the pursuit of all these aims."[4] Narcissistic rage is therefore a persistent and frequently chaotic pattern of aggression designed to reestablish self-esteem following humiliation. The hallmark of narcissistically motivated aggression is its disorganized nature, which may be understood best as the result of fragmentation of the self and subsequent impairment of such cognitive functions as logic, rational thinking, and judgment.

Kohut has attempted a psychological explanation for the response of rage to personal humiliation. He believes that rage can be understood in terms of the frustrated expectation of absolute power or omnipotence by the grandiose self. Hence, psychological mechanisms for regulating aggressions are mobilized in the service of achieving absolute control and mastery over the self-object, such as the feared and hated foreigners.[5] Acute narcissistic rage can give way to chronic narcissistic rage where the

---

[2]Heinz Kohut, *The Search for the Self* (New York: International Universities Press, 1978), p. 635.
[3]Ibid., p. 637.
[4]Ibid.
[5]Ibid., p. 656.

ego further relinquishes its reasoning capacity and even more persistently insists on the limitlessness of the power of the grandiose self. Through the defense mechanism of splitting, the self renounces any suggestion of inherent limitations and attributes all failures and weaknesses to others. The Ayatollah Khomeini's pronouncement, "Carter is the Devil," illustrates the form that this splitting can take.

NARCISSISM AND TERRORISM

The vicissitudes of the two narcissistic regressions, the grandiose self and the idealized parental imago, can be seen clearly in recent acts of terrorism. As a specific manifestation of narcissistic rage, terrorism occurs in the context of narcissistic injury. With respect to the Iranian situation, for example, various sources of humiliation can be identified. The Shi'ites in Iran have been traditionally considered outsiders and a disadvantaged group among the Moslem people as a whole. They are a minority and in concrete ways have been disenfranchised by other and more powerful sects of the Moslem religion. Their disadvantaged condition, which led to lowered self-esteem, was further aggravated by the autocratic and reportedly ruthless regime of the shah, who not only exerted extreme political and economic pressure on them but also, through his efforts to modernize Iran, violated basic religious tenets of that group. It can be argued that the Shi'ite people have developed a powerful chronic narcissistic rage in reaction to their disadvantaged condition. This aspect of Khomeini's revolution is clearly indicated by noting the Iranian reaction to it of nationalistic pride and a feeling of power, in contrast to the previously held self-image of chronic helplessness and shame.

NARCISSISTIC RAGE AND GROUP PSYCHOLOGY

Most terrorist activities are perpetrated by members of a group, and group dynamics play a central role in fostering terrorism. Kohut notes that some groups are held together by a shared grandiose self; that is, "by their shared ambitions rather than by their shared ideals."[6] Nationalistic pride can be a useful and constructive impetus to progress, but it can also be exploited for destructive ends, as was the case in Nazi Germany. A powerful charismatic leader is frequently at the head of these groups, as if

---

[6]Ibid., p. 658.

the group's shared grandiose self was personified by the leader. Kohut mentions two specific reasons for the idealization of the charismatic leader of the terrorist group, both of which are designed to protect the follower against the experience of painful narcissistic tensions. First, there is a genuine or nondefensive idealization in the form of meaningful high ideals, which protect the group members from experiencing shame. Second, the idealization of the group and its leader protects the individual members of the group against such intragroup feelings as envy, jealousy, and rage. Group cohesion and, equally important, individual cohesion further are facilitated by uniting to destroy a common foe. That foe, all bad, reinforces the group's sense of being right and good.

These group dynamics considerations are clearly illustrated in the Iranian situation. The ayatollah, as a leader of church and state, helps reduce the narcissistic tensions of the Iranian people by enabling them to share in his own grandiose ideals. There is a clear sense of rallying behind this charismatic figure as he defies the superpowers. Indeed, individuals throughout the Moslem world and even among other "disadvantaged" people, such as the American Nazi party, have rallied on behalf of the ayatollah. All of these groups find in Khomeini's opposition to the United States a source of narcissistic elevation. In addition, the group idealization of his movement tends to unify the Iranian people and reduce the probability of internal discord among them.

Kohut describes certain features of people who are suited to become charismatic leaders. They are "individuals who display an apparently unshakeable self-confidence and voice their opinions with absolute certainty." They do not feel ill, and their self-esteem is high, even though the maintenance of their own self-esteem might require use of manipulative strategies: 1) "of continually judging others," and 2) of establishing themselves "as the guides and leaders and gods of those who are in need of guidance, of leadership, and of a target for their reverence."[7] These individuals appear to have "fully identified themselves with either their grandiose self or their idealized superego. . . . The messianic figure . . . is done with the task of measuring himself against the ideals of his superego: his self and the idealized structure have become one."[8]

This leads to a serious inelasticity of personality. There is no longer the mobility that comes from reliance on several different sources of self-esteem. "The endopsychic equilibrium of the charismatic leader . . . seems to be of the all-or-nothing type. There are no survival potentialities between the extremes of utter firmness and strength on the one hand, and utter destruction (psychosis; suicide) on the other."[9] The average person

---

[7]Ibid., p. 826.
[8]Ibid.
[9]Ibid.

faced with the problem of maintaining self-esteem fulfills "ambitions nourished by the demands of the grandiose self . . . in a realistic way [by taking] into account the needs and feelings of others and of the fellow man with whom it is in empathic contact. The normal ego [also] attempts to exert its initiative and control in order to bring about behavior approaching that demanded by the idealized standards of the superego. In so doing it will compare the performance of the actual self with that demanded by the idealized standards and will acknowledge the fact that perfection cannot become reality."[10] Kohut describes charismatic leaders as having "no dynamically effective guilt feelings and never suffering any pangs of conscience about what they are doing. They are sensitive to injustices done to them, quick to accuse others—and also very persuasive in the expression of their accusations—and thus are able to evoke guilt feelings in others who tend to respond by becoming submissive and by allowing themselves to be treated tyrannically by them."[11]

Kohut suggests that some of these individuals are what Freud would have referred to as the exceptions. "Individuals who allow themselves immoral actions of many kinds are justified because they feel they have suffered an unjust punishment in childhood and have, therefore, ahead of time, expiated their later misdeeds."[12] This interpretation is readily applicable to the Iranian situation. The stated justification for Khomeini's reign of terror is that the people of Iran, and the ayatollah in particular, have been subjected already to terrorism by the shah and, therefore, have the moral right to perpetrate the crimes that they feel inclined to carry out.

Kohut disagrees with Freud about the origins of this stance. He would say that these are not individuals who have already suffered for their sins, but he thinks that they are individuals who have a stunted empathic capacity. They do not understand the wishes or the frustrations and disappointments of other people. At the same time, their sense of the legitimacy of their own wishes and their sensitivity to their own frustrations are intense.[13] Kohut's view is that the charismatic, messianic figure is one who has been traumatized by a failure of empathy from important individuals in earlier life. Here again the role of the shah as the unempathic figure is obvious. In Kohut's scheme, the individual, who has not been the object of sympathy, responds to early insults by assuming at too early a stage of development the management of his own self-esteem because of his desire to protect and shield himself from further trauma. He himself performs self-righteously the functions the other person was supposed to perform. He asserts his own perfection and demands full control over the other person.

---

[10]Ibid., p. 829.
[11]Ibid., p. 830.
[12]Ibid., pp. 829–30.
[13]Ibid., p. 850.

Khomeini is typical of the charismatic leader, toward whom disadvantaged, narcissistically vulnerable groups tend to gravitate. In addition, he may be further vulnerable to assuming his role as charismatic leader because of the additional narcissistic injuries of old age and of his long exile away from his homeland.

SOME IMPLICATIONS OF PSYCHOLOGY OF THE SELF

The object of terrorism clearly is one of humiliation. The special sense of outrage and terror evoked by acts of terrorism can best be understood as arising from their assault on our sense of "self," a concept closely related to our self-esteem and including other functions, such as those dealing with coherent and cohesive thought, feeling, and individual and group identity. The takeover of the American embassy in Tehran, a symbol of the group-self of the United States, is a good illustration of the way in which terrorism attempts to inflict narcissistic injury. The Iranians occupied the embassy, which presumably is inviolable territory of the United States. The intensity of the affective response of Americans to this action stems from the extent to which it is a narcissistic blow to the American self.

It is also interesting to examine the terrorists' victims from the point of view of the psychology of the self. Terrorist methods, such as brainwashing and the holding of hostages, also can be understood in terms of an assault on the victim's sense of a cohesive self. To deprive a person of contact with his family and country and to restrict his speech is to deprive that person of important sources of narcissistic equilibrium as well as individual and group identity. The captors require that hostages ask for everything, ask to be fed, ask to relieve themselves, ask to go to sleep. This reenacts the state of infant helplessness supported by an idealized parental imago. Not only are basic human needs met by the individuals in charge, but the individual's values and sense of self also are left to the captors. Others have discussed this phenomenon, the Stockholm Syndrome, in terms of an individual's so-called identification with the aggressor, which is thought to develop out of an unconscious sense of guilt. It seems more likely that this identification stems from a need to replace the lost sense of self with a new one, this time dictated by the captors.

CONCLUSION

The narcissistic aspects of terrorist behavior and the effects of that behavior on the victims mirror, in exaggerated form, features of normal emotional development. From the study of individuals with narcissistic rage, we may infer that a terrorist enterprise will not stop until the omnipotent grandiose strivings are given up. The narcissistically motivated terrorist would not stop if confronted with efforts to attempt to satisfy his grandiose aims through a policy of appeasement. Rather the terrorist challenges us to modulate effectively his narcissistic rage and channel it into constructive and useful ways. It is essential that terrorists "escape" from the crisis situation without further humiliation. Since the very basis for their activity stems from their sense of low self-esteem and humiliation, it is questionable whether an effective response could be based on further humiliating them by withholding food, arms, and contact with the outside world. A more effective method might be an appeal to the terrorists' sense of meaningful ideals.

This initial effort to apply the understanding of the psychology of the self to terrorist behavior should be considered an outline of areas for further study. Certainly the theoretical framework of this approach lends itself particularly well to the problem of terrorism. We need to know much more about the intrapsychic origins of terrorist behavior, but perhaps an even more important area for study is the interplay between these intra-individual factors and the workings of groups.

II.
THE TERRORIST
IN PROFILE

Profile of a Terrorist*

CHARLES A. RUSSELL and BOWMAN H. MILLER

Throughout the past decade, a steady and continued rise in terrorist activity within many nations of the world has generated a flood of academic, military, and journalistic studies on this subject. In most of these analyses, however, the primary focus has been on the mechanics of terrorism rather than the individuals involved. As a result, such subjects as the rural-to-urban shift in the locus of most terrorist and guerrilla operations as well as the structure, organization, financing, weaponry, strategy, and tactics of various terrorist groups all have been explored in some detail. In recent years, equally careful attention has been given to the problem of transnational terrorism and the increasingly close interrelationships existing between terrorist organizations in widely separated geographic areas of the world. However, until the well-publicized exploits of the now infamous Venezuelan terrorist "Carlos" (Illitch Ramirez Sanchez), considerably less attention was given to an examination of the individuals involved in terrorist activity. Nevertheless, as pointed out in the summary remarks of Dr. Chalmers Johnson at the 25–26 March 1976 Conference on International Terrorism held in Washington, DC, it is in this important area that additional knowledge is necessary.[1] Without knowledge as to the type of individuals engaged in urban terrorism and those factors motivating his or her actions, coping with the problems of both national and transnational terrorism will be increasingly difficult.

While this paper does not pretend to close the important research gap outlined above, it does represent an effort to determine if there are truly common characteristics and similarities in the social origin, political philosophy, education, age, and family background of those individuals engaged in terrorist activities within Latin America, Europe, Asia, and the

---

*A revised version of the article published in *Terrorism: An International Journal* 1, no. 1 (1977). Reprinted by permission.

[1]Conference on International Terrorism, 25–26 March 1976, Department of State Auditorium, Washington, DC. Conference panelists included representatives from the academic, industrial, journalistic, and governmental communities. Also present were speakers from the Federal Republic of Germany, Israel, and the United Kingdom.

Middle East. Based upon a compilation and analysis of published data regarding over 350 individual terrorist cadres and leaders from Palestinian, Japanese, German, Irish, Italian, Turkish, Spanish, Iranian, Argentinian, Brazilian, and Uruguayan terrorist groups active during the 1966–76 time span, an attempt is made to draw a sociological portrait or profile of the modern urban terrorist.[2] To ensure the greatest possible accuracy in this portrait, data were collected only on those individuals active in eighteen revolutionary groups known to specialize in urban terrorism as opposed to rural guerrilla warfare. Accordingly, among the Palestinians emphasis was placed on persons associated with the Popular Front for the Liberation of Palestine (PFLP) and the Black September Organization (BSO), whereas in Japan the Japanese Red Army (JRA), a group that has always operated outside that nation, was chosen. Within the Federal Republic of Germany, attention was given to the Movement Two June (M2J) and the Baader-Meinhof Gang (BM), whereas in Northern Ireland the Provisional Wing of the Irish Republican Army (IRA-P) was the target. In Italy similar emphasis was placed on the Red Brigades (RB) and the Armed Proletarian Nuclei (APN), whereas in Turkey the People's Liberation Army (TPLA) of the early 1970s was selected. For Spain, the Basque Fatherland and Liberty Movement, specifically ETA-V, and the Marxist influenced Anti-Fascist, Patriotic Revolutionary Front (FRAP) were used. Finally, in Latin America, the Argentine Montoneros and the Trotskyite People's Revolutionary Army (ERP) in that country, the Brazilian groups following Carlos Marighella and the Uruguayan Tupamaros were of particular interest.

In organizing information regarding personnel in the above-mentioned groups, data have been summarized under eight general headings entitled age, sex, marital status, rural versus urban origin, social and economic background, education or occupation, method and place of recruitment, and political philosophy. Within each category or heading, factors common to terrorists from various areas of the world are indicated as well as those that appear to vary depending upon national origin. The paper

---

[2]Most of the data used in this article was abstracted from general circulation English, French, German, Spanish, and Italian language newspapers, government documents, and research publications. In regard to Spain, Argentina, Brazil, Uruguay, the Federal Republic of Germany, and Japan, a substantial amount of government documentation on terrorist personalities and groups also was available. For Turkish, Irish, and Italian terrorist organizations and individuals, however, data was obtained primarily from newspaper reports and academic studies. In the case of the several Palestinian groups discussed, the authors are particularly indebted to Dr. Paul Jureidini, Vice President, Abbott Associates Inc., Alexandria, Virginia. A speaker on "Terrorism in the Middle East" at the above cited conference, Dr. Jureidini, a native of Lebanon, is the author of numerous classified and unclassified articles, research papers, and monographs on the Palestinian movement and is as well a consultant to several Department of Defense agencies. He is also a regular speaker at the USAF Special Operations School on Middle Eastern problems and insurgency.

concludes with a summary of commonalities and differences regarding terrorists from various geographic areas.

AGE[3]

Within the eighteen groups studied, the ages for active terrorist cadre members as opposed to leadership were remarkably consistent from group to group. Except for individuals affiliated with Palestinian, German, and Japanese organizations, the usual urban terrorist was between 22 and 25. Among the Uruguayan Tupamaros, a group particularly active in the 1966–71 time frame, the average age of arrested terrorists was 24.1. In neighboring Brazil, where revolutionary elements were very active in the late 1960s, and in Argentina, where terrorism has almost become a way of life since the early 1970s, individual terrorist cadres averaged 23 and 24 respectively. For other Latin nations such as Spain and Italy, almost identical figures were noted. In Spain, for example, arrested members of the Basque Fatherland and Liberty Movement averaged 23.2, and those associated with the Marxist-Communist Anti-Fascist, Patriotic Revolutionary Front were 24.6. Even in Iran, Turkey, and Northern Ireland, the same general pattern continued with ages averaging between 23 and 24. As indicated previously, only in Japanese, Palestinian, and West German groups was there an upward trend in cadre age. In Japan, based on arrested members of the Japanese Red Army, the average age was 28. For those affiliated with the Popular Front for the Liberation of Palestine and the Black September Organization, data on identified and arrested terrorists indicates most were in their late twenties. In the case of the Baader-Meinhof organization and the Berlin-based Movement Two June, data on over 100 individual cadre members reflected an average age of 31.3.

While a precise explanation is not readily available regarding the significantly older status of at least the Palestinian and West German terrorist cadre members, one possible reason may lie in composition of the

---

[3]The most fruitful sources of age data on terrorist cadres were governmental reports such as the Spanish *Terrorismo y Justicia en Espana* (Madrid: Centro Espa de Documentación, 1975). Also useful were academic analyses and chronologies such as Ernesto Mayans, "Los trabajos y los dias cronologia" (a day-by-day account of Tupamaro operations from 1962 through 1971) in Ernesto Mayans, ed., *Tupamaros: Antologia Documental* (Cuernavaca: Centro Intercultural de Documentación, 1971). Also useful were Foreign Broadcast Information Service reporting and the following newspapers: *The New York Times*; The London *Times*; *The Economist; Informaciones, Ya*, and *ABC* of Madrid; *La Nación* of Buenos Aires; *O Jornal do Brasil; Le Monde;* the English language *Turkish Daily News* of Ankara; *La Stampa* of Turin; *Il Messaggero* of Rome; *Corriere Della Serra* and *Il Giornale* of Milan; and *Die Welt* and *Frankfurter Allgemeine Zeitung* in West Germany.

groups themselves. In both cases, the terrorist organizations in question are not composed primarily of university students, both graduate and undergraduate, as is the case for many of the groups studied. Instead, many members of both Palestinian and West German organizations are university graduates who since have become junior professional people, doctors, lawyers, and so forth. By virtue of this fact alone, their average age is higher than that of the almost purely student groups.

While age trends for members of many terrorist groups have been relatively stable over the last decade, there are recent indications, particularly among the Spanish, Latin American, Irish, Iranian, and Turkish organizations, that the 22-to-25 age level may be dropping. In brief, it would appear that the often anarchistic-revolutionary philosophy heretofore largely a province of the university students has permeated into the secondary school level. Thus, arrests of Spanish ETA-V members in the spring of 1976 disclosed a number in their teens. Similar developments were evident in Argentina, Iran, and Turkey, while in Northern Ireland, some of the terrorists apprehended have been as young as 12 to 14. There are also signs that the age of Palestinian terrorists may be lowering. For example, those individuals involved in the 11 August 1976 attack on the Israeli El Al terminal in Istanbul's Yesilkoy Airport, for example, were 23 and 24.

Although terrorist cadres continue to fall into the early and midtwenties, the leadership level of many terrorist organizations is usually much older. In Brazil, during the late 1960s and early 1970s, Marighella and his successors often were in their late 40s or early 50s. Marighella himself, a man generally considered as the leading theoretician of urban terrorism, was 58 at the time of his death in November 1969. Among Argentine, Uruguayan, and Italian terrorist elements, leadership is or was in its mid-30s or early 40s. In Argentina, Mario Santucho, founder and leader of the highly effective People's Revolutionary Army, was 40 at the time of his July 1976 death in combat with government forces. His chief lieutenants, Enrique Gorriarán, José Urteaga, and Domingo Mena (also killed in July), were only slightly younger than Santucho. In a similar manner, Raul Sendic, chief of the Uruguayan Tupamaro organization, was 42 when his group began significant operations in the latter 1960s, whereas Renato Curcio, leader of the Italian Red Brigades, was 35 at the time of his arrest in early 1976. Within the Palestinian groups, policy level leaders are often in their late 40s or early 50s. Similarly, in Germany, Andreas Baader, founder of the Baader-Meinhof organization, is 33 and many of his group's current or former leaders (Horst Mahler, 40; Christa Eckes, 46; Gudrun Ensslin, 36; and Holger Meins, 35) are in their late 30s and early 40s. Ulrike Meinhof, the cofounder and chief ideologue of the Baader-Meinhof Gang, took her own life at the age of 42 in May 1972 while on trial in Stuttgart.

SEX[4]

Despite minor variations among some of the groups studied, urban terrorism remains a predominantly male phenomenon. During the period examined (1966–76), almost all significant terrorist operations (well over 80 percent) were directed, led, and executed by males. Within Latin American terrorist organizations (the Argentine Montoneros and ERP, the Brazilian successors to Marighella, and the Uruguayan Tupamaros), female membership was less than 16 percent, based on arrested-identified terrorist cadres. Among these organizations, the Tupamaros made perhaps the most use of females; however, with few exceptions, the role of these women was confined to intelligence collection, operations as couriers, duties as nurses and medical personnel, and in the maintenance of safe houses for terrorists sought by police and for the storage of weapons, propaganda, false documentation, funds, and other supplies.[5] Interestingly, the elusive Venezuelan terrorist "Carlos," an individual associated with Popular Front for the Liberation of Palestine operations in Europe, also used his female contacts in Paris almost solely for these purposes.[6] In Spanish, Italian, Turkish, and Iranian terrorist groups, this same predominantly support role for women has been noted.

Despite the support, as opposed to operational, roles assigned women in many terrorist organizations, there have been numerous well-known exceptions to this generalization. Thus, Leila Khalid and Fusako Shigenobu were highly effective leaders in the Popular Front for the Liberation of Palestine and the Japanese Red Army, respectively. Together, they were instrumental in arranging the initial PFLP training of JRA and West German cadres in Lebanon during the early 1970s. Today Shigenobu still is considered the actual leader and operational brains behind the JRA. Within Latin America, Norma Ester Arostito was a co-founder of the Argentine Montoneros and served as chief ideologue of that group until her death in 1976. In Spain, Genoveve Forest Tarat played a key role in the December 1973 ETA-V operation that resulted in the assassination of Spanish Premier Admiral Carrero Blanco as well as the 13 September 1974 bombing of a Madrid restaurant (Café Rolando), which resulted in eleven killed and more than seventy persons wounded.

---

[4]Sources were those cited in fn. 3.

[5]See "El papel de la mujer" in *Los Tupamaros en Acción* (Mexico, D.F.: Editorial Diogenes, 1972), pp. 56–62. This book, with a new prologue by Regis Debray, is a reprint of an earlier Tupamaro handbook published in Argentina under the title *Actas Tupamaros*.

[6]See "The Number 1 Terrorist," *Japanese Times Weekly* (Tokyo), 4 March 1975 and *Informaciones* (Madrid), 11 July 1975, pp. 2–3, articles entitled, "Carlos, el terrorista es miembro de FPLP'" and "La embajada cubana en Paris, complicada en el terrorismo," and the three-part series in *Der Spiegel*, 26 July, 2 and 9 August 1976.

In this same context, Margherita Cagol, the now-deceased wife of Italian Red Brigades leader Curcio, appears to have played an important role in that organization and quite possibly to have led the RB commando team that freed Curcio from Rome's Casale Monferrato jail on 8 February 1975.

While these and many other women have carried out key leadership or operational roles in varied terrorist groups, most female terrorists continue to function in a supportive capacity. Significantly, this frequent relegation of women to a support role is not the product of male chauvinism but rather practical experience. In the minds of most terrorist leaders, and as demonstrated by actual operations, women are simply more effective than men in such supporting activities. Several women living together (yet actually operating a safe house, weapons storage cache, or document fabrication facility) are infrequently seen by security personnel as something unusual, whereas a gathering of males in an apartment or house might well be viewed with substantial suspicion. Similarly, in the terrorist view, females—by virtue of their sex alone—are more adept at allaying the suspicions of security personnel. As a result, posing as wives or mothers, they often can enter areas that would be restricted to males, thereby obtaining useful intelligence information on government or business operations and activities.

Although women have functioned in a secondary role within most terrorist groups, they have occupied a very important position within the West German Baader-Meinhof organization as well as the Movement Two June. There, women constitute fully one-third of the operational, as opposed to support, personnel. In addition to the leading role of Ulrike Meinhof in founding the Baader-Meinhof Gang, nearly 60 percent of that organization and Movement Two June personnel at large as of August 1976 were women. Four of these women escaped from jail in West Berlin in June 1976. Several others were freed during the successful kidnapping of Peter Lorenz, Christian Democratic mayoral candidate in Berlin, by Movement Two June on 27 February 1975 and have since joined forces with the Popular Front for the Liberation of Palestine. In the West German context, there appears to be no real terrorist division of labor based on sex.[7] Women such as Meinhof, Ensslin, Ingrid Siepmann, Hanna Krabbe, Gabriele Kroecher-Tiedemann, and Angela Luther all

---

[7]See also Dr. Hans Josef Horchem, *Extremisten in einer selbsbewussten Demokratie* (Freiburg, 1975), pp. 26, 27. "Women are involved not only as helpers, informants, intelligence collectors but as active fighters who carry pistols up to 9 millimeter under their coats or in their purses which they readily use if necessary to avoid arrest. . . . Of the 22 activists of the RAF nucleus, 12 are women. Of the 20 activists who later augmented the RAF, eight are women. In the concept and activity of the RAF are also the result of an explosive emancipation of the participating female activists." (English trans. by Bowman H. Miller)

have been identified in leadership roles and as participants in robberies, burglaries, kidnappings, bombings, and other operations. In this context, Kroecher-Tiedemann was responsible for the "execution" of Austrian police official Anton Tichler during the December 1975 attack on the OPEC oil ministers meeting in Vienna, whereas Ilse Jandt, a former associate of the Movement Two June, planned and personally carried out the assassination of German terrorist turncoat Ulrich Schmuecker in West Berlin on 5 June 1974.[8]

MARITAL STATUS[9]

The unmarried terrorist is still the rule rather than the exception. Requirements for mobility, flexibility, initiative, security, and total dedication to a revolutionary cause all preclude encumbering family responsibilities and normally dictate single status for virtually all operational terrorist cadres. Statistics regarding arrested or identified terrorists in Latin America, Europe, the Middle East, and Asia reflect over 75–80 percent of the individuals involved were single. In the Federal Republic of Germany and West Berlin the 80 percent figure is also accurate. Some of the few married individuals involved in German terrorist activities (Mahler, Meinhof, and Luther) severed ties to spouses and children in order to pursue terrorist methods. Only in the case of the Uruguayan Tupamaros, a group that according to revolutionary theorist Regis Debray may have made the greatest use of women,[10] were a significant number (still less than 30 percent) of the terrorist cadre in a married status.[11] Of interest in regard to this group is the fact that the married status of many Tupamaros posed some significant operational problems for that group. In those instances where the wives of Tupamaros were arrested and subjected to interrogation, morale considerations almost compelled the group to seek their release. As a result, in operations such as the 8 March 1970 attack on the women's prison in Montevideo where the effort secured the release of thirteen women Tupamaros and was a propaganda/morale victory for the organization, the cost was high in casualties suffered by the attack team. Thus, the decision of most terrorist organizations to utilize unmarried or separated personnel appears sound from an operational point of view.

---

[8]*Innere Sicherheit* 27, Bonn, 14 April 1975.
[9]See fn. 3 for general source materials.
[10]"Prólogo" by Regis Debray in *Los Tupamaros en Acción*.
[11]Mayans, "Los trabajos y los dias cronologia."

RURAL VERSUS URBAN ORIGIN[12]

As pointed out so well by Marighella, probably the most widely read, known, and imitated theoretician and practitioner of urban guerrilla warfare, the terrorist must be intimately familiar with the terrain in which he or she operates.

> What matters is to know every path a guerrilla can use, every place he can hide, leaving the enemy at the mercy of his own ignorance. With his detailed knowledge of the streets, and all their nooks and crannies, of the rougher ground, the sewers, the wooded ground . . . urban guerrillas can easily elude the police, or surprise them in a trap or ambush. If he knows the ground well . . . he can always escape arrest.[13]

In view of the above, it is not at all surprising that most urban terrorists are natives or long-time residents of metropolitan areas, particularly the cities in which they operate. Within Argentina, where the ERP and Montoneros have been so successful in urban operations during the past six years, approximately 90 percent of their members are from the greater Buenos Aires area itself. In Brazil, the bulk of Marighella's followers and imitators came from Rio de Janeiro, São Paulo, Santos, and Recife, whereas in Uruguay over 70 percent of the Tupamaros were natives of Montevideo, their primary area of activity. Within Iran, Turkey, Italy, and the Federal Republic of Germany, most terrorists are from urban areas, particularly Tehran, Ankara, Rome, Milan, Genoa, West Berlin, and Hamburg. Similarly, a significant number of the Japanese Red Army members, who operated so effectively with European-based members of the Popular Front for the Liberation of Palestine during the years 1972–74, are from Tokyo, Kyoto, Osaka, or other Japanese metro-

---

[12]See fn. 3 for general source materials. See also Rolf Tophoven, *Guerrilla ohne Grenzen*, p. 127; "30 preguntas a un Tupamaro," *Punto Final* (Santiago), 2 July 1968, pp. 5–8; Andy Truskier, "The Politics of Violence: The Urban Guerrilla in Brazil," *Ramparts* 9 (October 1970): 30–34; "La actividad terrorista in Bresil," *Este & Oeste* (Caracas) 8, no. 132 (December 1969): 8–9; Charles A. Russell, James F. Schenkel, James A. Miller, "Urban Guerrillas in Argentina: A Select Bibliography," *Latin American Research Review* 9, no. 3 (Fall 1979): 53–89; *Il Messaggero* (Rome), 10 February 1976; Hubert O. Johnson, "Recent Opposition Movements in Iran" (Masters thesis, University of Utah, June 1975), pp. 305–20; Interviews with Dr. Paul Jureidini; *Terrorismo y Justicia en España;* Dr. Hans Josef Horchem, "West Germany: The Long March Through the Institutions," *Conflict Studies* 33 (London: Institute for the Study of Conflict, February 1973); Dr. Hans Josef Horchem, "West Germany's Red Army Anarchists," *Conflict Studies* 46 (London: Institute for the Study of Conflict, June 1974).

[13]Carlos Marighella, *For the Liberation of Brazil* (London: Cox and Wyman, 1971), pp. 74–75.

politan centers. Even in Spain this same trend is evident. There, however, although most members of the Communist FRAP are from larger cities such as Madrid or Barcelona, members of the Basque ETA-V generally come from smaller centers in the Basque region such as San Sebastián and Bilbao. In addition to an urban background, several European terrorist groups have tended to focus operations within a specific region or city of origin or in familiar nearby areas. Thus, in Italy, the Armed Proletarian Nuclei, which traditionally has operated in south and central Italy, focuses its activities in Naples, Reggio Calabria, and Rome while the Red Brigades, of northern Italian origin, have been most active in Milan, Genoa, Bologna, Turin, and Florence. Within Germany and Spain similar patterns are evident. In the Federal Republic, the Movement Two June—which originated in West Berlin—confined much of its activity to West Berlin, whereas the Baader-Meinhof organization, a group born in Frankfurt, operated primarily in the Frankfurt base area and surrounding cities. In Spain, with few exceptions, most activities of the Basque ETA-V have been in the Basque provinces and particularly the area surrounding the city of San Sebastián. In contrast, the FRAP, a group composed largely of Marxist students from Madrid and Barcelona, has tended to emphasize operations in their areas. Other identifiable patterns of this type are evident in Turkey, with the Ankara-based Turkish People's Liberation Army focusing on operations in that city, and in Iran, with the People's Strugglers and People's Sacrifice Guerrillas both stressing activities in Tehran and its environs.[14]

For the Palestinian organizations, particularly the Popular Front for the Liberation of Palestine, many members also appear to have been born in or lived for significant periods of time within major urban areas. In addition, many Palestinians, including some of those now affiliated with the PFLP, were educated abroad (in 1969 some 6,000 Palestinians were studying abroad).[15] Trained in European and various Middle Eastern universities located in such cities as Frankfurt, Stuttgart, Berlin, London, Cairo, Beirut, and Paris, these individuals were intimately familiar with urban life, normally spoke a foreign language, and were able to integrate into and live within any metropolitan area without difficulty. The success of Palestinian terrorist operations in Europe over the past four to five years attests readily to this fact.

---

[14]"El jefe de la brigada antiterrorista herido en un atentado," *Informaciones* (15 December 1976): 10; "Conmoción en Italia tras los recientes actos de terrorismo," *ABC* (16 December 1976): 27; "Tupamaro a la Italiana," *Cambio 16* (2–8 February 1976): 40–50.

[15]Barbara Anne Wilson, *Conflict in the Middle East: The Challenge of the Palestinian Movement* (Washington, DC: Center for Research in Social Systems, January 1969), pp. 20–30, 35–36.

SOCIAL AND ECONOMIC BACKGROUND[16]

In conjunction with their urban origin or long-time residence in metropolitan areas is the predominantly middle-class or even upper-class background of many terrorist cadres and leaders. A statistical review of data on arrested-identified terrorists associated with the eighteen groups mentioned earlier reflects well over two-thirds of these individuals came from the middle or upper classes in their respective nations or areas. In most instances their parents were professional people (doctors, lawyers, engineers, and so forth), governmental employees, diplomats, clergymen, military officers, or sometimes even police officials. Although these parents were part of the existing social and economic systems, many of them had been frustrated in their efforts to use them as vehicles for upward social and economic mobility. Liberal in political outlook, they also frequently advocated significant social and political change. When these parental views were coupled with the radical socioeconomic doctrines so popular in most university circles during the 1960s, this combination of forces—added to general student distrust of democratic institutions as effective media for implementing social change—may have moved some young people toward terrorism and guerrilla war as rapid methods of achieving the desired change or obtaining the power to implement such changes.

While space limitations do not permit a detailed case-by-case analysis of the more than 350 terrorists studied, even a cursory look at the background of some group leaders and cadres demonstrates their middle-class origin. Thus, in the case of the Baader-Meinhof organization and the Movement Two June in the Federal Republic of Germany, over 65 percent of the membership was from the middle class. Baader himself was the son of a historian, Meinhof the daughter of an art historian, Mahler the son of a dentist, Meins the son of a business manager, and Ensslin the daughter of a clergyman. In the Japanese Red Army a similar pattern was evident. There, even the leading female member, Shigenobu, was the daughter of an insurance executive while cadre members and leaders such as Maruoka Osamu, Hidaka Toshihiko, Nishikawa Jun, and others also were products of a middle-class environment. The same is evident among the Uruguayan Tupamaros, whose membership rarely included individuals from the working class and whose composition was over 90 percent middle- and upper-class students and young professionals. As pointed out

---

[16]See prior citations for source materials as well as Brian Crozier, ed., *Ulster: Politics and Terrorism* (London: Institute for the Study of Conflict, June 1973). See also Johnson, "Recent Opposition," pp. 259, 305, 331, 333, and the two *Conflict Studies* by Dr. Horchem.

very succinctly in November 1970 by then Uruguayan Chancellor Jorge Peirano Facio, "for each family of the upper social class there is a Tupamaro."[17] In Argentina, the same general situation prevails with members of the Trotskyite ERP and the radical Peronist Montoneros from these same general social levels. Even in areas such as Turkey, Iran, and among the Palestinian organizations, where one might expect some breakdown in the pattern, it remains generally consistent. Only in the ranks of the Provisional Wing of the Irish Republican Army is there a real deviation from the norm. To a significant degree this may result, as pointed out in several excellent studies on this organization by the London-based Institute for the Study of Conflict, from the fact that Catholic families in Northern Ireland traditionally have been relegated, by political means, to the lower economic and social levels through a process of deliberate discrimination. Accordingly, it is not surprising to find that many cadre members and the leadership within the IRA-P are not drawn from the middle and upper classes. This situation, however, stands out as almost the sole exception to an otherwise general and consistent pattern.

EDUCATION OR OCCUPATION[18]

As might be anticipated from comments made in preceding paragraphs, the vast majority of those individuals involved in terrorist activities as cadres or leaders is quite well educated. In fact, approximately two-thirds of those identified terrorists are persons with some university training, university graduates, or postgraduate students. Among the Latin American terrorist groups, particularly the Uruguayan Tupamaros and the Argentine People's Revolutionary Army and Montoneros, the figure neared 75 percent. Within even such essentially nationalist organizations as the Basque Fatherland and Liberty Movement, over 40 percent of the identified leaders and cadre members who have been arrested had some university training, and many were graduates. In the Federal Republic of Germany, the same pattern was evident with approximately 80 percent of the more than 100 identified terrorists involved in the Baader-Meinhof organization and Movement Two June having received at least some college education. For the latter group, the Free University of Berlin was a particularly fruitful recruiting ground.

---

[17]Mayans, "Los trabajos y los dias cronologia,"

[18]See also Mayans, *Tupamaros;* Johnson, "Recent Opposition," pp. 259–320, 331, 333, 334, *Arab World,* June 1973; "Secretly to Death," *Economist* (3 June 1972): 44; *Il Messaggero, Corriera della Sera, Il Giornale* (19 January 1976), *Daily American* (Rome), (20 January 1976), *Le Monde* (17 and 24 February 1972)).

Even in Turkey and Iran, university-trained terrorists were the rule rather than the exception. The Turkish People's Liberation Army, a group responsible for the March 1971 kidnapping of four U.S. Air Force airmen in Ankara and the subsequent March 1972 kidnapping and execution of three NATO technicians, was composed almost totally of students from the Middle Eastern Technical University (METU) in Ankara. Leading the TPLA group involved in this operation was Denis Gezmic, a METU graduate. Within Iran, a substantial number of those involved in terrorist activities were persons with university backgrounds. In Tehran, for example, Resa Resa'i, the 2 June 1973 assassin of U.S. Army Lt. Col. Lewis Hawkins, was a dentistry student at the time of his act. Other significant assassinations and terrorist acts in Iran, such as the attacks on the U.S. officers Price, Shaffer, and Turner, also were carried out in large part by Iranian university graduates.

For Palestinian groups, as pointed out by Dr. Paul Jureidini in his presentation on "Terrorism in the Middle East" at the Washington, DC, Conference on International Terrorism, most leading terrorist cadres are not only products of a middle-class environment but also university students or graduates. As early as 1969, as mentioned previously, over 6,000 Palestinians were studying abroad, particularly in Europe. Exposed to the Anarchist-Marxist ideas then so prevalent in European universities and active as members of the radical El Fatah-affiliated General Union of Palestinian Students (GUPS), individuals from this group constituted an important pool of educated manpower that was tapped frequently by BSO and PFLP recruiters.

Coupled with the generally high educational level of operational cadre members was an equally high level for group leaders. George Habbash, chief of the very active PFLP, is a medical doctor while his counterpart and frequent rival, Yasir Arafat, is a graduate engineer. Curcio, founder of the Italian Red Brigades, is a sociology graduate while Santucho (now deceased), former leader of the Argentine People's Revolutionary Army, was an economist, and Sendic, creator of the Tupamaros, is a lawyer. In the Federal Republic of Germany, Baader-Meinhof leader Mahler (now imprisoned) is a lawyer; Meinhof was a journalist, Ensslin and Luther teachers, and Jan-Carl Raspe a graduate sociologist. Practicing doctors and nurses also have been active terrorists in these West German groups.

Although spanning a rather wide educational spectrum, the formal training of both terrorist leaders and cadre members in most groups tended to focus on the humanities, with particular emphasis on law, history, economics, education, sociology, philosophy, and medicine. In contrast to this general arts and sciences curriculum, Iranian and Turkish terrorists tended to be educated in the more exact sciences, particularly in technical fields such as engineering. A general exception to the entire educational pattern, however, is the Provisional Wing of the Irish Republican Army, essentially for the reasons set forth in the earlier discussion of social origin. "The Provisional IRA, and the extremist Protestant groups which arose in reaction to it, are the only terrorist organizations in the world which even in their leadership have practically no intellectuals."[19]

As stated previously, particularly in regard to Latin American terrorists, the dominant occupation among these individuals is now and always has been that of student. Often in their lower twenties, Tupamaros, Montoneros, ERP members, and the various followers of Marighella frequently have conducted terrorist operations almost as a direct part of their college curricula. Operating from university centers, which by law and tradition were immune from government search, over 70 percent of the arrested-identified terrorists in Argentina and Uruguay were students, and in Brazil the percentage was well over 50. When older individuals also were active in these groups, they usually were white-collar workers and professionals such as doctors, bankers, lawyers, engineers, journalists, university professors, and mid-level government executives. Outside Latin America, although the percentage of students identified as terrorists was somewhat lower, this occupation remained important. Similarly, of the above professionals, lawyers, economists, and medical doctors were particularly prevalent among European and Middle Eastern terrorist leaders and cadres. In like manner, universities in West Berlin, Frankfurt, and Hamburg in Germany and elsewhere in Europe have served as operational bases for terrorist efforts.

METHOD AND PLACE OF RECRUITMENT[20]

Considering the important role played by students and university graduates (or dropouts) in most terrorist movements, it is not surprising that many large universities have been and now are primary recruiting grounds for operational terrorist cadres. Quite often young men and women first encounter Anarchist-Marxist doctrines upon entrance into a university where the prevalence of such concepts is often coupled with a strong Marxist bias on the part of professors and administrators. When these developments are linked with frequent Marxist domination of

---

[19]Richard Clutterbuck, *Terrorismus ohne Chance* (Stuttgart: Seewald Verlag, 1975), p. 174.

[20]See also "La universidad de la Republica y el Marxismo," *Este & Oeste* (Caracas) 14, no. 180 (October–November 1974): 1–6; "El problema de la Juventud Peronista," *Este & Oeste* (Caracas) 12, no. 177 (May 1974): 1–5: "El ERP y la subversión de Extrema Izquierda en Argentina," *Este & Oeste* (Caracas) 12, no. 177 (May 1974): 6–10.

student federations, it is not surprising that the university has become an ideological training ground for future terrorist cadres. Thus, for the Japanese Red Army, the universities of Tokyo, Rikkjo, and Kyoto have been very important. In Spain, both the Basque ETA-V and the Communist-supported FRAP have been staffed by graduates from the universities of Madrid and Barcelona. Within Italy, the universities of Rome, Turin, and Bologna are fertile recruiting grounds for Anarchist groups such as the Red Brigades. In Latin America, the National University in Montevideo, the University of Buenos Aires, and those in Brazil have supplied a substantial percentage of those individuals involved in urban terrorism. The pattern also continues in Iran, Turkey, and the Federal Republic of Germany. There, the universities in West Berlin, Frankfurt, Hamburg, Heidelberg, Munich, and Stuttgart have been the basic training centers for many German terrorist groups. Finally, even in the case of the Palestinians, many of whom were educated abroad, universities were frequent recruiting bases. Only in Northern Ireland and to some extent in the Basque ETA-V, as well as among certain Palestinian groups, is the pattern broken. In each of these cases, however, terrorist recruitment often is based on the primary appeal of nationalism rather than an Anarchist-Marxist political philosophy. For those few terrorist groups that include both intellectual and criminal elements, the place of initial recruitment for the latter is often a prison. Thus, the Italian Armed Proletarian Nuclei frequently makes initial contact with a potential terrorist while he or she is still serving a prison sentence. By facilitating the release of such an individual or providing assistance to him or her after release, APN is able to assess the individual's potential for terrorist activity. If useful to the organization, such a person often can be recruited without much difficulty. In this manner, Martino Zicchitella, the APN member killed in the 14 December 1976 assassination attempt against Rome's antiterrorist chief Alfonso Noce, apparently was drawn into the organization. The same has been true for the imprisoned Baader-Meinhof cadres whose stated objective is to politicize fellow inmates for the continued revolution once freed from confinement.[21]

POLITICAL PHILOSOPHY[22]

The question of a political philosophy is a most difficult one to treat, particularly as a category, since it defies a statistical response. Using the

---

[21]"El jefe de la brigada antiterrorista herido en un atentado," *Informaciones* (15 December 1976), p. 10.

[22]For a useful review of the political philosophy of terrorists and terrorist groups see Robert Moss, *The War for the Cities* (New York: Coward, McCann & Geoghegan Inc.,

basic definition of terrorism as a tactic used by weak groups against larger opposing forces in pursuit of political objectives, one can discard terrorism itself as meeting the criteria of a philosophy. Three basic ideological tendencies are at play among most major terrorist groups operating today: anarchism, Marxism-Leninism, and nationalism. It is the combination of these three in specific contexts that produces the variant left-extremist philosophies espoused by most terrorists today. Nationalism is rarely an important ingredient in such views. Of the eighteen organizations studied, it can be considered significant only in the case of three: the Basque ETA-V, the Irish Republican Army, and the Popular Front for the Liberation of Palestine. Even in these groups, however, it is strongly blended with Marxism. For most other organizations, such as the Japanese Red Army, the West German Baader-Meinhof Gang,[23] and the Movement Two June, the mixture is a combination of anarchism and Marxism with the latter as a predominant element.

Although basically Marxist, the majority of terrorist organizations today rejects the passive outlook of orthodox Soviet communism in favor of the revolutionary violence advocated by Marighella. In return, the orthodox Communists normally reject terrorists as bourgeois gangsters who lack a political foundation and have abandoned the tested social and political Communist party structure in favor of shortsighted and often counterproductive hooliganism. Accordingly, it should be no surprise that those terrorists discussed in this profile related more closely with the Trotskyite Fourth International than Soviet communism. "Trotsky's theory of 'permanent revolution' emphasizes, in its international aspects, the global nature of the phenomenon, the necessary links between revolution in one country with that elsewhere. Ethnic, cultural, and national distinctions will on this thesis be unable to withstand the revolutionary tide. . . ."[24] Thus, in the final analysis, the philosophical underpinnings of most modern terrorist groups may be found in a loose synthesis of the views developed by Mao, Trotsky, Marcuse, Fanon, and particularly those of Marighella.

In summation, one can draw a general composite picture into which fit the great majority of those terrorists from the eighteen urban guerrilla

---

1972), chap. 1 "The City and Revolution, Political Violence in Western Societies and the Roots of Revolution," pp. 17–30; Edward Hyams, *Terrorists and Terrorism* (New York: St. Martin's Press, 1974), pt I, "The Theorists," specifically chap. 1 through 4; and Paul Wilkenson, *Political Terrorism* (London: MacMillan Press Ltd., 1974), chap. 1 through 3.

[23]For detailed information on the political views of the Baader-Meinhof organization and leadership see *Dokumentation über Aktivitäten anarchistischer Gewalttäter in der Bundesrepublik Deutschland* (Documents on Anarchist Criminals in the Federal Republic of Germany), a compendium of confiscated Baader-Meinhof writings seized during raids on terrorists' cells in July 1973 and on 4 February 1974, published by the German Interior Ministry (in German) during 1974.

[24]Anthony Burton, *Urban Terrorism: Theory, Practice and Response* (New York: Free Press of Glencoe, 1976), p. 109.

groups examined here. To this point, they have been largely single males aged 22 to 24, with exceptions as previously noted, who have some university education, if not a college degree. The female terrorists, except for the West German groups and an occasional leading figure in the IRA, JRA, and PFLP, are preoccupied with support rather than operational roles. More often than not, these urban terrorists come from affluent, urban, middle-class families, many of whom enjoy considerable social prestige. Like their parents before them, many of the older terrorists have been trained for the medical, legal, engineering, and teaching professions, among others, and may have practiced these occupations prior to their commitment to a terrorist life. Whether having turned to terrorism as a university student or only later, most were provided an Anarchist or Marxist world view, as well as recruited into terrorist operations while in the university. It is within the universities that these young products of an affluent society were initially confronted with and provided Anarchist or Marxist ideological underpinnings for their otherwise unstructured frustrations and idealism.

While no international trend is as yet readily discernible, there are indicators that in a number of countries including Argentina, West Germany, Iran, and Spain, as well as the region of Northern Ireland, urban terrorist groups—or the phenomenon of urban terrorism itself—is recruiting younger and younger adherents. Increasing numbers also are drawn from those who are undergoing vocational training in preparation for work in skilled trades—electrician, gunsmith, mechanic, and printer—many of which are readily adaptable to terrorist requirements. To what extent this development may alter the composite picture sketched in this paper is a question deserving additional research and attention.

Infrastructures of Terrorist Organizations*

J. K. ZAWODNY

The purpose of this paper is to answer three questions: What is the main characteristic of terrorist organizations that affects their infrastructure? What does the infrastructure look like? How does this infrastructure affect the behavior of terrorists, on the analytical level of group dynamics?[1] Infrastructure in this context means an internal organizational structure, including formal and informal networks within that structure. It is this writer's thesis that this structure affects the behavior and activities of terrorists.

The data comes from nonclassified, open sources in five languages dealing with active terrorist movements in the United States and abroad, as of 1980. Since it is impossible, for security reasons, to acquire reliable information from first-hand interviews with terrorists, this paper relies on scattered data which in many instances defies verification. Nonetheless, for someone like this writer, who had five years of combat service as an urban guerrilla during World War II, the data provides a sufficient basis for conclusions to be drawn from uniformly present characteristics across several cultures.

WHAT IS THE MAIN CHARACTERISTIC OF TERRORIST ORGANIZATIONS THAT AFFECTS THEIR INFRASTRUCTURE?

The relatively small size of the group is the primary characteristic of a terrorist organization. By contrast, the European underground movements, so well developed during World War II and so efficient in their

---

*A revised version of the paper presented at the conference, "Psychopathology and Political Violence: Terrorism and Assassination," sponsored by the Institute of Social and Behavioral Pathology and the University of Chicago Department of Psychiatry, Chicago, Illinois, 16–17 November 1979.
[1]Those interested in motivational factors of an individual in regard to violence may refer to works by Bandura, Berkovitz, Ebbesen, Lawrence Z. Freedman, Freud, Hacker, Hokanson, Lorenz, Rutherford, and Walters.

systematic terrorist activities, were according to any standards huge organizations. For example, the Polish Underground Movement (*Armia Krajowa*) in 1944 had over 380,000 front-line troops plus at least an equal number of support members, totaling 760,000 people. The membership of the Italian Resistance was somewhere between 150,000–200,000; the French Forces of the Interior (FFI) for the northern and southern zones, about 425,000. Both effective management of the flow of communications up and down the chain of command and maintenance of the security for such masses of those involved demanded establishment of a rigid, hierarchical organizational structure patterned on military models. The smallest unit was a section of three to six persons; the members knew each other only by pseudonyms. In addition to his men, the leader of a section knew only four to six other section leaders of his platoon and his platoon commander. A platoon commander, usually a noncommissioned officer or a cadet, knew the section leaders of his platoon, the other platoon commanders, and his company commander. The company commander, usually a second or first lieutenant, knew only his platoon leaders, other company commanders, and his battalion commander, and so on up the ladder. Limiting the contacts and the circle within which each person interacted provided maximum security for those involved. However, this system made the process of communication slow. For an order from central headquarters to reach a private in a section, it had to descend through each level of the organization.[2]

In the United States, twelve to sixteen groups presently aspire to revolutionary change by violent means. Membership in each of them does not exceed forty to fifty people.[3] The Red Brigades in Italy are estimated by their own membership to number from four hundred to ten thousand, depending on who is counting and whether the sympathizers, who do not handle weapons, are also included. The Baader-Meinhof Gang was composed of approximately one hundred members. The Japanese Red Army fluctuates between thirty and forty members; the Palestinian group El Ansar, less than two hundred; Action Organization for the Liberation of Palestine, less than three hundred.

---

[2]In an urban setting, it took at least two to three days for an order from the commander in chief to reach a private in a section; an example was the order for mobilization to start the Uprising of Warsaw in 1944. This hierarchical organizational framework, cumbersome as it was, seemed the best under the circumstances when members numbered hundreds of thousands.

[3]Speech by William H. Webster, Director of the Federal Bureau of Investigation, at the World Affairs Council, Los Angeles, California, 27 November 1979.

WHAT DOES THE INFRASTRUCTURE LOOK LIKE?

A division of labor takes place among terrorists, and some structure is needed to channel communication and to coordinate activities. The small size of these groups imposes on them an infrastructure quite different from those of underground movements during World War II. On the basis of thirty years of studies of extralegal violent organizations, this writer would describe the typical contemporary terrorist infrastructure as centrifugal.

This centrifugal infrastructure resembles that of a solar system: the leader is the sun, and the members are surrounding planets, usually within the range of his direct impact. Thus, in the hierarchical system, the leader is at the top; in the centrifugal system, the leader is, so to speak, in the center. This arrangement has great consequences on the behavior of terrorists.

HOW DOES THIS INFRASTRUCTURE
AFFECT THE BEHAVIOR OF TERRORISTS?

Eleven patterns which are the direct results of centrifugal infrastructures are submitted here: ten are distinctly different from the behavior of hierarchical organizations, and one points to similarity.

1) The leaders of terrorist movements, by virtue of being in the center of their organizations, not only act as direct catalysts of actions, by planning and giving orders, but they are also participants in the actions. This arrangement is extremely important to the rank and file. Such an organizational structure provides the leaders with a high degree of visibility. They suffer equally with their fellow members all the consequences of action, including wounds and death. They share psychological stress beforehand and periods of decompression after action, with all its misery, floating anxieties, and tensions. These kinds of shared experiences build more intensely personalized loyalties than are characteristic in hierarchical organizations.

2) The centrifugal system secures more direct and rapid communication. This increases flexibility of action and success in combat operations, by allowing the leader himself to reassess the feasibility of an action on the basis of new and personally ascertained information. Moreover, it removes a common anxiety-producing dilemma among low-ranking leaders of a hierarchical organization: being required to execute a

plan that has been rendered unfeasible due to changed circumstances. Under these conditions, such leaders, as a rule, go ahead with the action, fearful of charges of disobeying orders, or of what to them is a worse punishment, criticism and ostracism by their peers.

3) Direct accessibility to the leader enables him to tap and react immediately to the most ingenious schemes conceived and the location of targets reported by rank and file. This further enhances tactical flexibility and allows terrorist groups to operate against targets of opportunity, a factor that is particularly important given the asymmetrical power relationship existing between the terrorists and the government they are attacking.

4) Another important feature of the centrifugal infrastructure is its independence from society's support. The hierarchical organization, by virtue of its very size and complexity, cannot exist without extensive social support. Moreover, it takes one to two years to develop such a complex network. By contrast, the centrifugal system is so small that it can exist independently of support networks; it is so mobile that it can be relocated quickly. But, above all, it can be created and mobilized instantaneously. Such a system has no files, no records, and no bureaucracy hindering its activities. An organization so independent of society that it has no fear of society's response presents a dangerous situation—the terrorists operate under no constraints.

In the case of a hierarchical organization, public opinion can hinder recruitment, thus causing its collapse. In a centrifugal system, the leader does not need public sentiment to provide adherents; he needs only the loyalty of his immediate followers. Even progressive annihilation of the immediate environment will not affect the physical integrity of a centrifugal unit—it will move to another area. During the five years of World War II, Polish society daily lost an average of three thousand people, killed by the Germans occupying central and western Poland.[4] This bloodletting had an immense effect on the structure of the Polish Underground. Under these circumstances, centrifugal organizations would remain relatively unaffected.

5) Direct access to the leader by the rank and file allows the latter to identify with the power of mythical and magical qualities usually attributed to the former and, as such, enables the followers to participate in his charisma.[5] The father-figure image, so eagerly instilled by leaders

---

[4]Eastern Poland was occupied by the Soviet army from September 1939 until the outbreak of war between Germany and the Soviet Union in June 1941.

[5]This writer knows from personal experience how prone under stress human beings are to ascribe magical qualities to their leaders. He remembers one incident, which illustrates the point, while he served as a second lieutenant and platoon leader of Polish insurgents in the Uprising of Warsaw in 1944. When women soldiers of his platoon had to leave the shelter of ruined buildings during the night for biological needs, they would invariably ask

among members, is reinforced; during Castro's early revolutionary activity, his Cuban followers sang a ditty: "Eisenhower, ha, ha, ha, Fidel Castro your papa!" Moreover, leaders have the opportunity to give direct moral dispensation for deeds which might otherwise be repudiated by certain standards of society or by the early upbringing of members. All these factors are helpful in freeing the members of internal dilemmas and in giving them self-images of heroes with a unity of purpose.

6) The leader also is directly involved in the selection and recruitment of new members to the group. The leader's personal role in recruitment is usually so magnetic and ego-gratifying to incoming members that such recruitment to the centrifugal organization is not related to the prospects of success of the organization. There too is some evidence that motivation behind joining a centrifugal organization is much less related to perception of threat than was the case with underground organizations in World War II.

7) Centrifugal groups tend to seek cooperation and allies not with stronger groups, but with those whom they can easily manipulate. Consequently, they coalesce on the peer level and are extremely wary of any involvements which may be powerful enough to impose demands on them and thus curb freedom of their activities. The major powers have perceived this tendency and have assisted terrorists indirectly, through smaller states: e.g., Czechoslovakia, North Korea, Cuba, Bulgaria, East Germany, Hungary, Iraq, and Syria. The countries of Algeria, Yemen, Libya, Uganda, Saudi Arabia, and Cyprus also have been involved in assisting and, in many instances, providing cover for the major or original sources of support.

This inclination of centrifugal terrorist organizations to ally with their peers has led to the development of informal networks and has influenced both training and operations. Both German and Japanese terrorists have received training in camps run by various Palestinian groups, and several leaders of Italy's Red Brigades were trained in Czechoslovakia. In one of the best known terrorist episodes, three members of the Japanese Red Army attacked Lod Airport outside Tel-Aviv in 1972 on behalf of the Palestinians, one faction of which—the Popular Front for the Liberation of Palestine—had provided them their training in Lebanon. Members of the Baader-Meinhof Gang helped hijack

---

him to escort them out "to protect them against artillery." It was true that the German artillery and mortars were pounding insurgents day and night, but it was also true that his presence against artillery explosions was absolutely useless. Yet, night after night his sleep was interrupted several times. He left the protection of the basement, to stand discreetly aside, waiting for the women to come back, meanwhile readying himself for death under these rather peculiar circumstances. The handling of his own fears was equally irrational. Whenever he was called to "go out," he would take along his machine pistol—mere psychological reassurance in that situation.

a French airliner bound for Israel and forced it to fly to Entebbe. Police have also established links between the Baader-Meinhof Gang and the Venezuelan terrorist "Carlos," the Red Brigades, and the Japanese Red Army.

In 1974, several representatives from terrorist organizations, including Basques, Irish, Croatians, Bretons, Welsh, and Catalans, gathered to discuss their mutual needs. Also in 1974, representatives of terrorist groups from Uruguay, Bolivia, and Chile met in Buenos Aires to establish a junta for revolutionary coordination. Paraguayans, Dominicans, Colombians, and Venezuelans joined the junta. Mutual exchanges of trained personnel, weapons, and money followed.[6] According to at least one source, it is reported that Libya, Iraq, and South Yemen provide money, weapons, and sanctuary for terrorist groups.[7]

8) Comparing the centrifugal vis-à-vis hierarchical extralegal violent organizations, this writer attempted also to ascertain to what degree the members of the centrifugal organization are able to maintain their anonymity. Presumably, this should be difficult in view of their direct accessibility to the leader. Anonymity is an important determining factor of terrorist behavior, because the less identity a terrorist has within the group, the less he feels personally responsible toward outsiders for the actions of the group. However, it was not possible to find sufficiently reliable data to submit to the reader any sound generalization.

9) There seems to be in all types of human organizations the need for the establishment of a working network within which, in time, a certain bureaucratic "bloat" takes place. Comparative studies of French, Italian, Polish, Soviet, and Vietnamese hierarchical clandestine organizations indicate over time the presence in their structures of these two bureaucratic phenomena: an increase in numbers of bureaucrats in excess of actual need; and the Peter Principle, or movement upward on the administrative ladder to the point where one reaches one's maximum level of incompetence.

This phenomenon is particularly true in hierarchical organizations. After World War II, the bureaucracy of the British Admiralty grew from 2000 to 3569 officials, while the Royal Navy's uniformed manpower decreased by one third and the number of ships in commission decreased by two thirds. A New York Police Department study in 1974 indicated that the force had grown by 55 percent over twenty years, but the number

---

[6]D. Anable, "Terrorism—Loose Net Links, Diverse Groups, No Central Plot," in John D. Elliot and Leslie K. Gibson, *Contemporary Terrorism* (Gaithersburg, MD: Bureau of Operations and Research, International Association of Chiefs of Police, 1978), *passim*.
    [7]Ibid., *passim*.

of policemen on the beat or cruising in cars remained the same. In 1974, the Italian Navy had more admirals than ships and one general for five thousand troops. In the same year, a French general or admiral commanded an average of seventeen hundred men.[8] Hierarchical clandestine organizations also are subject to considerable bloating, with a proliferation of secretaries, messengers, and bodyguards. There is no bloating in centrifugal organizations for two reason: such bloating would hamper the leader's direct exercise of power, and the small size of the organization mitigates against it. The result is enhanced efficiency.

10) The leader's direct control over membership is tremendously enhanced in centrifugal organizations. During World War II, the commander of the Resistance in Milan, when asked about the membership of his units and his control over them, said: "Six hundred if things are difficult, six thousand if things are not so difficult, and of course sixty thousand if things are easy."[9] This is not the case within the centrifugal system; here, members are within the direct range of the leader's vision. Control is exercised speedily and without mercy. As a result, it is much easier to join a terrorist organization than to withdraw from it.

11) Finally, one important similarity between hierarchical and centrifugal organizations should be mentioned. When either type of organization is threatened by stresses from within, their respective leaders will use external violence as a means of keeping the membership together. In other words, internal problems of the organization often serve as catalysts of external violence.[10] There are examples of this phenomenon, but, for understandable reasons, they are very difficult to prove and never officially admitted. Many actions have been ordered when there was no tactical, strategic, or political reason for using violence, except to fulfill the need perceived by a leader: either to distract the membership from internal problems, to restore cohesion, or for the leader's personal reasons, known only to him. These actions are always carried out under the label of a great cause.

Considering these eleven behavioral characteristics of contemporary terrorist organizations that are directly related to their infrastructure, what can we infer about trends for the future? First of all, according to statistics, the curve of frequency of world-wide attacks defies prognosis.

---

[8]Rafael Steinberg, *Man and the Organization* (Alexandria, VA: Time-Life Books, 1975), p. 77.

[9]Massimo Salvatori-Paleotti, "The Patriot Movement in Italy," *Foreign Affairs* 24 (April 1946): 545.

[10]See J. K. Zawodny, "Internal Organizational Problems and the Sources of Tensions of Terrorist Movements as Catalysts of Violence," *Terrorism: An International Journal* 1, nos. 3, 4 (1978): 277–85.

Frequency of Terrorist Attacks, 1968–78

Year	No. of Incidents
1968	111
1969	166
1970	282
1971	216
1972	269
1973	275
1974	382
1975	297
1976	413
1977	279
1978	353
	3,043 Total

It is safe to assume that many more incidents were not reported. During the same period, the total number of people killed by terrorists was 2,102; the wounded numbered 5,078. On the other hand, figures for the United States and Canada for the period 1975–78 show a steady decrease in the number of terrorist incidents.[11] It is not necessarily correct, however, to conclude that the diminishing frequency of terrorist activities in this country has decreased the threat of terrorism to society. In fact, as much, if not more, harm is resulting from greater selectivity and sensitivity in choosing objects of attack.

It might be useful to readers to take a closer look at the domestic situation. By any criteria, we Americans live in an extremely violent culture. In 1978, there was one murder every 27 minutes. In the same year, one million violent acts were committed.[12] We are subjected daily to violence in the media. In 1973, 70 percent of programs on television depicted acts of violence.[13] By the time an average American youngster reaches his eighteenth birthday, he will have witnessed 18 thousand murders on television.[14] Undoubtedly, this has some effect on our capacity to accept violence as a problem-solving mechanism, and sensitivities toward the sanctity of human life are dulled by such exposure. The rate of

---

[11]National Foreign Assessment Center, *International Terrorism in 1978: A Research Paper* (Information as of 14 January 1979), RP79-10149, March 1979, *passim*. U.S.-Canadian figures, 1975–78, are 51 in 1975, 37 in 1976, 23 in 1977, and 19 in 1978.

[12]Presentation by Steven Gremminger, International Affairs Staff, Law Enforcement Assistance Administration, U.S. Department of Justice, "Research on Terrorism: An Overview," at the conference, "Psychopathology and Political Violence: Terrorism and Assassination," Chicago, 16–17 November 1979.

[13]Ronald H. Bailey, *Violence and Aggression* (Alexandria, VA: Time-Life Books, 1977), p. 61.

[14]Ibid., p. 61.

homicides has been climbing consistently since 1963.[15] The sex of the perpetrators of violence also reflects cultural values—four out of five homicides and nine out of ten robberies in the United States are committed by males, although the rate of increase in female participation in violent acts is increasing more rapidly than that for men.[16]

The large number of illegal aliens in the United States also is relevant as a potential source of violence. Estimated to be between 6 and 12 million, they come from fifty-one nations. Their illegal entry into this country makes them vulnerable to police harassment and provides fertile ground for illegal organized violence. Some scientists speculate that the perception of threat can easily induce human beings to violent aggressive behavior.

Thus, the question is raised: in light of the high visibility of violence and the potential for violence in the United States, why do we have so relatively few and small terrorist groups, and why are their activities diminishing? A reason is that, with all the shortcomings of our democratic procedures, our political system provides two ways in which violence is diffused prophylactically before it emerges. The first is the vast network of formal and informal channels through which grievances can be voiced and, at least, given the impression of being considered. The terrorist usually "shoots in the direction from which there is no hope"; in our system, there always seems to be an alternative action promising hope for peaceful settlement of grievances. The second way involves the abundance of opportunities to exercise a relatively high degree of violence without repercussions from society, such as restraint or punishment. Catharsis is provided by sublimation, transference, and diffusion of violent aggression in such socially acceptable modes as sports, televised dramatic violence, and the news media.

The question remains: How to combat terrorism? One may follow the French scientist, Henri Laborit, who maintains that to deal with human violence in general, "a start must be made . . . [to see] that society's rewards no longer go to its least compassionate members. There is no other way . . . to avoid . . . violence, exploitation, warfare, and genocide. Up to the present, humanism itself has always been in the service of predatory groups that seek to dominate others and are convinced of their right to do so: it has never served the human race as a whole."[17]

One may say that such a statement is for dreamers, and that present-day policymakers are concerned with suppression of terrorism in order to

---

[15]Ibid., p. 16 and *passim*.
[16]Ibid., p. 27.
[17]Henri Laborit, "The Biological and Sociological Mechanisms of Aggression," *International Social Science Journal* 30, no. 4 (1978): 746–47.

secure and preserve democratic procedures and processes for settling social grievances. This writer understands their position and their concern and can only suggest keeping in mind that "a terrorist may be completely wrong about what he is fighting for, but he is not likely to be so wrong about what he is fighting against."

Women as Terrorists

DANIEL E. GEORGES-ABEYIE

Twenty-four Sandinista guerrillas struck Nicaragua's National Palace in Managua at midday in late August 1979. Their leader was Commandante Zero, the forty-two-year-old student-turned-revolutionary, Eden Pastora Gomez; the second in command appeared to be twenty-two-year-old Commandante Two, Dora Maria Telles Arguello. Thus for the second time within one year, a woman terrorist seized world attention, and again the question arose, how prominent are women as terrorists?[1]

With a few notable exceptions, women have played a relatively minor role in terrorist violence in the last thirty years, although conditions now are favorable for their greater involvement as free-lance nonmovement-oriented terrorists as well as members of terrorist organizations. The first type refers to the individuals who commit terrorist acts, yet are not members of terrorist groups.

There is no universally accepted definition of terrorist violence, as opposed to certain types of collective and criminal violence that at times are labeled nonpolitical or quasi-terrorist. For the sake of uniformity in approach and clarity, let us accept the definitions of political (true) terrorism, nonpolitical terrorism, and quasi-terrorism offered in the report on terrorism by the National Advisory Committee on Criminal Justice Standards and Goals. More specifically, let us focus on those types of incidents which the report has labelled political terrorism:

> violent, criminal behavior designed primarily to generate fear in the community, or a substantial segment of it, for political purposes. Excluded from this definition are acts or threats of a purely personal

---

[1]The first instance occurred earlier in 1979; a woman terrorist, apparently the *ad hoc* leader of an ill-fated El Fatah raid which had lost its male commander before even setting foot on Israeli land, or Israeli-occupied territory, was killed in a blazing gun battle in a bus on the outskirts of Tel Aviv. The year 1980 was highlighted by a hostage situation in which the U.S. Ambassador to Colombia, along with other high-ranking diplomats, was held hostage by leftist M-19 guerrillas. A woman guerrilla appeared to play a major role in the actual hostage negotiation process.

character and those which are psychopathological and have no intended sociopolitical significance.[2]

Included in this definition is the threat as well as the actualization of criminal violence. Of essence, in regard to this definition and its application as a guide to the study of women as terrorists, is the utilization of criminal violence or the threat of criminal violence as a means to change governmental policy, if not the government itself.

Information on women as terrorists is sketchy at best. Walter Laqueur takes cognizance of the fact that women have participated in almost all guerrilla movements but have been most prominent in small urban guerrilla groups in the United States and West Germany, and particularly in Korea, where they constituted more than a quarter of the Communist revolutionary cadre.[3] W. Middendorff and D. Middendorff note the dearth of reliable criminological studies of German terrorists and suggest two reasons for this absence of information:

> firstly because there are not enough terrorists to enable statistical empirical research and secondly because the terrorists constantly resist any psychological and psychiatric examination, and they completely refuse to answer any questions. . . .[4]

Charles A. Russell and Bowman H. Miller's excellent study in this volume provides one of the most comprehensive reviews of variables associated with terrorism.

Various mass-media sources as well as social-control sources, primarily the Federal Bureau of Investigation (FBI) and the International

---

[2]National Advisory Committee on Criminal Justice Standards and Goals, *Report on Civil Disorders and Terrorism* (Washington, DC: Government Printing Office, 1976), pp. 3–6. The committee defined nonpolitical terrorism as acts that exhibit a conscious design to create and maintain a high degree of fear for coercive processes, but the end of which is individual or collective gain rather than achievement of a political objective. Quasiterrorism is a description applied to those activities incidental to the commission of crimes of violence that are similar in form and method to true terrorism but lack its essential ingredient, the true political motive. The following works also explore the definitional parameters of the terms terrorist, guerrilla, and insurrectionist: Walter Laqueur, *Guerrilla* (Boston, 1976); S. Sarkesian., ed., *Revolutionary Guerrilla Warfare* (Chicago, 1975); Y. Alexander and S. Finger, eds., *Terrorism: Interdisciplinary Perspectives* (New York, 1977). See also U.S., House of Representatives, 93rd Cong., 2d Sess., 1 August 1974, Committee on Internal Security, *Terrorism* (Washington, DC: Government Printing Office).

[3]Laqueur, *Guerrilla*, p. 398. No distinct break exists between terrorism and guerrilla warfare; some may argue that the two forms of violence vary in regard to object of attack (there being no clear distinction between civilian and noncivilian guerrilla campaigns in the military or police forces) or in regard to goals. A terrorist campaign attempts to change one or more government policies, while a guerrilla campaign attempts to control territory and ultimately topple the present government.

[4]W. Middendorff and D. Middendorff, "Changing Patterns of Female Criminality," mimeograph (Freiburg, n.d.).

Association of Chiefs of Police (IACP), also concluded that women have played a relatively secondary role in terrorist violence, as well as in terrorist groups, although there have been some notable exceptions.[5] These exceptions are discussed by Russell and Miller, who note that women have occupied an important position in West German terrorist movements, especially in the Baader-Meinhof organization and the Movement Two June where they have constituted one-third of the operational personnel.

Other exceptions to the relatively low-level participation of women as terrorist leaders or as members of terrorist groups include:

1) Leila Khalid and Fusako Shigenobu, leaders in the Popular Front for the Liberation of Palestine (PFLP) and the Japanese Red Army (JRA), respectively. Together they were instrumental in arranging the initial PFLP training of JRA and West German cadres in Lebanon during the early 1970s.

2) Ellen Mary Margaret McKearney, a runner for the Irish Republican Army (IRA) bombers operating in England.

3) Norma Ester Arostito, cofounder of the Argentine Montoneros. She also served as their chief ideologue until her death in 1976.

4) Genoveve Forest Tarat, who played a key role in the 12 December 1973 Basque Fatherland and Liberty Movement (ETA-V) operation that resulted in the assassination of Spanish Premier Admiral Carrero Blanco. She also participated in the 13 September 1974 bombing of a Madrid restaurant, the Café Rolando, which resulted in eleven dead and seventy wounded.

5) Margherita Cagol, the now-deceased wife of Italian Red Brigades leader Renato Curcio, who played an important role in the organization and quite possibly led the Red Brigades commando team that freed Curcio from Rome's Casale Monferrato jail on 8 February 1975.

6) Bernardine (Bernadette) Rae Dohrn, active in the Weather Underground (WU).

7) Mario Torres, wife of Carlos Torres, of the Armed Forces of National Liberation (FALN). They were possibly coleaders and cofounders of this Puerto Rican movement.

8) The Symbionese Liberation Army (SLA) women, including Angela Atwood, Camilla Christine Hall, Emily Mantague Schwartz Harris, Nancy Ling Perry, Mary Alice Landles, and Patricia Solytsik (alias Mizmoon-Zoya). The latter is believed to be the theoretician and homosexual lover of Camilla Hall. Both the FBI and the IACP contend that the SLA, like the Weather Underground, was an organization in

---

[5]Federal Bureau of Investigation, *Uniform Crime Reports* (Washington, DC: U.S. Department of Justice, 1977). In 1978 the FBI noted that the percent change for violent crime perpetrated by women over the time span 1968–77 was +72.0, while the respective percent change for property crime was +121.3.

which homosexuality–bisexuality and pansexuality were common, characteristics present in both the ideology and practice within middle-class terrorist organizations with considerable white female input. The homosexual relationship between Hall and Solytsik is cited as an example of homosexual/feminist orientation common within American white terrorist organizations. The SLA history also reveals a tie between white radical support of black prisoner organizations, a vague anarchic-socialist political economic orientation, feminism, and gay rights.

The Weather Underground, a group splintered from the Students for a Democratic Society (SDS), included Dohrn, one of America's most sought-after terrorists.[6] Of special interest is the fact that women factions within the WU became quite powerful and, in fact, moved into the leadership of that organization. The WU also openly espoused the need for the decline of the nuclear family and for homosexual love—both physical and emotional—to free women from male psychic and physical domination. The Weather Underground, like the SLA, espoused and practiced a program of extreme feminism, homosexuality-bisexuality, gay rights, and socialism.

Chart 1 reveals by region and country terrorist groups that either had female leadership or a sizable female component in their cadres.

**Chart 1. Terrorist Organizations with Women as Leaders
or Sizable Numbers of Women as Cadre***

North America
United States

Symbionese Liberation Army (SLA)	Extremist	Inactive after May 1974
Armed Forces of National Liberation (FALN)	Puerto Rican Separatist	Active
Weather Underground (WU)	Extremist	Active

South America
Argentina

Fuerzas Armed Revolutionaries (FAR)	Peronist	Merged with Montoneros in 1973 making strongest Peronist group
Montoneros	Peronist	Active with FAR

---

[6]H. Jacobs, ed., *Weathermen* (Palo Alto, CA, 1971). Another source on the Weathermen is U.S., Senate, 94th Cong., 1st Sess., January 1975, Committee on the Judiciary, *The Weather Underground: Report of the Sub-Committee to Investigate the Administration of the Internal Security Laws* (Washington, DC: Government Printing Office).

*Sizable number of women cadre does not mean that the female membership exceeds one-third; in most cases the women constitute less than one-fifth of the active membership.

Chart 1 (continued)

Uruguay

Tupamaros or Movimento de Liberaction Nacional (MLN)	Castroite, now eclectic	Broken up by security forces but formed links with guerrillas in neighboring communities—Inactive in 1976

Europe
Great Britain

Angry Brigade	Extremist	Defunct

Ireland

Irish Republican Army (IRA) Provisional wings	Catholic nationalist but officially under Marxist control	Active in shootings and bombings

Italy

Red Brigades or Brigate Rosse	Maoist	Active in street violence

Spain

Euzkadita Azkatasuna (ETA)	Basque Separatist	Active (approximate strength 200)

West Germany

Movement Two June	Left-Wing Anarchist	Active
Red Army Faction	Left-Wing Anarchist	Active

Source: Compilation of information gathered from an extensive review of mass-media data, discussions with officials in the FBI, state and local police, and federal government officials.

All of these groups were Marxist or Anarchist oriented even when primarily nationalistic in regard to propaganda. Considerable female input in terrorist groups, though often apparent in nations with strong feminist movements, is not confined to such nations; for example, Spain, Argentina, Uruguay, Italy, and Northern Ireland lack a strong feminist tradition yet have had considerable feminist input in terrorist organizations. Role-set instability tied to economic progress—the stage of industrialization—also appears to be as relevant as feminism as an associative variable tied to women as terrorists. We must note, however, that such technologically backward societies as pre-Communist Korea also had significant numbers of female cadres. Thus, a multidimensional perspective is called for when identifying causative and associative variables linked with significant female input in terrorist organizations.

Before citing explanations for female membership in contemporary terrorist groups, we should note too that women have played a role in revolutionary and terrorist violence in the past. The following section provides a brief introduction to past incidents of terrorism by women.

FEMALE INVOLVEMENT IN TERRORIST ACTS AND GROUPS: THE PAST

According to Middendorff and Middendorff, terrorism and political murder are old forms of criminality, and female participation, at least in isolated instances, is not all that new. These two authors discuss the position that women have held in Russian revolutionary and terrorist violence.[7] R. Gaucher points out that women played an important role in all Russian revolutionary organizations, and not only in the areas of propaganda, organization, liaison, information, and assistance: some took a direct part in terrorism.[8] Included are four examples of violent revolutionary activities perpetrated by women, as cited by Gaucher and Middendorff and Middendorff: Tatiana Leontiev's assassination in Switzerland of a Frenchman whom she believed to be the Russian minister of the interior; Lydia Sture's attempted shooting of a policeman who tried to arrest her; Vera Zasulich's attempted assassination of Governor Trepov; and Vera Figner's laying of mines along a route to be taken by the czar.

Thus, one can note isolated instances of terrorist violence by women, if we examine the literature and the times of the great revolutionary upheavals. But these were isolated instances of primarily middle-class women engaged in revolutionary or terrorist violence. This class factor is a variable that holds in contemporary times as well, if we exclude the primarily lower-class nationalistic struggles of the Irish Catholics in Northern Ireland, the Basque revolutionaries in Northern Spain, and the various nationalistic struggles of East, South, and Central Africa, as demonstrated in FRELIMO's struggle in Mozambique; UNITA, MPLA, and other revolutionary groups in Angola; and the various revolutionary groups that comprised the Patriotic Front in Zimbabwe.

Middendorff and Middendorff's excellent review of changing patterns of female criminality also highlights many of the similarities and some of the differences which exist between past and contemporary female terrorists. Their comparison of Russian revolutionary women of the pre-World War I period and the German terrorists of today brings out three points: both groups of terrorists were ideologists and tried to change

---

[7]Middendorff and Middendorff, "Changing Patterns," p. 4.
[8]R. Gaucher, *The Terrorists* (Great Britain, 1968), pp. 54, 55.

the course of history, although without success; both groups were from middle- and upper-class families; and the Russian terrorist's demeanor in court was refined, courageous, and dignified, while the German terrorist in court exhibited extreme hostility, profanity, and discourtesy.[9]

EXPLANATIONS FOR FEMALE MEMBERSHIP IN
TERRORIST ORGANIZATIONS

Many varied, and at times, extreme explanations have been offered for female involvement in terrorist activities. Here are the most common: 1) revolutionary and terrorist activity offers excitement; 2) danger is both an attraction as well as a repellant; 3) terrorist violence is tied to causes which initially may appear legitimate; 4) terrorist organizations provide an opportunity for upward mobility, in leadership and in an active role in formulating the group's policies, opportunities that are absent or extremely limited in the white male-dominated world of legitimate activity; 5) terrorist organizations offer change and a renunciation of the current male-dominated chauvinistic mores; 6) the traditional American stereotype of women as weak, supportive, submissive, silent, and of lower intelligence and drive is absent in the philosophies of many terrorist organizations; 7) membership in a terrorist organization is the natural outgrowth of membership in extreme feminist organizations; 8) women are by nature more violent and dangerous than men, and terrorist organizations provide an outlet for this tendency; 9) women are rejecting stereotypic roles and thus adopting traditional male roles that include revolutionary and terrorist violence; 10) hormonal disturbances, caused by excessive sexual freedom and particularly by having sexual relations before maturity, affect these women; 11) economic, political, and familial liberation due to the trend toward greater justice and equality for women plays a role; 12) a continuation of natural selection, or the survival of the fittest, has an influence; 13) middle-class white Anglo-Saxon Protestant (WASP) restraints, in regard to mind-sets (ideas and attitudes) as well as behavior, are rejected.

Many of these explanations appear extreme and even laughable. But, perhaps, there is some merit to a less extreme interpretation of some of the correlates to these and other theories of this specific form of female criminality. There can be little doubt that the North American and Western European terrorist organizations with female leadership or sizable numbers of female cadres proselytized female homosexuality and bisexuality as well as pansexualism and feminist ideology—factors not

---

[9]Middendorff and Middendorff, "Changing Patterns," p. 5.

present in most South American, African, Asian, and Eastern European terrorist groups. We must not, however, confuse associative factors for causal models. Unfortunately, the data in respect to female involvement in terrorist and guerrilla organizations is rudimentary at best. Each of the above-cited explanations can and should be developed into hypotheses and tested by means of various social science research techniques. Several of the previously cited explanations grounded in the changing socio-economic role-set ascribed to women offer fruitful areas for social science research. This writer would also contend that terrorism by women may, in part, be tied to the same systemic structural-funtional changes in society that have brought about uncertainty in female role-sets and a possible increase in female criminality in general.

WOMEN AS CRIMINALS: THEORETICAL PERSPECTIVES

Countless theories have been offered in an attempt to explain female criminality. Dorie Klein's excellent short review of these theoretical perspectives is certainly worth reading. It is that author's view that the same factors that have challenged and destabilized the expected traditional role-set assigned to women also have fostered terrorist activity by women.[10]

Before going further, a brief summary of the most popular past and present theories that have attempted to explain female criminality is in order. Most of the early attempts at theory building tried to explain female criminality in terms of physiological or psychological characteristics of individuals, with little or no emphasis on sociocultural factors; these attempts included the theoretical work of Freud, Cesare Lombroso, and Kingsley Davis. On the other hand, W.I. Thomas and Otto Pollak created a bridge between these two broad perspectives. Chart 2 provides a summation of major theoretical perspectives of female criminality. It reveals a number of interesting perspectives shared by various social-control agencies in regard to women as terrorists: the belief that they exhibit masculine body types and psychological profiles; and the belief that many, if not most, of their acts are emotive rather than instrumental, i.e., emotional rather than well-thought-out acts with a rational program of action not tied to a love interest, such as an attempt to free a captured husband or lover from police or army custody. Social-control personnel often state that female terrorists are more likely to engage in acts of senseless or nongoal-oriented violence than are their male counterparts, a

---

[10]Dorie Klein, "The Etiology of Female Crime: A Review of the Literature," *Issues in Criminology* 8 (1973): 3–30.

Chart 2. Theoretical Perspectives of Female Criminality

Theorist	*Orientation*	*Title of Major Work*
Cesare Lombroso	Crime as an atavism (survival of primitive traits in individuals, e.g., considerable body hair) Lower intelligence Lack of passion	*The Female Offender* (New York, 1903)
W.I. Thomas	Psychological passivity Physiological immobility Women are cold and calculating Female amorality Women driven by basic wishes to manipulate the male sex Drive to achieve ulterior motives Individual accommodation to social surroundings	*The Unadjusted Girl* (New York, 1923)
Sigmund Freud	Psychological passivity Physiological immobility Penis envy Women are anatomically inferior The deviant is attempt to be a man	"Anatomy is Destiny," Lectures on Psychoanalysis (New York, 1933)
E. Kingsley Davis	Demands for sexual novelty are not fulfilled in marriage Some males are cut off from sexual partners because they are unmarried, ugly, and/or deformed Some males are cut off from sexual partners because of some other sexually competitive disadvantage	"The Sociology of Prostitutes," *American Sociological Review* 2 (October 1937): 744–55
Otto Pollak	Hidden female crime Rising crime rate among females is the result of sexual emancipation Women are as criminal as men When their criminality is detected, they may still avoid arrest	*The Criminality of Women* (Philadelphia, 1950)

Chart 2 (continued)

Female crime is tied to
  socialization
Some biological factors are
  tied to female criminality,
  e.g., lesser physical
  strength than men
Psychological concomitants
  of menstruation, preg-
  nancy, and menopause are
  tied to the etiology of
  female crime

M. Rappaport	Female offenders are psy-chological misfits	"The Psychology of the Female Offender," *NPAA Journal* 3 (January 1957): 7–12.
G. Gisela Konopka	Emotional problem: loneliness and dependency	*Adolescent Girls in Conflict* (Englewood Cliffs, NJ, 1966)
J. Cowie, V. Cowie, and E. Slater	Chromosomal explanation of female delinquency Female offenders are different physiologically and psychologically from the normal girl Delinquent girls are more masculine than the normal girl	*Delinquency in Girls* (London, 1968)
H.C. Vedder and D. Sommerville	Female delinquency seen as blocked access or mal-adjustment to the normal feminine role	*The Delinquent Girl* (Springfield, IL, 1970)
D. Hoffman-Bustamente	Women's crimes are the result of five major factors: 1) differential sex role expectations 2) sex differences in socio-logical patterns and application of social control 3) differential opportunities to engage in crime 4) differential access to criminal subcultures and careers 5) sex differences built into crime categories	"The Nature of Female Crim-inality," *Issues in Criminology* 8 (Fall 1973): 117–36.

Chart 2 (continued)

F. Adler	Greater female assertiveness Spinoff of the women's libera- tion movement Breakdown in prevailing pat- terns of sexual inequality	*Sisters in Crime* (New York, 1975)
R. Simon	Breakdown in prevailing pat- terns of sexual inequality Greater labor force participa- tion of females has led to increased opportunities for crime Female criminality shall not increase drastically (Adler disagrees)	*Women and Crime* (Lexington, MA, 1975)

factor that likely would place a disproportionate number of female terrorists into Frederick Hacker's category of crazies.[11]

TOWARD A THEORY OF WOMEN AS TERRORISTS

The following is a rudimentary attempt at a formulation of a theory of women as terrorists. It must be stressed that this theory is rudimentary at best, but it does present the known variables associated with female terrorist behavior.

Proposition One: *Women, except for a few notable exceptions, have played a relatively minor role in terrorist violence in the last thirty years.* Official arrest and suspect data reveal a relatively minor level of female participation in terrorist activity.

Proposition Two: *Although women, except for a few notable exceptions, have played a relatively minor role in terrorist violence in the last thirty years, one may expect female participation, both as free-lance nonmovement-oriented terrorists as well as members of terrorist organizations, in terrorist incidents to increase dramatically in the future.* Changing role-sets ascribed to women will place them more directly into the mainstream of academia and corporate enterprise. These changes in the expected belief and activity patterns of women will result in direct conflict with the more traditional female role-sets: wife, mother, and passive, gentle, noncompetitive beauties of moderate or low intelligence and low aspirations. With women entering the labor force as well as the

[11]Frederick Hacker, *Crusaders, Criminals, Crazies* (New York, 1976).

academic world at an accelerating rate, the system with its limited resources and rewards will frustrate women who have attained all of the socially defined attributes usually tied to success, such as proper speech, aggressive personalities, superior technical training, and high levels of education; these highly skilled women will perceive the reality of blocked opportunity while becoming more conscious of their unique exclusion from the system of rewards, thus fostering and reinforcing demands for sociostructural change of both a socialist and feminist nature.

We must also realize that as new employment fields open up for women, they will acquire new skills, some of which may be used in terrorist acts. Combat or combat-support units in the "New Army" train women to shoot guns and handle explosives, while new opportunities in various local, state, and federal-level control agencies also open up similar training. Women currently taught to work on farms, in forests, and in mines learn skills in the storage and discharge of explosives.

Proposition Three: *Female input in terrorist acts is tied in part to feminist demands and practices.* Feminist organizations, or organizations with socialistic principles, allow for increased opportunities to women for upward mobility. This upward mobility more likely is determined by a woman's innate or learned skills and leadership qualities than by the sex-linked, stereotyped characteristics often found in more traditional male-dominated organizations. Female input in groups that champion feminist and socialistic objectives is likely to be considerable. If such demands should exceed society's capacity to deliver reform, then violence or the threat of violence is probable by radical organizations.

Proposition Four: *Contemporary female terrorists are likely to exhibit male personality or physical traits.* The demand for immediate change and the ability to compete forcefully in the labor market and in the classroom are traits often viewed as masculine. Thus, those who assert markedly radical demands for structural-functional change in regard to role-sets assigned to women, or any oppressed majority or minority, may be viewed as masculine in character. Women who lack the characteristics and traits that society considers appropriate—gentleness, passivity, non-violent personalities, seductiveness, physically attractive faces and figures—may seek success in some non-feminine realm, by displaying aggression, unadorned faces and bodies, toughness, or other masculine qualities.

Masculine or feminine characteristics are often culturally defined. Female terrorists of the future can be expected to exhibit fewer of the characteristics usually defined as masculine, because clear divisions between sex-linked roles no longer will exist.

Proposition Five: *Terrorist acts by females now and in the future will become more instrumental and less expressive.* There can be little doubt that terrorist acts by females have often been expressive in character. However, as more women join terrorist groups with well-defined political goals and objectives, women will carry out fewer incidents of so-called expressive violence, or violence that does not appear to be conducive to goal achievement. There is no reason to believe that trained female terrorists will function in a manner different from trained male terrorists.

The claim that terrorism by women is often tied to the liberation of their imprisoned mates is no different from much of the terrorism perpetrated by their male counterparts. In fact, most acts of terrorism by either female or male terrorists have not been tied to the liberation of loved ones. However, male terrorism has not been totally immune to the act of struggling for the liberation of imprisoned lovers: one must recall that the Uruguayan government's most effective counterterrorism strategy against the Tupamaros, or Movimento de Liberacion Nacional (MLN), was the wholesale arrest of the loved ones, wives, and families of the male-dominated guerrillas of the MLN movement. The government then waited for the Tupamaros to attack the jails and prisons which held their families, on the theory that during the attack the guerrillas would be slaughtered.

A theory, therefore, that attempts to explain women as terrorists would read as follows: one may expect a considerable amount of female terrorists in organizations that exhibit and preach feminist or socialistic principles. These organizations and, thus, sizable numbers of female cadres may exist in societies undergoing dramatic challenge to, or change in, their present economic system. Trained female terrorists can be expected to function in a manner similar to their male counterparts. And female terrorists most likely will serve as integrated cadres in both socialistic and nationalistic struggles, and not as autonomous legions of Amazon-oriented warriors.

THE OUTLOOK FOR FEMALE PARTICIPATION IN TERRORISM

Most criminal-justice experts who specialize in the study of terrorism agree that conditions are favorable for increased terrorist activity throughout much of the world and that women will play an increasingly dynamic and important role. What is debatable is whether or not female terrorism is and will continue to be more emotive and less instrumental than male terrorism, or terrorism that is carried out by groups predominantly male in both ideology and membership. The emancipation of women from the household and related domestic functions, their increased opportunity and expectations in the worlds of enterprise and academia brought about by the reorganization of the workplace, and feminist pressures on women's role in the nuclear family will no doubt produce a woman who is both willing and able to take her rightful place in all aspects of society and culture, including revolutionary and terrorist activities.

The classic factors conducive to terrorist violence remain: 1) a self-conscious, segregated, ethnic, cultural or religious minority;[12] 2) which feels itself to be economically deprived or politically oppressed—a feeling exacerbated by the effect of modern communications—with poor job opportunities, lacking in voting rights, but encouraged to believe that change is coming and then is disappointed; 3) in a situation of unemployment or inflation; 4) externally encouraged; 5) with an historical "them" to blame; 6) and with frustrated elites to provide leadership and to overcome the natural distaste, of all save the psychopathic fringe, to initiate violence by giving it an ideological justification; 7) in a society with at least an oral tradition of democracy and upward mobility.[13]

To these factors we must add feminist demands, both logical and irrational, requiring serious response and gratification by societies with a history of nonresponse to nonviolent pressure, including the so-called western democracies. If we are to comprehend more fully the role of women as terrorists, we must recognize that women comprise a self-conscious, dynamic sector of our society which often perceives itself to be an oppressed majority—a majority oppressed not only because of race, religion, ethnicity, or national origin but also because of sex. That oppression mirrors all of the factors that Burton and Laqueur have listed as classic conditions conducive of terrorist violence. Future research might attempt to examine more fully the correlates of female terrorism, the conditions conducive to terrorist and revolutionary violence, feminism, socialism, and the traditional and changing modes of female criminality.

---

[12]A. Burton, *Urban Terrorism: Theory, Practice and Response* (New York: 1975), p. 249.
[13]Walter Laqueur, *Terrorism* (Boston, 1977).

A Chapter in the History of Individual Terror:
Andrey Zhelyabov

Writing in his memoirs about a meeting that took place at the end of 1878, Andrey Ivanovich Zhelyabov, the architect of the *Narodnaya Volya* (People's Will) strategy, explained what he learned from his own experience of "going to the people." After working hard in the village for some sixteen hours a day, he felt every night in his bones how he was increasingly turning into an automaton.

> It was then that I grasped the fact that as long as the peasant is forced to sweat and tire himself out in earning just enough for his daily crust and essential livelihood, just sufficient to satisfy the most basic and modest needs of life, then one cannot expect of him anything other than that he will devote himself to fulfilling his biological desires and pursuing the means of their satisfaction. The suspicious, distrustful peasant regards every stranger with dislike, seeing him as a competitor or as an agent of the state intent on increasing his burden.

Zhelyabov drew the conclusion that "history moves frighteningly slowly, one has to give it a push."[1] When he was asked to assess the chances of some constitutional change, he replied that this too was a possibility but that, whatever the case, the overriding aim was "to give history a push."

A number of factors had led him to this conclusion: the blind alley in which the "going to the people" movement had been trapped; the encounter with the impenetrability, suspicion, and ignorance of the admired same people; the risk of sinking into the mire of the loathed reality; the feeling that the mills of history ground far too slowly; the clash with the "force of habit that exists among millions—tens of millions"; the exploding of the populist myths and the pent-up fury of years of imprisonment, persecutions, and executions. Hence, a way out had to be found to break the vicious circle, to push history forward, and thereby jump over certain of its stages. In one of the few Zhelyabov documents to survive, he wrote on 12 May 1880 to M.P. Dragomanov, the intellectual leader of the

---

[1] P. Semyenuta, "Iz vospominanyi ob A. Zhelyabove," *Byloye 1906* 4: 219–25.

Ukrainian democratic movement, that the government's situation had been clearly spelled out to it. The regime's days were numbered, and it was felt that it had no social or moral hinterland. All that kept it alive was fear, greed, and the inability to organize for concerted action. The demand for concessions while there was still time was a demand for political logic, but this was neither what the "power-loving old man," Czar Alexander II, wanted, nor was it the policy of the czarevich. This accounted for the hesitations and paralysis of the government. Therefore, "two or three good pushes are likely to topple the regime."[2]

ZHELYABOV'S PERSONALITY AND EARLY YEARS

Zhelyabov was no legalist or publicist. He participated actively in all the *Narodnaya Volya* actions and clashes with the authorities and had no time to spare for wording programs and writing articles. Yet his memoirs, the "Program of the Working Section of the Narodnaya Volya," the "Preparatory Work of the Party," his trial confession together with that of Nicolai Ivanovich Rysakov, whose views reflected his own, all reveal his basic ideas. There is no doubt that he was one of the leading personalities in the Executive Committee of *Narodnaya Volya* and one of the most important persons in the Russian revolutionary movement. Lev Tikhomirov, one of the editors of *Zemlya Volya*, described him as "one of the greatest Russians of the last twenty-five years," one of those "who took upon their own shoulders the burden of an entire generation."[3]

The son of peasants, Zhelyabov possessed unusual physical strength; he was tall, had finely sculpted features, and was a brilliant speaker. All these characteristics were combined with a sharp intellect and a brave heart. Mikhail Fedorovich Frolenko tells of a bet Zhelyabov made on the way to the Lipetsk meeting, that he could stop a laden coach by taking hold of its back axle; Zhelyabov was as good as his word and even managed to stop the galloping horse. Another story tells of how he quieted a mad bull by wrestling him by the horns.[4] The chief of the gendarmerie, Shebeko, was impressed by Zhelyabov's calm, his inner tranquility, and his self-control in prison, during the trial and just before his execution. Rysakov, Zhelyabov's protégé, who himself broke down under investigation, said in his confession that there was no one to equal Zhelyabov in

---

[2]M. P. Dragomanov, *Sobranye polit. sochimenyi* II (Paris, 1906), pp. 414–18; "Pismo A. Zhelyabova M. Dragomanovu," *Byloye 1906* 3: 71–72.

[3]L. Tikhomirov, *A. Zhelyabov* (Geneva, 1899), p. 30

[4]M. F. Frolenko, "Lipetskij i voronezhkij syezoy," *Byloye 1907* 1: 69, 74; L. G. Deych, *Delo i-go marta* (St. Petersburg, 1906), p. 408.

"controlling his thoughts, feelings, and aspirations."[5] Elemental strength, the Russian peasant's ability to suffer and persist, joy in life and optimism even in the darkest of times, and an iron will: these were the qualities that made Zhelyabov a leader. Tikhomirov claimed that there were many better terrorists than Zhelyabov on the Executive Committee, but there was none to equal him in the *Narodnaya Volya* for power of persuasion, oratorical fire, and authority.[6]

It is doubtful whether any other group throughout the entire history of the Russian revolutionary movement could boast the degree of responsibility, authority, and sense of personal obligation that marked the central nucleus and leadership of the Executive Committee of the *Narodnaya Volya*; among this group, Zhelyabov was certainly the most outstanding. Georgi Valentinovich Plekhanov, who left the Narodniki in 1879 because of his opposition to terror, considered Zhelyabov a far-sighted man, an outstanding representative of western European radicalism. "The Russian revolution," he wrote, "was for him not an enterprise that would free just the peasants and the labouring classes, but one that would bring a new life to the entire Russian people."[7]

Zhelyabov was born in 1850 to a family of serfs in the province of Feodosia, close to Simferopol in the south. In the conditions of serfdom that obtained before the emancipation, Zhelyabov was born a slave. One of the most painful episodes of his life was the rape of his aunt by the local bailiff. The brand of shame this stamped on him was never erased and, in a much later letter to a friend he wrote, "I was a child then, twelve years old, yet even so, I swore I would kill Lorentsov [the bailiff] when I grew up." The local landowner first noticed Zhelyabov's abilities and provided him an education. He went first to the Simferopol school and then enrolled as a law student in the university at Odessa. Here he was seized by the revolutionary mood and soon became one of the influential activists among the students. His reaction to the manner in which a student was insulted brought about his expulsion from the university, and he then joined the ranks of that group which both nourished the revolutionary movement and served as a principal cause of the revolution—the group of expelled students.[8]

Unlike most members of the "circles" of the 1870s, Zhelyabov saw the trial of the Nechaev group, which had attempted to incite peasant

---

[5] "Pokazanya pervomartovtsev," *Byloye 1918* 10–11: 275. For G.D. Goldenberg's confessions, see S. Volk, *Narodnaya volya 1879–1882* (Moscow-Leningrad, 1966), p. 90. On Zhelyabov's personality, see also the report of General Shebeko, *Khronika revolutsyonnogo dviznenya v rossiyi 1878–1887* (Moscow, 1906), pp. 159–60.

[6] Tikhomirov, *A. Zhelyabov*, pp. 47–48.

[7] A. Tun, *Istorya revolutsyonnykh dvizhenyj v rossiyi, izd. proletaryi 1924,* Plekhanov's introduction, pp. 30–31.

[8] Tikhomirov, *A. Zhelyabov*, pp. 62–74.

revolution, as a sign of things to come. He departed from sentimentalism for revolutionary activity and, after some hesitation, he joined the underground. When it was suggested that he join the Volkhovsky group, he was doubtful: "What would you do if you had responsibility for a beloved family, with a father and mother dependent on you, and you knew that by joining an underground movement there was a danger that you would no longer be able to help them?" But when he finally came to a decision, he burned all his bridges behind him and became entirely absorbed in the matter at hand. Despite his marriage in 1873 to Olga Semenovna Yanenko, the daughter of an Odessa merchant and member of the city council, he was thrice arrested in the following year and released.[9] "In 1874 we were anarchists in our political outlook," he declared at his trial in 1881. "My whole intent was to work through peaceful means. But I became wiser in prison. It was here that I became a revolutionary." In May 1878, he was brought to trial with the 193, and after his acquittal sank into a depression from which he tried to shake himself free by means of hard physical labor. He rented a garden in the Kamenetz-Podolsk region and engaged in propaganda work among the peasants. In the autumn, he returned to Odessa where he dissociated himself from Valerian Andreyevich Osinsky, the first man to organize widespread terrorism in southern Russia, and his friends but nevertheless learned the use of sea mines.

JOINING THE TERROR

Lev Grigorevich Deych, the rebel leader in Kiev and later Social Democrat, wrote about a meeting that took place in the home of Sofya Perovskaya, later to be Zhelyabov's common-law wife and his comrade on the Executive Committee. He was most impressed by Zhelyabov's personality, which immediately excited attention. The meeting took place at a time when Perovskaya herself was fiercely opposed to terror. Also present were Vera Ivanova Zasulich, who began her terrorist career in Kiev; Zundelevich, who was to be arrested in 1879 and sentenced to life imprisonment at hard labor for establishing clandestine presses; Alexander Alexandrovich Kviatkovsky, who later attempted to blow up the Winter Palace and was hanged in 1881; Alexander Dmitrievich Mikhilov; Yakov Vasilevich Stefanovich, the Kievan revolutionary and peasant organizer; and Plekhanov. Zhelyabov spoke in a full, quiet, bass voice, pleading for the necessity of terror and warning against further involvement in the

---

[9]His father-in-law, Yanenko, was a wealthy and distinguished citizen of Odessa but not mayor of the city, as mistakenly noted in F. Venturi, *Roots of Revolution* (New York: Grosset & Dunlap, 1966), p. 645. See also Tikhomirov, *A. Zhelyabov*, pp. 17–18.

"going to the people" movement. Revolutionaries, he said, must "pull the trigger" in the struggle for political freedom, but they must not remain isolated and lacking in a hinterland. Thus, he stressed the need for action among more advanced sections of the population and for winning the support of the liberal groups. He was a very talented speaker, Deych reports, but Plekhanov was better in polemic because, unlike Zhelyabov, he had a taste for sharp personal attack.

Zhelyabov gave the terrorist movement its first injection of real system.[10] It was Frolenko who, in his memoirs, took credit for bringing Zhelyabov to the Lipetsk conference, although from another source we learn that Zundelevich was the man responsible for discovering Zhelyabov and recruiting him into the founding core of the *Narodnaya Volya*.[11] At all events, Zhelyabov was the central figure at Lipetsk. It was he who set forth the broad outlines of the strategy and political orientation. Before coming to Lipetsk, he had laid down a condition for his participation—the murder of the czar—but he soon became immersed totally in the strategy of terror. His acceptance of terror amazed many who had known him as a man of balanced views who had taken a stand against violence. Frolenko explains the change by Zhelyabov's sense of realism. David Footman, in *Red Prelude*, offers another explanation: he suggests that Zhelyabov's immense vitality found in the *Narodnaya Volya* an outlet that absolutely suited it, "for it gave him all that any man of his temperament could ask for—a complete break with the failures and humiliations of the past, a leading role in a movement that had been his dream since childhood, the confidence that his part was well within his powers, and a vast Empire waiting to be conquered."[12]

Another factor should be taken into consideration. Zhelyabov was sincere in his objections to the writings of Nicolai Morosov, one of the editors of *Zemlya Volya*, for he saw terrorism as a passing means to an end, a one-time tool that would serve only as a single link in the strategic chain of events that made up political struggle. Although he engaged in active terror, according to Rysakov, "he continued to see the light through the smokescreen of the mines and the bombs." Zhelyabov always kept before him the vision of a great historic movement, and it was this great movement that he sought to unite and advance. Terror was to be the first step in a sequence that would lead to an uprising among the urban masses, the army, and the peasants; to a liberal opposition; and to social ferment. Thus he drew in and organized the working-class periphery, the military, and the student organizations. At the same time, he was convinced that terror meant partisan warfare, struggle that depended for its success on a

---

[10]Deych, *Delo i-go marta*, pp. 408–12.
[11]P. S. Ivanovskaya, "Neskolko slov ob A. Zhelyabove," *Narodovoltsy* (Moscow, 1931), p. 20.
[12]David Footman, *Red Prelude* (London, 1944), pp. 141–42.

constant effort, carried out unhesitantly and with the utmost devotion. With this in mind, he opposed efforts wasted on fruitless projects. Possibly he attached more importance to sowing terror and shaking the regime than to the execution of any individual act in all its details: the attack on the railway line near Alexandrovsk was marred by a failure whose exact character was never made clear, while the bombing of the Winter Palace failed because the dynamite charge was insufficient. Speaking at a conference in Kharkov, Zhelyabov propounded the idea that the regime must be attacked again and again until it was forced to grant political freedom, by which it would be possible to engage in peaceful propaganda activities.[13] For him, the government itself was the proper object of terror.

Zhelyabov viewed with concern the manner in which the Executive Committee became increasingly involved with terror pure and simple. Polonskaya (Oshanina) describes the feverish and unusually strained atmosphere in which the discussions on the eve of 1 March 1881 took place. The meeting also took note of the need to fill the ranks of the Executive Committee following inroads on it made by casualties among many of its members, but no one could concentrate on this point. After the meeting, Zhelyabov approached her and asked for details about people who might be suitable for membership in the Executive Committee. Speaking to Tikhomirov, Zhelyabov expressed concern that they were dissipating all their capital in their terrorist campaign. Polonskaya notes that initially there were no real disagreements on the subject of terror, but that, as the actions became more extreme, it became clear that terrorism was being conducted at the expense of other activities. It was then that some people advanced the claim that more attention should be paid to organization and propaganda.

> Truth to tell, not everyone was pleased with the fact that terror was swallowing up so much of our strength. They would have preferred that more of our strength be channelled into organization and propaganda, but this proved to be impossible. Terror took up so much of our strength simply because otherwise there would have been no terror at all.[14]

TESTIMONY OF RYSAKOV AND HRINEVITSKI

The human factor, more than any strategic considerations or programmatic guidelines, was of prime importance in this fatal preoccupation

---

[13] *Vospominanya russkikh revolutsyonerov*, Stein ed. (Berlin, n.d.), pp. 88, 91.
[14] "Pokazanya M. Polonskoy," *Byloye 1907* 6:5–7.

with terrorism. As Footman points out, "Terrorism, even more than war, requires meticulous training and an iron discipline to enable human nature to support the strain."[15] The tension of face-to-face confrontation, the repeated attacks, and the losses sustained among the organization's elite had other effects: human feelings, such as the desire for revenge, for some reward, for some action that would defend the honor of the party, for some relief of the tension, all made inroads into the considerations of caution and intelligent strategy. Terrorist warfare is marked by a suicidal trend, which becomes stronger as the struggle itself sharpens. The same morale, dedication, readiness to sacrifice, and conviction of the justice of the cause, which are the strengths of a terrorist underground, are also its weaknesses. For the government, while it is more vulnerable than the underground, finds it easier to absorb shocks, since it is staffed by a reserve of men hungry for honor and power and the privileges these bring. The same cannot be said of the terrorist party. The Executive Committee was both more sensitive and more vulnerable, and its reactions were more susceptible to the human element. An analysis of the circumstances surrounding the assassination of Alexander II on 1 March shows that, on the one hand, the human element was all important in enabling the terrorists to carry out the impossible, but, on the other hand, the limitations of the human element later were responsible for the movement's inability to continue and measure up to the impossible. Terrorism consumes its capital, since it gambles everything on one card, and that card is an illusion.

In the historical literature, insufficient attention has been paid to the confession made by Rysakov.[16] A member of the fighting battalion of the Workers' Section of the *Narodnaya Volya*, he was chosen by Zhelyabov to take part in the assassination of the czar. He was then nineteen. Caught immediately after he had thrown the first bomb and hearing the czar say that he was "thank God" still alive and well, Rysakov shouted after him that "it's too early yet to thank God!" The bomb then thrown by Hrinevitski, which ended the monarch's life, echoed the youngster's words. After his arrest, Rysakov was handed over to Dobrinski, "a consummate soul destroyer," who had been the interrogator of Grigory Davidovich Goldenberg, when the putative assassin of Alexander II betrayed his comrades. Afraid of dying, cut off from his surroundings, and shocked by the fact that his hero and leader Zhelyabov had fallen captive to the authorities. Rysakov was unable to put up any resistance. His interrogator managed to make him feel that his behavior under cross-examination would influence the regime's future path and hence the fate of

---

[15] Footman, *Red Prelude*, p. 139.

[16] "Pokazanya pervomartovtsev," *Byloye 1918* 10–11: 230–311. This document was revealed only in 1917.

all others who sought the good of the people, that baring his soul and revealing his ideas were of the utmost political importance. The result was the document known as the "Rysakov Confession."

On 8 March, Rysakov delivered this ideological credo, which mirrored Zhelyabov's attitudes. He described terrorism as a merely defensive instrument, designed to build up and develop strength and the legend of strength. Zhelyabov's aim, so it seems, was to crystallize some strength, using controlled terrorist activities, and not be drawn into any decisive clash before the time should be ripe. Behind this was the thought that it would be possible to move into offensive terror when sufficient power had been built up. Rysakov quoted Zhelyabov as telling him a little while before the assassination, that "now we are stronger, and so we don't have to behave any longer as helpless people."

Next Rysakov expounded the inevitability of terror in the Russian reality. "It was not we who prepared the ground for terror," he claimed. The party had no monopoly on terror; it was mentioned in the villages as well. Here too one could hear murmurs that it was necessary to take "action from the side" against the representatives of the regime who were squeezing and suppressing the people. Rysakov expressed fear of the dangers of a spontaneous uprising: a movement that had no framework would snowball in utter confusion without anyone being able to control it; also, a peasant revolutionary movement might join up with the terrorist movement and serve as the latter's roving battalions, in other words engage in partisan warfare. As Rysakov put it, the Goldenberg episode proved just how baseless were the hopes of arriving at an accommodation with the authorities. The expectation of change from above amounted to reconciling oneself to unbearable conditions. Yet in his later confessions, Rysakov followed Goldenberg, saying that he, Goldenberg, the experienced terrorist, was right in changing his attitude. Terror was useful to the party, but it should not have had as its sole aim the killing of the czar.

Here he takes issue with Zhelyabov's stand, although without mentioning him by name. The assassination of Alexander II had one clear purpose: "To put an end to terror and bring about a real improvement in the lives of the peasants and the workers." As for himself, said Rysakov, "I never saw the attack as a murder. Never in my life did I envisage myself face to face with blood, the groans of the wounded, and such like; as I saw it, the attack would be a marvellous act that would lead society into a new life." Under Zhelyabov's influence, he saw himself as a partner in the attainment of the good, happy to sacrifice his life to this end. He adds, "Even as I threw the bomb, I felt no hatred of the Tzar." Thus, in the confession of young Rysakov, whose spirit was broken by interrogation, the whole tragedy of individual terror is expressed.

The second assailant, Hrinevitski, also left a confession in the form of a will prepared before he set out. Speaking in the spirit of Zhelyabov, Hrinevitski says:

Alexander II has to die. His days are numbered; I, or someone coming after me, must be charged with dealing the final awful blow which will echo, like thunder, throughout all Russia, even as far as its furthest corners. This the near future will prove. The Tzar will die and with him—we, ourselves, his enemies, his murderers. This act is essential for the cause of freedom, for it will deal a mighty blow to that system which some sly souls term "absolute monarchy" and we ourselves term tyranny ... I shall not be privileged to witness the last battle. Fate has decreed me an early passing and thus I shall not see the victory, shall not feel, not even for as little as a single day, a single hour, the hours of the glorious festival. Yet, for all that, I feel convinced that in my death I shall be doing all that I have to do, and more than that no man can ask. A revolutionary party must devote itself to igniting the glowing tinder, setting the spark to the gunpowder, taking all steps to ensure that the movement which serves as redeemer shall also reap the victory and not end with the destruction of all the best of the country's sons. . . ."[17]

PROGRAM OF THE WORKERS' SECTION

Hrinevitski. and Rysakov both were protégés of Zhelyabov and members of the fighting battalion of the Workers' Section of the *Narodnaya Volya*, to whose development he devoted such massive efforts. Its program was one of the few documents from his pen that have survived. Compiled in November 1880, it was sent at Zhelyabov's initiative to Karl Marx, who added certain comments. It is most singular that the problem of the terrorist struggle was mentioned only as the merest hint. The program's concern was an outline for the socialist revolution in Russia. The Social Revolutionary party, with a membership drawn from all strata and classes of the empire, was presented as the sole and faithful ally of the masses. The document also emphasized that "all those who exist at the expense of the people, that is to say, the authorities, the landowners, the industrialists and factory owners, the kulaks, all these will never of their own free will relinquish that which makes their life easy." On the other hand, the program also stressed that among the ranks of the intelligentsia were to be found natural allies for the overthrow of the regime, since this class too was oppressed by the authorities. Democratic changes in the regime were bound to bring reality closer to the socialist order. In a possible uprising, the workers' associations were assigned the role of constituting an armed force ready to support the revolution when it broke out in response to the will of the people. To quote the program itself:

---

[17]*Literatura narodnoy voli* (Paris, 1905), p. 971.

The blow at the enemy with a hope of victory can only be struck by the Social Revolutionary party, with the workers' section being an integral part of that body. The party is recruiting from among the people and society the forces to carry out the revolution, it is establishing associations among the peasants and the urban workers, the army and other strata of society. The party is establishing the battle organization that is to strike at the regime, to overturn it and set it in confusion until it loses its balance, thus rendering it easier for all those who are dissatisfied—the people, the workers, and all who wish for their good—to rise up and carry out a general revolution.[18]

With this concept of the party as the shock force of the revolution, the program gave a special place and role to the urban workers. It stressed the importance of controlling the large cities and the need to ensure that the fruits of the revolution of the masses, won by their own labor and blood, not fall into the hands of the bourgeoisie. Thus the people would have to establish immediately a provisional government, although such a government would certainly be composed of the educated strata and classes. There followed an appeal that might have been taken from "The Address of the Central Bureau to the Communist League," written by Marx in 1850. It was stated in "The Address" that "the workers are following the provisional government with keen attention and forcing it to work for the good of the people." The constituent assembly would be called only when "the uprising is crowned with complete success and when the transfer of land and factories to the hands of the masses shall be accomplished, and when there shall be no other military force in the country than that of the enlisted people's army."

In the Zhelyabov program, consideration also was given to the other possibility that, in the pressure of the struggle and with the threat of a rebellion, the authorities might decide to consider concessions and grant a constitution to the people. It was to this goal that the entire terrorist strategy of the blow at the center, or the final blow, was in fact geared. If this end could be achieved, the workers were to participate in the parliament and maintain the class struggle, by strengthening their demands through mass declarations and demonstrations. The *Narodnaya Volya* party, by maintaining continual pressure on the authorities and building up strength, was "getting ready for the moment when the old order would no longer be able to withstand the claims of the people, when the revolution would take place with a hope of total success."

---

[18]Ibid., pp. 878–86; also *Revolutsyonnoye narodnichestvo* Godov XIX Veka T. II (Moscow-Leningrad, 1965), pp. 184–91. The photocopy of Marx's remarks is also published here.

WORST POSSIBLE ALTERNATIVE IN
THE WORST POSSIBLE CIRCUMSTANCES

Two strategic concepts emerge from Zhelyabov and the majority of the *Narodnaya Volya* membership: 1) that a constitutional regime would come into being, putting an end to the need for terror and revolutionary activity, and 2) that a revolution would have to be effected at any cost, and that the right moment for revolution would have to be precipitated even under the worst of circumstances. It was for this reason that the Blanquist-Jacobin element of the party grew more powerful after the czar's assassination, as all hopes of a constitutional government faded. Both attitudes, the constitutional and the Blanquist alike, were the result of strategic considerations springing from the changing circumstances produced by events. Thus, when Pavel Axelrod writes in his memoirs that Zhelyabov saw the attainment of a democratic constitution as the entire purpose of the struggle,[19] and when Plekhanov describes Zhelyabov's appearance at Voronezh as one who was advocating "abandoning all thought of the class struggle,"[20] they were stressing merely a single facet in the overall, long-term strategy advanced by Zhelyabov: to unite all the forces opposed to czarist absolutism.

The revolutionaries saw terror as the salient, though not the sole, weapon of the political struggle. However, it was the tragedy of the *Narodnaya Volya*, and of the Socialist Revolutionaries after them, that terrorist activities sapped their strength. The terrorist nucleus, the "fighting organization," the clashes, and the "blow at the center" influenced all other considerations and frustrated all the programmatic statements. "The worst possible circumstances" that created the terror also determined its progress and sealed its fate. In the autumn of 1880, at one of the most critical moments of the terrorist struggle, Zhelyabov called a meeting of the Executive Committee and asked permission to go to the Volga region where millions of peasants were dying of hunger after a severe drought and there to head a peasant uprising. He argued that if the party stood aside at this point and did not come to the aid of the people in overthrowing the "regime of stranglers," it would lose all credibility in the eyes of the people and "would never again regain it." "I know what is in your minds," said Zhelyabov. "The coming attempt on the Emperor—do I propose to cancel it? No, most emphatically I do not. I am only asking for a postponement." There was general silence. Anna Pribyleva-Korba reports, "This silence was by way of being a vote, and Zhelyabov left the meeting without

---

[19]P. Axelrod, *Perezhitoye i peredumannoye* (Berlin, 1930), p. 362.
[20]Tun, *Istorya*, p. 31.

putting his proposal to a formal vote."[21] Zhelyabov also was the first to consider organizing the army officers and made the initial contact with them even before the *Narodnaya Volya* party came into being. N.E. Sukhanov, the naval officer, and one of the leaders of the *Narodnaya Volya* as well as a member of the Executive Committee, describes the immense impression Zhelyabov made when he appeared at a naval officers' gathering in Kronstadt.[22]

In the critical early days of 1881, the murder of the czar became a specter haunting the entire Executive Committee, after the execution of Kviatkovsky and the arrests of Stepan Grigorevich Shirayev, Alexander Ivanovich Barranikov, Zundelevich, Mikhailov, and others. Zhelyabov was still insisting on the need to rescue Nechaev, although it was clear to him that "the party's honour demands that the Tzar be murdered" and that the assassination plans must have top priority. He planned the 1 March operation as a hunt from which the czar would be unable to escape. Three courses of action were planned: the mining of a tunnel that had been dug beneath the czar's route; a bombing squad which would operate if the czar traveled by a different route; and, should both these fail, the stabbing of the czar by Zhelyabov himself. On 27 February, Zhelyabov was caught in a trap laid for him as a result of revelations made by one of his own protégés from among the Workers' Section of the *Narodnaya Volya*. The assassination was carried out without his aid, but it was accomplished in accordance with the strategy and organization that he had readied.[23]

---

[21]A. Pribyleva-Korba, "K. biyografyi A. I. Zhelyabova," in *Narodovoltsy* 3 (Moscow, 1934), p. 17–20.

[22]Volk, *Narodnaya volya*, p. 315.

[23]Zhelyabov had been arrested on 27 February. About the accomplished assassination, he learned only when the investigators brought Rysakov to confront him. He then declared that this was a great day for the revolutionary movement and a step ahead in advancing the people's liberation.

III.
HOSTAGE TAKING AND
ITS AFTERMATH

Political Hostage Taking in Western Europe: A Statistical Analysis

CLIVE C. ASTON

The taking of hostages in Western Europe has had a long association with insurgency and warfare.[1] As early as 197 B.C., the Romans put down Indibilus's revolt in Further Spain and required the defeated tribes to give hostages as a guarantee of their future good conduct.[2] During the Earl of Tyrone's rebellion in Ireland at the end of the sixteenth century and again during the counterrevolution in the Vendée in the French Revolution, this tactic was employed by the governments with equal success. In more recent times, during World War II the German High Command in Paris issued a circular on 12 September 1940 authorising local commanders to take hostages in retaliation for acts of sabotage.[3] Even today, nuclear strategy based on the so-called balance of terror "is simply a massive and modern version of an ancient institution: the exchange of hostages."[4]

A new qualitative distinction between the types of potential hostages began to emerge by the twelfth century.[5] A single, important nobleman came to be deemed as effective a bargaining chip as multiple, less

---

[1]Western Europe hereafter will be defined as that geographical area composed of the twenty-one member states of the Council of Europe: Austria, Belgium, Cyprus, Denmark, France, West Germany, Greece, Iceland, the Republic of Ireland, Italy, Liechtenstein, Luxembourg, Malta, the Netherlands, Norway, Portugal, Spain, Sweden, Switzerland, Turkey, and the United Kingdom. Although the Council of Europe was only composed of eighteen member states in 1968, the current membership of twenty-one will be utilized.

[2]Appian, *Appian's Roman History* (London: William Heinemann, 1964) quoted in Robert B. Asprey, *War in the Shadows: The Guerrilla in History* (London: MacDonald and Jane's, 1975), p. 20.

[3]M.R.D. Foot, *SOE in France* (London: Her Majesty's Stationery Office, 1976), p. 148.

[4]Thomas C. Schelling, *The Strategy of Conflict* (London: Oxford University Press, 1973), p. 239.

[5]It has also been noted that, by the Middle Ages, not only were hostages being taken by warring nations or parties but "creditors sometimes took voluntary hostages who guaranteed to ensure that the debtor paid his debts." Henri Souchon, "Hostage-Taking: Its Evolution and Significance," unpublished paper presented at the Journée des Otages held at the Ecole Nationale Supérieure de Police 24 February 1976, p. 2.

important hostages taken from among the peasantry. For example, the abduction of Richard the Lionhearted by Duke Leopold of Austria in 1193 secured the duke a vast ransom from England, whereas Barbarossa seized 300 hostages in order to obtain a favorable peace treaty with Milan in 1158.[6] This pattern has continued to the present day, although it is only within the past decade that hostage taking by nonstate actors to achieve political ends has become widespread in Western Europe.

The major difficulty in compiling an accurate chronology of contemporary political hostage incidents is the lack of reliable data. INTERPOL, although perceiving itself to be a clearinghouse for information of this kind, is forbidden by Article 3 of its constitution from involvement in any incident of a political, military, religious, or racial nature. The Central Intelligence Agency (CIA) data set entitled *International Terrorism: Attributes of Terrorist Events* (ITERATE) is concerned with general terrorist incidents from a global perspective and tends to ignore less spectacular hostage incidents or ones that are less evidently political. Even assuming that the other reports on terrorism published so far by the CIA are any more reliable, they are derived from a data base approximately two years out of date and even then are confined to incidents of an arbitrarily defined international nature.[7]

An attempt to ascertain the exact number of politically motivated kidnappings in Italy provides a useful illustration of the problems encountered in compiling a chronology. Roughly 5 percent of all kidnappings in that country are politically motivated.[8] It should be a simple task of calculating 5 percent of the yearly totals to arrive at an approximate figure for political kidnappings. However, to do this the various yearly totals available must be both accurate and congruent, which they are not. The Italian Interior Ministry lists a total of thirty-five kidnappings for 1974, whereas INTERPOL records forty-one. The figures arrived at by the major international newspapers are no more congruent. On 28 November 1974, the *International Herald Tribune* stated that the kidnapping of Ilaria Melloni was the forty-second of the year, and *The Times Index* for 1974 recorded a final total of forty-five.

Smaller, regional newspapers tend to be more accurate for local events, and greater reliance must be placed on them. But even here, once an event has ceased to be newsworthy, it is relegated to the back pages, if it is reported at all. As a result, the precise duration of some incidents is either unknown or unclear, as was the case with the kidnapping on 4 April

[6]Wolf Middendorf, "Geiselnahme und Kidnapping," *Kriminalistik* 26, no. 12 (December 1972): 559.

[7]See *International and Transnational Terrorism: Diagnosis and Prognosis* (Washington, DC: CIA, April 1976) and *International Terrorism in 1976–1978*, 3 vols. (Washington, DC: CIA, July 1977–March 1979).

[8]*New York Times Magazine*, 20 November 1977.

1971 of two members of a wealthy family in Ankara; they were released after the payment of a ransom, but the date of their release is unclear. Every effort has been made to verify the facts of each incident utilized in this data base from at least two separate sources, such as newspapers and other data sets.[9] However, in numerous cases this proved to be too exacting a criterion, and verification from a second source was impossible. Undoubtedly, a great deal more information exists within the files of police departments and government agencies, but these records generally are not available.

GEOGRAPHICAL DISTRIBUTION

Brian Jenkins has suggested that "kidnappings are more likely in countries where the terrorists are operating on home terrain and have an underground organization . . . [and] . . . barricade and hostage incidents are more likely when the terrorists are operating abroad or in countries where they lack the capability for sustaining underground operations."[10] Although this may be a matter of expediency more than anything else, the experience of Western Europe does appear to bear this out. Of the twenty-one incidents that can be attributed to groups operating abroad, sixteen

---

[9]The newspapers utilized here were: *Corriere Della Sera, La Stampa,* and *L'Unità* of Italy; *El Pais* of Spain; *Le Monde, L'Express, Le Figaro, International Herald Tribune,* and *Christian Science Monitor* of France; *Frankfurter Allgemeine Zeitung, Die Welt,* and *Die Zeit* of West Germany; *Lloyd's List, The Times, The Financial Times, The Sunday Times, Daily Telegraph, Sunday Telegraph, Observer, Guardian,* and *Daily Mail* of the United Kingdom; *The New York Times* and *Washington Post* of the United States; *Egyptian Gazette, Egyptian Mail, al-Ahram,* and *al-Gumhuriyah* of Egypt; *al-Nahar* and *al-Safa* of Lebanon; and *Jerusalem Post* of Israel. The magazines were: *Time; Newsweek; Economist; Life; 8 Days; Arab Report and Record; Events; Arab World; Stern; U.S. News and Foreign Report;* and *al-Hawadess* of Beirut. Miscellaneous sources were: *The Times Index; Keesing's Contemporary Archives; The Annual of Power and Conflict,* ed. by Brian Crozier (London: Institute for the Study of Conflict, 1971–79); Lester A. Sobel, ed., *Political Terrorism,* 2 vols. (Oxford: Clio Press, 1978); Brian Michael Jenkins and Janera Johnson, *International Terrorism: A Chronology, 1968–1974* (Santa Monica: Rand Corporation, R-1597-DOS/Arpa, March 1975); Brian Jenkins, Janera Johnson, and David Ronfeldt, *Numbered Lives: Some Statistical Observations from 77 International Hostage Episodes* (Santa Monica: Rand Corporation, P-5905, July 1977); U.S., House of Representatives, 93rd Cong., 1st Sess., *Political Kidnappings, 1968–73,* a staff study prepared by the Committee on Internal Security (Washington, DC: Government Printing Office, August 1973); *Chronology of Attacks upon Non-Official American Citizens, 1971–75* (Washington, DC: U.S. Department of State, 20 January 1976); *Chronology of Significant Terrorist Incidents Involving U.S. Diplomatic/Official Personnel, 1963–75* (Washington, DC: U.S. Department of State, 20 January 1976); *Foreign Broadcast Intercept Service;* and *Summary of World Broadcasts.*

[10]Jenkins, et al., *Numbered Lives,* p. 1.

were sieges and five were kidnappings. Similarly, the South Moluccans, who generally have not integrated into Dutch society and do not possess any real underground network outside their own communities, have conducted only sieges. However, there are some notable exceptions. The various Palestinian groups, for example, possess an undeniable organizational ability and an effective, albeit generally known, underground capability throughout Western Europe, but they have never engaged in kidnapping outside Lebanon. The Red Army Faction (RAF), on the other hand, apparently has abandoned sieges in favor of kidnappings, following the abortive attack by one of their splinter groups on the West German embassy in Stockholm in 1975. Furthermore, with the possible exception of the South Moluccans, groups operating in Western Europe have employed hostage taking as only one of their many tactics, which include bombings and assassinations. Indeed, many groups now appear to have abandoned hostage taking in favor of these other tactics.

Nine countries of Western Europe have escaped being the targets of demands or of being hosts to a political hostage incident between 1 January 1968 and 31 December 1978.[11] Of the remaining twelve countries listed in Table 1, there does not appear to have been any correlation between the type of government in power at the time of the incident and the frequency or form of the incident. Hostage-taking incidents have occurred in countries ruled by a Socialist party, such as Sweden under Olaf Palme, and in countries ruled by a right-wing regime, such as Spain under Francisco Franco. Similarly, some countries, such as Greece and the Netherlands, have experienced only one form of a political-hostage incident, while others, such as France and Italy, have had both. Any explanations for this are bound to be empirical and only germane for a particular country at a particular time. Austria and West Germany, for example, now have both adopted hard-line positions in dealing with political-hostage incidents, and yet the incidents continue to occur. Turkey, on the other hand, always has maintained a no-concessions policy and had not had a hostage incident for over six years, until the Eagles of the Palestinian Revolution took over the Egyptian embassy in Ankara on 13 July 1979 and demanded the revocation of the newly signed Israeli-Egyptian peace agreement.

One interesting correlation can be made. Indigenous separatist groups and exile-minority communities generally have been responsible for the majority of political-hostage incidents within their respective host countries. The Basque separatist group ETA, for example, has been responsible for nineteen out of twenty-four incidents that have occurred in Spain; the Provisional Irish Republican Army (PIRA) has been responsible for six of the seven incidents in the United Kingdom but for the

---

[11]No political hostage incidents occurred during the first two years of this time frame.

Table 1. Geographical Distribution of Political Hostage Incidents in Western Europe

	1970	1971	1972	1973	1974	1975	1976	1977	1978
Austria.............	—	—	—	A/S,S	—	S	—	2K	—
Cyprus.............	—	—	—	—	—	—	—	K	S
France.............	—	—	K	S	K	K/S,3K,3S	—	K,S	2S
Federal Republic of Germany...........	—	—	4P/K,S	—	—	P/S,K	P/K,K	K	—
Greece.............	—	—	—	2S	K	—	—	—	—
Republic of Ireland.....	—	—	—	—	—	K/S	—	—	—
Italy..............	—	—	3K	K,S	4P/K,2K	K/S,K	3K,S	2K	K,S
Netherlands........	S	—	—	—	A/K,S	P/S,A/S,2S	—	P/S,2S	S
Spain.............	K	A/K	K	K,S	—	2S	K/S,4K	K/S,K	4A/K,5K,S
Sweden............	S	AK/S,S	—	—	—	S	—	A/K	—
Turkey............	—	6K,S	A/K,K/S	—	—	S	—	K	—
United Kingdom......	—	—	—	K,S	—	—	—	—	3K

K—Kidnapping
S—Siege
K/S—Kidnap/Siege
A/K—Attempted Kidnapping
A/S—Attempted Siege
AK/S—Attempted Kidnapping/Siege
P/K—Planned Kidnapping
P/S—Planned Siege

only two incidents in the Republic of Ireland; the EOKA-B for two of the three incidents in Cyprus; and the Action pour la Renaissance de la Corse (ARC) and the Front de la Libération de la Corse were each responsible for one of the only two incidents in Corsica. Similarly, the South Moluccans have been responsible for nine of the eleven incidents that have occurred in the Netherlands; the Ustashi have been responsible for two of the five incidents in Sweden; and the Harkis for five of the fourteen incidents in France. There are exceptions. France, for example, also is faced with a separatist movement in Brittany, but the members have never engaged in hostage taking. Neither have the various exile-minority communities in the United Kingdom, such as the White Russians and East European émigré groups.

FORM OF HOSTAGE INCIDENT

The usual classification of hostage incidents into sieges and kidnappings can be taken a stage further by dividing them into those that were successful, those that were attempted, and those that were merely planned. A successful hostage incident is one in which a hostage was in fact seized; an attempted hostage incident is one in which the seizure was foiled for one reason or another, usually through the intervention of the police or other government agents; and a planned hostage incident is one that was foiled or abandoned before it could be put into effect. Utilizing this tripartite schema, as illustrated by Table 2, 81 percent of all known incidents were successful (91 out of 113), 9 percent were foiled (10 out of 113), and a final 11 percent were never put into effect (12 out of 113). Kidnapping—either successful, attempted, or planned—accounted for 60 percent of all known incidents (68 out of 113).

Another variant of the barricade-and-hostage situation also must be considered a siege. A kidnap/siege, as it will be termed, occurs when the responding authorities locate the hideout where the kidnap victim is being held and surround it as they would for a siege, as has been the case with six incidents. A variation of the kidnap/siege occurs after an attempted kidnapping when, for example, the police respond too quickly for the hostage takers to escape with their victim or when the hostage takers are delayed by the potential victim for a length of time sufficient to allow the police to arrive. The sole example of this type occurred with the attempted kidnapping/siege at the Yugoslav embassy in Stockholm by the Ustashi on 7 April 1971.

Table 2. Form of Hostage Incident

	1970	1971	1972	1973	1974	1975	1976	1977	1978	Total
Kidnap	1	6	5	4	4	5	8	9	9	51
Attempted Kidnap	—	1	1	—	1	—	—	1	4	8
Planned Kidnap	—	—	4	—	4	—	1	—	—	9
Siege	2	3	2	7	9	13	2	4	6	40
Attempted Siege	—	—	—	1	—	1	—	—	—	2
Planned Siege	—	—	—	—	—	2	—	1	—	3

YEARLY NUMBER OF INCIDENTS OF ANY FORM

There appears to have been little correlation between the frequency of one type of incident and the frequency of the other. For example, it cannot be assumed that merely because a high number of kidnappings occurred in any one year, then also a high number of sieges occurred in the same year. On the other hand, it cannot be assumed that the inverse is true and that if there were a high number of kidnappings, then there were a low number of sieges, or vice versa. The second highest number of any form of a kidnapping occurred in 1972 with ten recorded incidents, but only two of any form of a siege were recorded in the same year. Similarly, the highest number of any form of a kidnapping occurred in 1978 with thirteen recorded incidents, and yet the same year also witnessed the third highest number of any form of a siege with six recorded incidents.

YEARLY SUCCESS RATES OF INCIDENTS

There appears as well to have been little correlation between the yearly success rates of either type of incident. However, these figures may be misleading empirically due to the small number of incidents recorded in some years. For example, there is a success rate of 100 percent for kidnappings and sieges in 1970, and yet there were only one kidnapping and two sieges in that year. On aggregate, a hostage taker had a 75 percent chance of seizing hostages in kidnappings and an 89 percent chance in sieges. Interestingly enough, these figures on the yearly success rates probably are indicative of the impact of the learning process taking place within governments, which have slowly learned how to respond to a hostage incident, and within the terrorist community, whose members have learned how to counteract that response.

LOCATION AND DURATION OF SUCCESSFUL INCIDENTS

The locations of successful kidnappings only were reported in twenty-two incidents, but of these, 45 percent involved an abduction from cars, 36 percent from the hostages' homes, and 5 percent each from a military base, a hostel, and a university. Excluding the ten incidents in which the duration is unknown or uncertain, the average length of the remaining forty-one successful kidnappings was 12.5 days and the median

Table 3. Location of Successful Sieges

	1970	1971	1972	1973	1974	1975	1976	1977	1978	Total
Embassy/Inviolable Premise	2	2	—	2	1	5	1	—	1	14
Train	—	—	—	1	—	1	—	1	—	3
Private Residence	—	1	1	—	—	3	1	1	—	7
Commercial Premise	—	—	1	4	—	3	—	—	2	9
Other	—	—	1	—	—	1	—	2	3	7
										40

5. The longest period during which a hostage was held was ninety-one days and began on 13 April 1977, when M. Revelli-Beaumont was kidnapped from his Paris home by the Committee for Revolutionary Socialist Unity (CRSU).

The locations of successful sieges, which are always reported because of their very nature, are illustrated in Table 3. The most common location, an embassy or other inviolable premise, such as a consulate or a diplomat's residence, has accounted for 35 percent of all sieges.

The average duration was 138 hours (5.8 days) and the median 17–18 hours. However, these figures are slightly misleading due to the inclusion of the seven kidnap/sieges, which are likely to be of longer duration because of their very nature. By removing these, the average duration now becomes 68 hours and the median 15. The seven kidnap/sieges produced an average duration of 468 hours (19.5 days) and a median of 120 hours (5 days). The longest a siege lasted was 20 days, and two such sieges began on 23 May 1977 with the South Moluccan takeovers of a train near Onnan and an elementary school in Bovensmilde.

NATURE OF GROUPS ENGAGED IN POLITICAL HOSTAGE TAKING

Groups that have engaged in political hostage taking can be classified according to various criteria, such as ideology, tactical and strategic objectives, structural size, or sociological composition.[12] Some groups, such as the Harkis or the ARC in France, are either not overly politicized or have an unclear, even confused, ideology. Other groups, such as the United Red Army and the Italian Armed Proletarian Nuclei, or Nuclei Armati Proletari (NAP), are avowedly Marxist or even Anarchist, whereas still others, such as the Mussolini Action Squads or the Swedish Ustashi, are right wing. Interestingly enough, the PIRA seemed only to adopt a left-wing stance when it became apparent that their sources of arms from the United States were drying up, and they would need to turn to other groups to replenish their supplies. Similarly, the tactical and strategic objectives of groups engaged in political hostage taking vary

---

[12]For useful typologies of terrorist groups, see Brian Crozier's testimony in *Hearings Before the Sub-committee to Investigate the Administration of the Internal Security Act and other Internal Security Laws, of the Committee on the Judiciary*, U.S., Senate, 94th Cong., 2nd Sess., Part 4 (Washington, DC: Government Printing Office, 14 May 1975), pp. 182–83; Paul Wilkinson, *Political Terrorism* (London: Macmillan Press, 1974), pp. 32–44; and Richard Schultz, "Conceptualizing Political Terrorism: A Typology," *Journal of International Affairs* 32, no. 1 (1978): 9–10.

considerably from the Palestinian Liberation Organization (PLO), which is recognized by the United Nations as a national liberation movement, to the Fighters for the Defense of Israel, which appears to exist solely to combat the Palestinians. The structural size of groups also varies from the Italian Red Brigades, with an identified active membership of about 460,[13] to Black December, whose membership consisted only of the three hostage takers involved in the siege of the Indian High Commission in London on 20 January 1973. Even the sociological composition of groups is dissimilar and ranges from the German Movement 2 June, or Bewegung 2 Juni, wherein over 65 percent of the membership was from the middle class,[14] to the PIRA, whose membership is predominantly from the lower or working class.

As Table 4 illustrates, responsibility for taking hostages for political gain has been claimed by twenty-six different, though not necessarily autonomous, groups and factions. The occupation of embassies by students as a form of protest has occurred on seven occasions, although in only two were hostages taken. In one kidnapping, that of Revelli-Beaumont, "for the first time in a major European incident, a Latin-American connection with left-wing Argentinian Peronists was disclosed."[15] On the other hand, the kidnapping of Father Hugh Murphy in Ulster by the Ulster Freedom Fighters on 18 June 1978 actually was conducted by two members of the Royal Ulster Constabulary who merely posed as members of the group.

FATE OF THE HOSTAGE TAKERS

Of the two types of incidents, kidnappings are not only more common, they are also safer for the hostage takers.[16] In fact, the tactic is so safe that precise figures for the number of hostage takers involved in forty-one of the fifty-one kidnappings are unavailable. Seen from this perspective, the hostage takers had an 80 percent chance of escaping identification during a kidnapping. Nonetheless, a total of forty-two hostage takers was arrested, shot, or identified as active participants in the remaining ten incidents, thus producing an average and a median of four participants per incident.

---

[13]"Dossier of Terror," *Police* 10, no. 10 (June 1978): 26.
[14]Charles A. Russell and Bowman H. Miller, "Profile of a Terrorist," in this volume.
[15]Crozier, *Annual of Power and Conflict* (1977), p. 26.
[16]Hereafter, all statistics are only those which refer to successful incidents.

Table 4. Nature of Groups Engaged in Political Hostage Taking

	1970	1971	1972	1973	1974	1975	1976	1977	1978
ARC	—	—	—	—	—	S	—	—	—
Black December	—	—	—	S	—	—	—	—	—
CRSU	—	—	—	—	—	—	—	K	—
EOKA-B	—	—	K	K	—	—	—	K	—
ETA	K	A/K	K	K,S	—	—	4K	K	4A/K,5K
Fighters for the Defense of Israel	—	—	—	—	—	—	—	—	S
FLNC	—	—	—	—	—	—	—	S	—
Grupos de Acción Revolucionaria Internacionalista (GARI)	—	—	—	—	K	—	—	—	—
Grupo de Resistencia Antifascista Primero de Octubre (GRAPO)	—	—	—	—	—	3K,S,K/S	K/S	K/S	—
Harkis	—	—	—	—	—	—	—	—	—

K—Kidnapping
S—Siege
K/S—Kidnap/Siege
A/K—Attemped Kidnapping
A/S—Attempted Siege
AK/S—Attempted Kidnapping/Siege
P/K—Planned Kidnapping
P/S—Planned Siege

Table 4 (continued)

Movimiento para la Auto-determinación e Independencia del Archipielago de las Canarias (MPAIAC)....	—	—	—	—	—	—	—	S
Mussolini Action Squads....	—	—	—	4P/K	—	—	—	—
Nouvelle Résistance Populaire (NRP).........	—	K	—	K	K	—	K	—
NAP.................	—	—	—	K	—	—	—	—
Palestinians/Black September/PFLP...........	—	S	5S,A/S	—	3S,A/S	S	—	2S
PIRA................	—	—	K	K	S,K/S	—	K	2K
RAF/Holger Meins Commando/Movement 2 June........	—	4P/K	—	—	K,S,A/S	P/K,K	A/K,3K	—
Red Brigades..........	—	3K	K	K	K/S	K	K	K
South Moluccans........	S	—	—	A/K	P/S,2S	—	P/S,2S	S

K—Kidnapping
S—Siege
K/S—Kidnap/Siege
A/K—Attemped Kidnapping
A/S—Attempted Siege
AK/S—Attempted Kidnapping/Siege
P/K—Planned Kidnapping
P/S—Planned Siege

111

Table 4 (continued)

	1970	1971	1972	1973	1974	1975	1976	1977	1978
Squadre Armati Comunista (Armed Communist Units)	—	—	—	—	—	—	2K	—	—
Squadre Proletarie di Combattimento (Fighting Proletarian Squads)	—	—	—	—	—	—	—	—	S
Students	S	K	—	—	—	S	—	—	—
Turkish People's Liberation Army	—	5K,S	A/K,K/S	—	—	—	—	—	—
Ulster Freedom Fighters	—	—	—	—	—	—	—	—	K
United Red Army	—	—	—	—	S	—	—	—	—
Ustashi	—	AK/S,S	—	—	—	—	—	—	—

K—Kidnapping
S—Siege
K/S—Kidnap/Siege
A/K—Attempted Kidnapping
A/S—Attempted Siege
AK/S—Attempted Kidnapping/Siege
P/K—Planned Kidnapping
P/S—Planned Siege

112

Sieges are far more costly for the hostage takers. As Table 5 illustrates, of the 363 active participants in the forty sieges, only 25 escaped without the aid of the authorities. However, 21 of these escaped because the hostages were taken only incidentally to prevent them from becoming a hindrance to the main attack, and the authorities did not become involved until after the attack was over and the hostages already released. Excluding these, the hostage takers had only a 1.2 percent chance of escaping identification once the authorities responded; although 179, of the 288 arrested, were immediately released following their identification by police.

Any attempt to calculate an average number of participants for each of the forty sieges is largely misleading, due to the two embassy occupations by thirty and fifty students, respectively, and a further three incidents involving thirty-five, fifty, and fifty participants, respectively. However, when all incidents are combined, this results in a median of five hostage takers per siege.

NATURE OF HOSTAGES

Historically, hostages were chosen either according to their quality or their quantity. This latter group still accounts for the largest proportion of hostages seized in Western Europe and are best classified as "innocents." In fact, 66 percent of all hostages seized in Western Europe can be placed in this category. However, some groups argue that there is no such thing as an innocent victim. For example, the three Jewish emigrants taken from the Chopin Express train in 1973 were seen to be legitimate targets by the Eagles of the Palestinian Revolution because they were Jewish and, more importantly, they were emigrating to Israel. Nonetheless, there are other victims, such as hotel guests and airline passengers, whose only "crime" appears to have been that they were in the wrong place at the wrong time. The other four categories depicted in Tables 6 and 7 are self-explanatory and are merely refinements of the original nobleman or quality classification.

Fewer persons per incident are taken in kidnap situations. However, there was one incident in which 5 people were seized and two incidents each involving the abduction of 3 and 4 people respectively. This results in an average of 1.3 hostages taken in each of the fifty-one kidnappings and a median of 1. Significantly, as Table 6 illustrates, 51 percent of all kidnap victims have been from the capitalist category. Perhaps surprisingly, the second largest group has been those referred to as innocents, although nine of the fourteen of these were Algerian workers abducted by the Harkis in 1975 to pressure the Algerian government into capitulating to

Table 5. Fate of Hostage Takers Involved in Sieges

	1970	1971	1972	1973	1974	1975	1976	1977	1978	Total
Arrested	65	4	3	8	—	177	7	11	5	280
(Wounded)	—	1	—	—	—	5	—	1	1	8
Killed	—	1	15	2	—	2	—	6	—	26
Granted Safe Conduct	—	—	—	8	3	13	—	—	—	24
Escaped	—	—	—	6	—	—	—	6	13	25

Table 6. Nature of Kidnap Victims

	1970	1971	1972	1973	1974	1975	1976	1977	1978	Total
Diplomats	1	—	—	1	—	1	—	—	1	4
Police/Servicemen	—	5	—	—	—	—	1	1	1	8
Capitalists	—	3	5	2	4	—	9	6	4	33
Innocents	—	1	—	—	—	9	—	2	2	14
Government Officials	—	—	—	1	1	2	—	—	2	6
										65

Table 7. Nature of Siege Victims

	1970	1971	1972	1973	1974	1975	1976	1977	1978	Total
Diplomats	9	5	—	21	11	123	5	—	8	182
Police/Servicemen	1	—	3	5	—	—	—	4	—	13
Capitalists	—	—	—	—	—	2	—	—	—	2
Innocents	—	3	9	200	—	137	—	185	93	627
Government Officials	—	—	—	1	—	1	1	1	73	77
										901

their demands. Perhaps also surprisingly, the smallest group has consisted of the four diplomats.

As Table 7 illustrates, by far the largest group of siege victims has been the innocents, accounting for 70 percent of the hostages. The second largest group has been composed of diplomats with 182 hostages taken in the fourteen sieges of an inviolable premise. The smallest group has consisted of the 2 capitalists who were originally kidnap victims but whose hideout was discovered by police and surrounded. An average of 26.9 hostages was taken in each of the thirty-three sieges and an average of 1.9 in each of the seven kidnap/sieges. However, a median of 10–11 hostages was seized in each of the sieges and 1 in each of the kidnap/sieges.

FATE OF THE HOSTAGES

As Table 8 illustrates, the fate of two of the sixty-five kidnap victims is unknown. However, the outcomes of these (the kidnapping of a police inspector by the Basque ETA in 1976 and the kidnapping of Renato Penterioni in Rome by the Armed Communist Units on 16 June 1976) probably have never been reported. The fate of the remaining 63 hostages is depicted as it relates to the response to the hostage takers' demands. Fewer hostages have been killed if demands were granted. In terms of a ratio between total hostage deaths and the total number of those released, 14 percent have been killed.

As Table 9 illustrates, 22 siege victims managed to escape, but 1 of these died and 2 others were wounded in the process. The fate of the remaining 879 hostages is depicted as it relates to the response to the hostage takers' demands. In those incidents in which no demands were presented, 130 of the hostages were released and only 4 killed. In those incidents in which demands were granted, 210 of the hostages were released but 1 was killed anyway. In those incidents in which demands were not granted and the hostage takers surrendered, 163 of the hostages were still released and only 5 were killed. However, in those incidents in which demands were not granted and the incident was terminated by assault, 12 of the hostages were killed and a further 13 wounded, but 341 hostages were rescued unharmed. In terms of a ratio between those killed and those released for each of the four categories, 3 percent, 0.5 percent, 3 percent, and 3.3 percent respectively have been killed.[17] Accordingly, and in common with kidnappings, fewer hostages have been killed if demands were granted. If demands were refused, a marginally higher ratio of

---

[17]Nine targeted hostages were killed during the initial attack, before hostages had been seized.

Table 8. Fate of Kidnap Victims

	1970	1971	1972	1973	1974	1975	1976	1977	1978	Total
No Demands										
Released	1	2	2	1	2	—	—	—	4	12
Killed	—	—	—	1	—	—	—	1	2	4
Demands Granted										
Released	—	3	2	1	1	11	6	5	1	30
Killed	—	—	—	—	—	—	—	1	—	1
Demands Refused										
Released	—	4	1	1	2	1	1	1	1	12
Killed	—	1	—	—	—	—	1	1	1	4
Fate Unknown	—	—	—	—	—	—	2	—	—	2
										65

Table 9. Fate of Siege Victims

	1970	1971	1972	1973	1974	1975	1976	1977	1978	Total
No Demands										
Released	3	1	—	100	—	2	5	4	15	130
Killed	—	1	3	—	—	—	—	—	—	4
Demands Granted										
Released	—	—	—	63	11	136	—	—	—	210
Killed	—	—	—	1	—	—	—	—	—	1
Demands Refused; Hostage Takers Surrendered										
Released	7	3	—	49	—	96	—	—	8	163
Killed	—	—	—	1	—	4	—	—	—	5
Demands Refused; Assault										
Released	—	3	—	8	—	8	1	177	144	341
Killed	—	—	9	—	—	—	—	2	1	12
Wounded	—	—	—	—	—	—	—	7	6	13
Escaped										
Unharmed	—	—	—	3	—	16	—	—	—	19
Injured	—	—	—	2	—	—	—	—	—	2
Died	—	—	—	—	—	1	—	—	—	1
										901

hostage deaths has occurred if the incident was terminated by assault (3.3 percent) than if the hostage takers were allowed to surrender on their own accord (3 percent). In terms of a ratio between total hostage deaths and the total number of those released, only 2.5 percent have been killed.

NATURE OF DIRECT TARGET OF DEMANDS

As Table 10 illustrates, 39 percent of all kidnappings in which the direct primary target was within the private sector produced demands. Perhaps surprisingly, the second most common occurrence was for no demands to be presented, as happened in 31 percent of the kidnappings. However, the second most common direct primary target was the host government, as occurred in 24 percent of the incidents. Algeria was the direct target in the three incidents in which demands were aimed at a foreign government.

As Table 11 illustrates, 40 percent of all sieges produced demands directed primarily against the host government. Again, the second most common occurrence was for no demands to be presented, as happened in 33 percent of the sieges. However, the second most common direct primary target for demands was a combination of the host government and a foreign government, as occurred in 20 percent of the incidents. These and the ones from the foreign government category were Algeria (twice), Austria (twice), Egypt (twice), France (three times), Indonesia, Israel (twice), the Netherlands (twice), the United Kingdom, West Germany (twice), and Yugoslavia (twice).

NATURE OF DEMANDS

As Table 12 illustrates, 29 percent of all kidnappings were conducted solely for a monetary ransom. A further 12 percent produced a combination of demands, of which 6 percent were for the release of prisoners and a monetary ransom; 2 percent for the release of prisoners and safe conduct; 2 percent for the release of prisoners, a monetary ransom, and safe conduct; and last, 2 percent for the transfer of prisoners from one jail to another and the publication of a manifesto. There were an additional 14 percent solely for the release of prisoners, and another 6 percent for specific political changes. A further 8 percent were aimed at producing specific corporate policy changes within the private sector, and a final 16 incidents produced no demands at all.

Table 13 shows that 33 percent of all sieges produced a combination of demands. These can be broken down into 18 percent for the release of

Table 10. Nature of Direct Target of Demands from Kidnappings

	1970	1971	1972	1973	1974	1975	1976	1977	1978	Total
Host Government	—	2	1	1	2	2	—	2	2	12
Foreign Government	—	—	—	—	—	2	—	—	—	2
Combination	—	—	—	—	—	1	—	—	—	1
Private Sector	—	2	2	1	1	—	7	6	1	20
No/Unclear Demands	1	2	2	2	1	—	1	1	6	16

Table 11. Nature of Direct Target of Demands from Sieges

	1970	1971	1972	1973	1974	1975	1976	1977	1978	Total
Host Government	—	1	—	4	—	5	1	3	2	16
Foreign Government	—	1	—	—	—	2	—	—	—	3
Combination	1	—	1	1	1	3	—	—	1	8
Private Sector	—	—	—	—	—	—	—	—	—	0
No/Unclear Demands	1	1	1	2	—	3	1	1	3	13

Table 12. Nature of Demands from Kidnappings

	1970	1971	1972	1973	1974	1975	1976	1977	1978	Total
Specific Political Changes	—	—	—	1	—	1	—	—	1	3
Release Prisoners	—	1	1	—	1	2	—	1	1	7
Ransom	—	2	1	—	—	—	5	6	1	15
Escape	—	—	—	—	—	—	—	—	—	0
Combination of These	—	1	—	1	2	2	—	—	—	6
Specific Corporate Policy Changes	—	—	1	1	—	—	2	—	—	4
No Demands	1	2	2	2	1	—	1	1	6	16

prisoners and safe conduct out of the country; 8 percent for specific political changes and safe conduct; and last, 8 percent for the release of prisoners, a monetary ransom, and safe conduct. In another 18 percent of the sieges, the sole demand was for safe conduct; in 10 percent, for specific political changes; and in 8 percent, for the release of prisoners. In a final thirteen incidents, there were no demands at all.

RESPONSE TO DEMANDS

Table 14 indicates that no demands were made in sixteen kidnappings, so no response was required, and in one the response is unknown. Of the remaining thirty-four incidents, demands were granted in 59 percent, partially granted in 6 percent, and rejected outright in 35 percent.

As Table 15 illustrates, no demands were made in thirteen sieges, so no response was required. Of the remaining twenty-seven incidents, demands were granted in 19 percent, partially granted in 7 percent, and rejected outright in 74 percent.

RESPONSE OF DIRECT TARGET TO SPECIFIC DEMANDS

It is possible to break down Tables 14 and 15 even further and to examine the nexus between specific demands, the nature of the target, and the response. Of the two kidnappings in which the primary target was a foreign government (here Algeria), the sole demand was for the release of a prisoner being held in that country, and both incidents succeeded in getting the prisoner released; however, the two incidents occurred a day apart and were for the release of the same prisoner. Of the three sieges in which the primary target was a foreign government, one (here Yugoslavia) refused to release a prisoner, and in the other two (both involving Egypt), demands for specific changes in political policy similarly were refused.

The situation is far more complex when demands are directed at a combination of primary and secondary targets. There was one kidnapping in which demands were of this type, but neither the primary target (here Algeria) nor the secondary target (here France) agreed even to enter into negotiations with the hostage takers until the hostage was released. Of the eight sieges in which demands were of this type, only one resulted in both the primary target (here France) and the secondary target (here the Netherlands) agreeing to grant demands for the release of a prisoner, a

Table 13. Nature of Demands from Sieges

	1970	1971	1972	1973	1974	1975	1976	1977	1978	Total
Specific Political Changes	1	—	—	—	—	3	—	—	—	4
Release Prisoners	—	1	—	—	—	—	1	1	—	3
Ransom	—	—	—	—	—	—	—	—	—	0
Escape	—	1	—	3	—	2	—	—	1	7
Combination of These	—	—	1	2	1	5	—	2	2	13
Specific Corporate Policy Changes	—	—	—	—	—	—	—	—	—	0
No Demands	1	1	1	2	—	3	1	1	3	13

Table 14. Response to Demands from Kidnappings

	1970	1971	1972	1973	1974	1975	1976	1977	1978	Total
Granted	—	2	1	1	1	4	4	6	1	20
Partially Granted	—	—	1	1	—	—	—	—	—	2
Rejected	1	2	1	2	2	1	2	1	—	12
No Demands	—	2	2	1	1	1	1	2	6	16
Unknown	—	—	—	—	—	—	1	—	—	1

Table 15. Response to Demands from Sieges

	1970	1971	1972	1973	1974	1975	1976	1977	1978	Total
Granted	—	—	—	3	1	1	—	—	—	5
Partially Granted	—	—	1	—	—	1	—	—	—	2
Rejected	1	2	1	1	—	8	1	3	3	20
No Demands	1	1	1	2	—	3	1	1	3	13

monetary ransom, and safe conduct out of the country. There were four incidents in which the primary target refused to release prisoners, and in three of these, safe conduct was refused by the secondary target but granted in the fourth. Finally, there were three incidents in which the primary target refused to initiate any specific political changes; in two of these, safe conduct was granted by the secondary target but refused in the third incident, when demands called for specific internal political changes.

Table 16 demonstrates that 70 percent of kidnappings in which the private sector was the primary target have resulted in demands being granted.[18] The most common demand was solely for ransom and was granted in 93 percent of the incidents in which demands were of this type. The second most common demand was for a specific change in corporate policy. These were partially granted in 50 percent of the appropriate incidents and rejected in 25 percent; in the final incident, the response is unknown. The other demand directed against the private sector involved a ransom and the release of prisoners which, as the primary target in this incident had no ability to grant, were rejected.

As Table 17 illustrates, 77 percent of kidnappings in which the host government has been the primary target have resulted in demands being rejected, regardless of their content. The most common demand was solely for the release of prisoners and was granted in only 20 percent of the incidents. The second most common demand was for specific political changes, and these were rejected in every case.

Table 18 indicates that 81 percent of sieges in which the host government was the primary target have resulted in demands being rejected, regardless of their content. The most common demand was solely for escape and was only granted in 43 percent of the incidents. The two second most common demands were for the release of prisoners and for the release of prisoners and escape; these were rejected in every case.

GLOBAL VERSUS REGIONAL EXPERIENCE

There are certain inherent difficulties in attempting to compare the above findings with those arrived at by three similar studies of the same phenomenon, but from a global perspective.[19] Primarily, the definitional

---

[18]There were no sieges in which the private sector was the primary target, and accordingly there will be no table to illustrate the modalities of this occurrence.

[19]Jenkins, et al., *Numbered Lives*, pp. 33–47; Edward F. Mickolus, "Negotiating for Hostages: A Policy Dilemma," *Orbis* 19, no. 4 (Winter 1976): 1311; and Paul Wilkinson, "Terrorism: International Dimensions," *Conflict Study No. 113* (London: Institute for the Study of Conflict, November 1979), p. 2.

Table 16. Response by Private Sector to Specific Demands from Kidnappings

	1970	1971	1972	1973	1974	1975	1976	1977	1978
Ransom	—	2G	G	—	—	—	4G,R	6G	G
Ransom and Release of Prisoners	—	—	—	—	R	—	—	—	—
Specific Corporate Policy Changes	—	—	PG	PG	—	—	UK,R	—	—

G—Granted
R—Rejected
PG—Partially Granted
UK—Unknown

Table 17. Response by Host Government to Specific Demands from Kidnappings

	1970	1971	1972	1973	1974	1975	1976	1977	1978
Specific Political Changes	—	—	—	—	—	R	—	—	R
Release Prisoners	—	R	R	R	G	—	—	R	R
Release Prisoners and Ransom	—	R	—	—	—	—	—	—	—
Release Prisoners and Escape	—	—	—	—	R	—	—	—	—
Release Prisoners, Ransom, and Escape	—	—	—	—	—	G	—	R	—
Transfer of Prisoners and Publication of Manifesto	—	—	—	—	—	G	—	—	—

G—Granted
R—Rejected

Table 18. Response by Host Government to Specific Demands from Sieges

	1970	1971	1972	1973	1974	1975	1976	1977	1978
Release Prisoners	—	R	—	—	—	—	—	—	—
Escape	—	—	—	—	—	R	R	R	R
Release Prisoners and Escape	—	—	—	2G,R	—	G,R	—	—	R
Release Prisoners, Ransom, and Escape	—	—	—	—	—	2R	—	2R	—
Specific Political Changes and Escape	—	—	—	G	—	—	—	—	—

G—Granted
R—Rejected

Table 19. Global Versus Regional Yearly Number of Kidnappings

	1968	1969	1970	1971	1972	1973	1974	1975	1976	1977	1978
Jenkins	1	3	23	6	1	6	4	9	—	—	—
Mickolus	2	3	33	13	11	30	10	32	—	—	—
Wilkinson	1	3	32	17	11	37	25	38	30	22	29
(Average)	—	—	29.3	12	7.7	24.3	13	—	—	—	—
Western Europe	—	—	1	7	6	4	5	5	8	10	13

124

criteria employed by the other studies does not appear to be exactly the same and not as rigid as that employed here. The focus here has been on all political-hostage incidents that have been conducted within Western Europe by nonstate actors and included those with both an intranational and an international character. However, the other three only focused on those with an international element. Two of them excluded cross-border incidents, whereas Paul Wilkinson included them. Consequently, discrepancies in total figures are inevitable. Similarly, the temporal parameters are different. Brian Jenkins, for example, utilized incidents which occurred between August 1968 and June 1975, whereas Edward F. Mickolus utilized those between 1 January 1968 and 31 December 1975. On the other hand, Wilkinson and this study employed a data base which extended throughout the entire decade from 1 January 1968 until 31 December 1978. As a result, total figures for the occurrence of each type of incident again are bound to be different. Finally, the degree and form of analysis in each study is also dissimilar. Only Jenkins and this study analyzed the content of each incident, including the nature of the demands, the response, and the fate of the hostages. Nonetheless, certain comparisons are still possible. It should, for example, be possible to compare roughly the yearly totals of incidents in those years mutually covered by all four studies (1969–74) by calculating an average yearly total from the other three studies and comparing that figure with the one arrived at here for Western Europe. However, it must be remembered that Western Europe is also included in the other studies and, as such, it will affect the yearly totals. As the other studies employed a different data base for Western Europe than that employed here, discrepancies are again inevitable. As a result, a precise comparison becomes impossible because of a lack of a consensus of the extent of the experience of Western Europe, and it is with a certain reservation that the following comparisons are made.

YEARLY NUMBER OF INCIDENTS

Table 19 indicates that the highest number of kidnappings in the rest of the world occurred in 1970, with an average between the three studies of 29.3. However, 1970 represented the second lowest year for Western Europe, with only one kidnapping. Similarly, the second highest number of kidnappings in the rest of the world occurred in 1973 with an average between the three studies of 24.3, but the same year represented the third lowest for Western Europe with only four kidnappings. Interestingly enough, this same inverse correlation existed in the opposite direction. The highest number of kidnappings in Western Europe occurred in 1971 with six. However, 1971 represented the third lowest year for the rest of the world with an average between the three studies of twelve kidnappings. Similarly, the second highest number of kidnappings in Western Europe occurred in 1972 with 6, but the same year represented the second lowest for the rest of the world with an average between the three studies of 7.7. However, this inverse correlation cannot be expressed as a generalization in terms of a high number of kidnappings in Western Europe will necessarily have meant a low number of kidnappings in the rest of the world, or vice versa. For example, the third highest number of kidnappings in Western Europe and the rest of the world both occurred in 1974 with five and thirteen respectively.

Table 20 shows that the highest number of sieges in the rest of the world occurred in 1974, with an average between the three studies of 10.3. However, 1974 represented the second lowest year for Western Europe with only 1 siege. The second lowest number of sieges in the rest of the world occurred in 1971 with an average between the three studies of 0.7, but the same year represented the second highest for Western Europe with 3. However, the remaining four years mutually covered by all four studies involved a fairly close degree of congruence between Western Europe and the rest of the world: no sieges occurred anywhere in 1969; 2 and 2 respectively in 1970; 2 and 2.7 respectively in 1972; and 8 and 7.7 respectively in 1973.

CONTENT OF THE INCIDENTS

It is also worthwhile to compare the analysis of the content of the incidents as undertaken by Jenkins and by this study. Specific findings, such as the nature and response to demands or the identity of the hostage takers, are obviously not amenable to comparison due to the different temporal and geographical limits of each study. However, general trends or findings, such as percentile probabilities, are readily adaptable to such a comparison.

The first category worthy of comparison is the overall breakdown of incidents:

	Jenkins[20]	Western Europe
Kidnaps	42	51
Attempted Kidnaps	6	8
Sieges	16	33
Attempted Sieges	5	2
Kidnap/Sieges	4	7
Unplanned Sieges	4	5

[20] Jenkins, et al., *Numbered Lives*, p. 10.

Table 20. Global Versus Regional Yearly Number of Sieges

	1968	1969	1970	1971	1972	1973	1974	1975	1976	1977	1978
Jenkins	—	—	—	—	2	7	11	5	—	—	—
Mickolus	—	—	1	1	3	8	11	18	—	—	8
Wilkinson	—	—	5	1	3	8	9	14	4	5	8
(Average)	—	—	2	0.7	2.7	7.7	10.3	—	—	—	—
Western Europe	—	—	2	3	2	8	1	14	2	4	6

Although there is a discrepancy in the total number of incidents, the general pattern is the same; kidnappings and attempted kidnappings have accounted for approximately 60 percent of all political-hostage incidents. While the number of hostages who have been seized in kidnappings is roughly the same, the number of those taken in sieges has been quite different:

	Jenkins[21]	Western Europe
Kidnap Victims		
Average	1.4	1.3
Median	1.0	1.0
Siege Victims		
Average	14.0	26.9
Median	6.0	10–11

The duration of the two types of incident has also been quite different:

	Jenkins[22]	Western Europe
Kidnappings		
Average	38 days	12.5 days
Median	4–5 days	5 days
Sieges		
Average	47 hours	138 hours

The figures on the fate of the hostages have also been quite dissimilar:

	Jenkins[23]	Western Europe
Siege victims released	72.0%	95.0%
Kidnap victims killed	16.0	14.0
Siege victims killed	15.0	2.4
Total hostages executed	3.0	3.2
Total hostages killed during assaults	12.0	1.3

However, a comparison of the payoff/risk calculations indicates a fairly close degree of congruence in all but the final category:

[21] Ibid., p. 11.
[22] Ibid., p. 13.
[23] Ibid., pp. 25–27.

	Jenkins[24]	Western Europe
Probability of seizing hostages	90%	81%
Probability that all kidnappers will escape, whether or not they seize hostages	77	80
Probability that all or some of the demands other than safe conduct will be met	40	44
Probability of full compliance with such demands	36	40
Probability of full compliance when safe conduct is the sole demand	86	43

The experience of Western Europe, therefore, appears to have been both similar and dissimilar to that of the rest of the world. Certain categories, such as the ratio of kidnappings to sieges and four of the five payoff/risk calculations, have exhibited a high degree of congruence. The majority of categories, on the other hand, has been quite dissimilar: more hostages involved in sieges in Western Europe; kidnappings shorter in duration and sieges longer; a greater percentage of siege victims released unharmed; a lower percentage of all kidnap and siege victims killed; a lower percentage of hostages killed during assaults; and a far lower probability of full compliance with demands for safe conduct. Furthermore, the yearly number of political-hostage incidents of either type does not appear to have borne any correlation to the experience of the rest of the world. A higher number of incidents that has been experienced in any given year by the rest of the world may or may not have been mirrored by the experience of Western Europe for that particular year, and vice versa.

Regardless of how typical or atypical the experience of Western Europe has been, numerous conclusions can be drawn from the above. Undoubtedly, the most interesting concerns the fate of the hostages, and indeed it now becomes possible to correct earlier delusive impressions. For example, in his letter of 28 September 1976 to the secretary-general of the United Nations requesting the inclusion of an additional item in the agenda of the 31st session of the General Assembly entitled "Drafting of an international convention against the taking of hostages," Hans-Dietrich Genscher, the West German foreign minister, stated that in "many cases the incident ends with the deliberate killing of the hostages."[25] However, of the fifty-eight incidents that had occurred in Western Europe between 1968 and the time of his letter, only 7 percent had ended in the deliberate killing of the hostages—2 kidnappings and 2 sieges. In fact, only 3.2

---

[24]Ibid., p. 24.
[25]General Assembly, Official Records, 31st Sess., Annexes, A/31/242, p. 1, para. 1.

percent of all hostages have been killed in Western Europe. Moreover, in strict statistical terms, more hostages have been killed during assaults than if the hostage takers had been allowed to surrender on their own accord. It is also interesting to note that while the most common primary target of all demands has been the host government, marginally more incidents have resulted in no demands being presented—28 versus 29 incidents respectively. The most common type of demands has been for a combination of specific political changes, the release of prisoners, payment of a monetary ransom, and safe conduct out of the country, as has occurred in 31 percent of the incidents in which demands were presented. Of the sixty-one incidents in which demands were presented and the response is known, they were only granted 41 percent of the time, partially granted 7 percent, and rejected outright in 52 percent.

Hostage Taking: The Dutch Experience

ROBERT HAUBEN

Between 1974 and 1977, there were seven episodes in which 283 individuals were taken hostage for varying periods of time in the Netherlands. This paper is an attempt to summarize the rather extensive data amassed by the various Dutch mental health disciplines in the management of these episodes.[1] We can review them through a recitation of the episodes themselves; discussions of coping and affiliation; a compilation of the aftereffects noted; an explanation of the different types and degrees of aftercare offered, with the results to date; and an attempt to extract from these experiences information, knowledge, and conclusions which might be of use in other situations or other cultures.

EPISODES

Occupation of the French Embassy in The Hague, 13 September 1974
    Three Japanese nationals, members of the Japanese Red Army, held the embassy for four days. Eleven persons were in the building at the time of the occupation: seven Dutch and four French citizens. On 15 September, two women were released, and on 17 September the rest of the hostages were let go when demands of the terrorists were met: ransom, the

    [1]The conclusions and information in this paper are based upon six months of research by the writer in the Netherlands. This time was spent in interviews in Dutch with ex-hostages, therapists, and negotiators, together with a study of the Dutch literature, most of which has not been translated. Other sources were family doctors, social workers, and members of the Central Steering and Support Committee (CBOG). Of importance also were statistical studies by the Dutch Ministry of Public Health in its report, *Psychological Examination of the Consequences of Being Held Hostage in the Netherlands, 1974–1977;* J. Bastiaans, et al., *Psychologisch Onderzoek naar de Gevolgen van Gijzelingen in Nederland, 1974–1977* (The Hague: Staatsuitgeverij, 1979); C. Kho-So, "Naar een Diagnose van het Gijzeligssyndroom en Psychotherapie van Gegijzelden," *Tijdschrift v. Psychotherapie* 3 (1977): 206–13; H. C. Schouwenburg, "Het Klachtenpatroon bij 'somatiserende' patienten," *Ned Tijdschrift v. Genees* 32 (1977): 91–99.

131

release of a comrade in a French prison, and a plane in which to leave the country.

Incident at the Scheveningen Prison, 26 October 1974

Four prisoners took twenty-two persons captive during a church service. These hostages were members of a choir who came to the prison weekly, along with the organist and two guards. Four children and three adults were released on the first day; the rest were freed on 31 October following an assault by Dutch marines, who overpowered the convicts.

Capture of the Train at Wijster, 21 December 1975

A two-part train with no through connection was captured on that date. In the first part of the train, thirty-five persons were held by the same number of Moluccans. In the second part, twenty-four were held hostage even though they had no direct contact with the Moluccans. The second group escaped unharmed from the train in the course of the first two days. During the first three days, three hostages were killed, two others escaped, and five were released. On 31 December, the captors freed the remaining hostages.

Takeover of the Indonesian Consulate in Amsterdam, 4 December 1975

The building was occupied by a group of Moluccans who held thirty-six hostages, including fourteen children from a school within the consulate, personnel from a travel agency, teachers, consular employees, and several visitors. The children and some adults were released in the first few days. The hostages gave up on 19 December.

Hijacking of an Airplane, 4 September 1976

Three Palestinians skyjacked a KLM DC-9 en route to Amsterdam from Nice. Five crew members and eighty passengers, fifty of whom were Dutch, were aboard. Nineteen hours later, the hostages were released in Cyprus in return for a promise of safe conduct for the terrorists. Little information is available about this episode, because KLM put a lid of secrecy on it to avoid legal tangles.

Capture of a Train at the Punt, 23 May 1977

Nine Moluccans took over a train between Assen and Groningen with ninety-six passengers on board. Within the first hour, forty-two were released; on 5 June, two women; and on 8 June, one more man. On 11 June, nineteen days later, marines stormed the train and liberated forty-nine passengers. Two hostages as well as six terrorists were killed; three terrorists were arrested.

Capture of the School at Bovensmilde, 23 May 1977

Almost simultaneously with the train at the Punt, four Moluccans occupied an elementary school with five teachers and 125 pupils. Twenty Moluccan children attending were released promptly. Several of the Dutch children began to show signs of a viral disease, and by 28 May all the children were released; only the five teachers remained in captivity. On 11 June, at the same time as the attack on the train, marines invaded the school, liberated the teachers, and arrested the perpetrators. No one was hurt.

	Number of Persons	Duration of Episode (Days)
French Embassy	11	4
Scheveningen Prison	22	5
Wijster Train	35 (+24)	10
Indonesian Consulate	36	15
KLM Plane	85	1
Punt Train	96	19
Bovensmilde School	131	19

These brief descriptions show that Dutch officials did not react to the hostage situations in the same way. Similarly, treatment, preparation for the reception of the hostages, ongoing work with the families, and aftercare showed no unified principles.

COPING

The relations to stress situations observed were placed in three groups: adaptation, defense mechanisms, and coping. Adaptation, or adjustment, comprises all reactions used by victims to reduce stress and increase the chances for survival. Defense mechanisms are unconscious means of adjusting, such as repression, counterphobic reactions, and reaction-formation. Coping is derived from the French verb *couper*, "to cut," and refers to a special form of adjustment, often conscious, whereby a well-learned and trusted mechanism of adjustment is applied to an atypical situation. Hamburg has described a good coper as one who can reasonably solve crisis and stress situations, restrict increasing anxiety to reasonable bounds, maintain self-esteem, and develop and maintain relationships. Successful coping is not only a factor of intelligence. The key issue is the ability to estimate a new and threatening situation and to bring Hamburg's four factors into play.

When a severe stress situation faces an individual, his primary reactions are those of alarm heightened by arousal reactions or alertness states, thus allowing the most efficacious action. The first such reaction is anxiety, which if excessive is not helpful but rather impedes the adjustment. It is understandable that denial is a favored second line of defense. Diminution of the level of consciousness into twilight states, dreamlike states, depersonalization, withdrawal from reality, and even psychotic reactions is such a mechanism. Another reaction to severe stress is the optimal self-control of thoughts and feelings; it can produce heightened self-esteem, flight reactions, or identification with the aggressor.[2] This also can take the form of affiliation—making contact with the terrorists or other hostages—which will be explored later.

Coping by the hostage during captivity can be accomplished through several means: diversions (engaging in games, handcrafts, study, reading); positive thinking (talking to oneself and imparting courage or tranquility to oneself and others); humor; rationalization (regarding the situation strictly rationally, without feelings); fatalism (accepting one's lot); denial of the situation; religion and prayer; cooperation; and affiliation. On the other hand, coping by family members can be handled by the following: seeking information; maintaining the normal daily routine; seeking diversion; affiliation; turning to the church and prayer; positive thinking; fatalism; and activist role assumption.

Some forms of successful coping noted were:

1) Cognitive appraisal: a term coined by Lazarus which he uses to analyze emotional reactions to stress. This appraisal is a function of the situation as well as the individual's convictions, cognitive style, and personality traits.

2) Learned helplessness: a term coined by Seligman to describe the situation whereby the negative aspects of an aversive event render an individual not in control, but where he imagines he does have control. The realization that he has no control can produce a neurotic reaction; the idea that he can do nothing causes the learned helplessness and depressive reactions. From this information, we can hope to arrive at a happy mix of self-control and control.

3) Preventative training: so-called stress inoculation procedures are primary here. These are training procedures in which high-risk candidates (military, business, diplomatic, et al.) are taught prophylactic measures through positive (systematic) thinking. To avoid being overwhelmed by events, the hostage should have hope and faith, the capacity to relativate, the ability to know why he keeps going:[3] all these can increase his chances for survival.

---

[2]The Latin source, *aggredo*, means in a positive sense to approach a person or task.
[3]For example, Viktor Frankl's existentialism.

There are already discernible reactions between the individuals involved in captivity and emergency situations. Teichman and Kligger (1975) describe two stages: in the first few hours or days, the hostage searches for information, exchanges information and goods, and helps his fellows; after five or six days, he attains an individual function or status in the group and develops new friendships and relationships.

AFFILIATION

Formation of contacts is seen between the hostage and the other hostages as well as between the hostage and the terrorists. Affiliation with fellow hostages can generate mutual support, encouragement, and reassurance. Affiliation with terrorists takes different forms, which include the use of the captors as a source of information: what are their attitudes, intentions, ideology? Affiliation is distinguished from identification with the aggressor, a defense mechanism whose name was changed at the Evian Conference to "identification with the controller." This has been described as the Stockholm Syndrome, a strong sympathy or even love by a female hostage for her captor. In the case of Patty Hearst, we saw her make a 180-degree about-face from sympathy and complicity with the terrorists to complete identification with the FBI. We can add her subsequent marriage to her former bodyguard, a policeman.

Van Dyke believes that the Stockholm Syndrome is due to two factors: identification with the aggressor and negative attitudes toward authority. Symonds thinks that more is involved in these symptoms than mere identification with the aggressor. He believes this syndrome is due to a traumatic infantilism along with pathological transference; that is, an identification with the terrorists plus an attempt to relate to an individual who threatens the hostage's existence.

AFTEREFFECTS

The Dutch found a direct correlation between the length of captivity and the severity, degree, and/or number of complaints. The chief findings in short-term hostage episodes seen in the first few weeks were both negative and positive. Negative sequelae as a result of being held hostage included tension, anxiety, phobias, disturbed sleep, somatic complaints, irritability, depression, poor concentration, and thought or speech preoccupation. Positive sequelae were relativation, heightened enjoyment, more intense interpersonal contact, and heightened self-esteem. However, the long-term effects were similar: anxiety, phobias, psychosomatic complaints, disturbed sleep, nightmares, irritability, lability, and depression; added to these were long-term consequences of aggression, feeling misunderstood, insecurity, and disturbed concentration. Nearly a third (32 percent) of the hostages claimed no long-term aftereffects. There seemed to be few long-term positive effects, although several hostages cited greater self-esteem, enjoyed more attention, and were more attentive. However, this positive value decreased with the passage of time.

Bastiaans describes a delayed Disaster Syndrome. After years of tremendous pressure in youth, there can be years of adequate functioning before this syndrome appears, usually at about age fifty. Physical and psychological symptoms include much rumination about the past, more guilt "memory of fatigue" (fatigue from the past recalled and reexperienced), a higher frequency of illness, but not a higher frequency of earlier death. The individual often cannot work or function. No one knows why this syndrome arises, but it is thought that the central nervous system is less resilient with age.

Family members of the hostages also were affected by the hostage taking. The main short-term effects were tension, sleep disturbances, anxiety, phobias, vague somatic complaints, preoccupation, irritability, and depression. Longer-term effects included sleep disturbances, preoccupation, anxiety, phobias, psychosomatic complaints, irritability, lability, aggression, and depression. Some 39 percent claimed no negative aftereffects. Of those who acknowledged complaints, 88 percent believed that their problems had not previously existed; that is, 12 percent thought the complaints were exacerbations of previous ones.

A number of other factors correlated highly with the appearance of negative sequelae after the hostage episode. It was found that the following could be used during captivity as predictors of negative consequences: more negative experiences, younger age of the hostage, less education, greater degree of affiliation, greater amount of pairing off, poor bodily functions prior to captivity, severe anxiety, hyperactivity, duration of captivity, and rigidity. A number of factors, of which some were related to these determinants of hostage outcomes, also could be used to predict the outcome of families to the hostage episode. The variables found to be of importance, or of a predictive value, included age, prior education, duration of captivity, degree of stress experience both at the start and end of the captivity, expectations about the resolution of the situation, somatic complaints, disturbance of the daily rhythm, eating patterns, anxiety, prior psychosocial problems, and level of functioning. The tendency was noted that when more of these factors were present, more negative aftereffects prevailed. Thus more negative expectations, less education, and longer duration of captivity seemed to correlate with negative outcomes after liberation.

CARE AND AFTERCARE

These terms refer to help offered during, directly after, and long-term to the ex-hostage and his family. It is important to note that of the 123 individuals who responded to this inquiry, 41 percent (51 persons) did not avail themselves at all of the aid offered, or did only once. Only 17 percent (21) used the services occasionally, 25 percent (30) availed themselves of it quite often, and 17 percent (21) used it regularly.

Before discussing this care, it must be mentioned that both traditionally and through the socialized medicine system, the family doctor, or general practitioner, is the central figure in Dutch medical services; he is the sole person who can refer a patient to a specialist. Although there has been a gradual shift away from this system in recent years, the family doctor is a strong father figure and the person to whom the patient always will turn first. This hierarchy was maintained in the treatment of the ex-hostages and their families. Some mental health specialists (psychiatrists, psychologists, and social workers) were called in, but for a variety of reasons the ex-hostages were seen primarily by their family doctors. Also, these people came from widespread areas of the country, so that centralized medical treatment was not possible. Family doctors played a primary care role with families during the captivity as well. And to a lesser degree, visits by the clergy were valued.

Psychotherapy is not strongly developed in the Netherlands, and the services available generally are uneven in quality.[4] Psychiatrists tend to be somatically oriented, but this is not the primary orientation desired in such cases. Only 14 percent of ex-hostages and 11 percent of family members showed a preference for a trained psychologist or psychiatrist, while 37 percent showed no preference at all for the professional's background.

The nature of Dutch mental health is brought home emphatically by the following simple statistics: of 161 ex-hostages, only one was treated by a certified psychologist or psychiatrist; of 123 family members, three were seen by these disciplines. All the rest were seen by social workers, family doctors, or were not seen at all. Of those who did seek help, only 68 percent of hostages as well as family members sought it up to three months after liberation.

---

[4]There are significant differences between Dutch and American psychiatry, although it is beyond the scope of this paper to examine them further. The delivery of psychiatric services in the Netherlands relies upon a system of social psychiatrists, who are municipal employees and serve the Dutch population at home or in designated out-patient clinics. Hospital psychiatrists deal with the in-patient population. The chief treatment modalities are supportive talks and extensive use of medications, many of which are unknown or not licensed for use in the United States.

In reflecting about the types of aftercare offered, two basic principles emerge and can be generalized as active or passive approaches. These delineate two different philosophies relating to the delivery of mental health services: the passive represents the patient's being present or available but showing no initiative, while the active represents an aggressive or even intrusive approach. In general, active refers to approaching the ex-hostage or the family and visiting and maintaining contact with them; passive is a holding-back attitude which lets the individual determine the presence or absence, type, and frequency of the contact. It was found that 85 percent of the ex-hostages and 90 percent of the family members favored an active attitude. The medical thinking was best summarized by the expression, "be available but not pushy."

The factor of continuity with aftercare was at least as important as the question of care or not. Some 86 percent of the ex-hostages believed that guidance was needed directly after liberation; they expected the person who offered help to continue in further aftercare. One ex-hostage commented, "you had just established a bit of trust in the relationship when it ended, and you had to start all over again." Besides continuity of care, there were other points of agreement: a well-organized reception center, delayed contact with the police and press, and early physical examination and care.

In long-term adjustment, we probably have the most critical and most poorly understood area of aftercare. There is fairly widespread unanimity among ex-hostages, their families, the population at large, and mental health professionals that the patient should forget, let bygones be bygones, and return to normal life as soon as possible. This view is absolutely wrong.

A greater and greater mass of evidence is appearing in the literature on the occurrence of delayed symptoms, even when no problems were obvious during the initial period after liberation. Evidence now is overwhelming that a victim of disaster, whether man-made or natural wherein he perceives his life to be threatened or endangered, takes on symptoms to one degree or another in later years. There can be speculation on the reasons for this Disaster Syndrome, and even arguments that it is impossible to show a cause-and-effect relationship between events and sequelae separated by many years. This is simply not true. When we repeatedly and consistently show a correlation in such a population, we must expand our thinking.

The Dutch follow-up report in 1979 examined the late effects of the different hostage episodes five, four, three, and two years after the actual incidents of captivity. It must be stated that 43 percent of the hostages then claimed that they had either no aftereffects or only very slight ones. While perhaps not accurate, this percentage is nevertheless their personal assessment. Some 27 percent believed that they had severe complaints, while 30 percent were in the mid-range. Unfortunately, no effort was made to analyse these assessments and self-evaluations, and our inclination is not to accept them at face value.

Those individuals with whom the writer spoke personally either had had early complaints or none at all; some had had no treatment or were still in treatment; all were still suffering considerably and attributed their symptoms directly to their experiences during captivity. Strong repression and a lack of reactions shortly after release were the two main factors which heightened the chances of long-term negative consequences.

In aftercare, reactions to the authorities and the media are two important matters to consider. The authorities were thought to have reacted well by 40 percent, but poorly by 24 percent, an interesting statistic that probably reflects judgments of dispositions made after liberation rather than during captivity. In the case of the Dutch hostages, much weight was given to financial considerations; almost 60 percent used the services offered from zero to a few times and then stopped. With the exception of a few individuals who became involved in further efforts to help others, there was uniformly some dissatisfaction with the way things were handled before, during, and after captivity. When aftercare was less, complaints were greater, and vice versa; the writer did not encounter a single person who thought that everything that could have been done was done. Other areas of dissatisfaction were in nonmaterial support (psychiatric and/or psychological care, family help, etc.), and 70 percent reproached the government for its failure to prevent such terrorist episodes.

The issue of the media is crucial. Problems begin with the terrorist act and the intervention of the press at the site of captivity. Excessive questioning of members of the family by newsmen reaches the point of badgering, with little or no consideration for their own crisis. During captivity, 43 percent of the studied group were not approached by the press, 36 percent were approached but rejected any contact, and 21 percent had several meetings with the press, even though the family realized that press contacts and interviews could lead to negative consequences for the hostages. Of the 21 percent who had contacts with the media, 62 percent were negatively disposed, 23 percent were neutral, and only 15 percent positive.

An interesting footnote to these reactions is that one striking motive of terrorists is to gain publicity for their cause or ideals, and therefore the press, either indirectly or unwittingly, aids this purpose. It is a curiosity of Dutch society that neither the families, the ex-hostages, nor the authorities recognized this point and interceded in contacts between these groups. After release of the hostages, 18 percent had no contact with the press, 30 percent were approached but rejected the contact, and 52 percent had multiple contacts with the media.

One of the major problems with the press, aside from intrusion, was the fact that the ex-hostages and/or family members spoke emotionally, impulsively, and as the result of complex intrapsychic turmoil, especially shortly after liberation. For example, a man stated to the press as he was being released by the Moluccans, "They're really not such bad young men." At this, his wise wife said to him, "Keep quiet, you've said enough. Now let's go home." Such remarks later would have repercussions.

CONCLUSIONS

The various Dutch experiences have led to a number of conclusions at this time. While Dutch cannot be translated literally into American equivalents, lessons can be learned and points made.

First, some statistics: the total ex-hostage Dutch population was 283 persons. Of these, 59 percent (168) cooperated in the study by being interviewed, 5 percent (13) refused an interview, and 17 percent (50) were sent questionnaires of which fifteen were returned completed. As for the rest, 19 percent (52) could not cooperate because they had died, their whereabouts were unknown, or they did not speak Dutch. Almost all the ex-hostages believed that the terrorists acted correctly and politely, but all were puzzled why they had resorted to violent means to realize their political goals.

Second, many individuals, having been taken hostage and having had their lives threatened, suffered long-lasting negative effects; some suffered immediately, others showed only delayed reactions, and some experienced both. Short-term effects (within four weeks) were most often tenseness, insomnia, fears, and phobias. Women's reactions were more severe than men's. Long-term effects (after four weeks) were found in two thirds of the ex-hostages and included irritability, increased lability of moods, fears, phobias, and in some cases vague physical complaints, insomnia, feelings of being threatened or misunderstood, and great preoccupation with the hostage experience. The younger and less educated experienced these effects the most, together with those who were held captive longest. Some short- and long-term effects were noted: an ability to see things more relatively; a feeling of well-being; better interpersonal relationships, especially with the immediate family; and more emotional involvement with others.

Third, several recommendations for treatment may be made to the therapist:

1) Do not adopt the usual waiting stance familiar to psychotherapy. Do not force yourself upon the ex-hostage or his family but rather "be available but not pushy."

2) After five days, keep in regular touch with the patient. Appropriate questions to him might run in this vein: "Hello, how are you? What's new? Is there anything I can do for you?" These all show concern and interest but avoid giving the message, "You are sick and really need my help."

3) Be aware of what Hoppe has called the master-slave situation, which may develop between the therapist and patient as a continuation of the latter's relationship with his captors during captivity.

4) Keep in mind that the pat-on-the-shoulder, get-back-to-normal-as-soon-as-possible attitude on the part of the therapist is the wrong approach.

5) Find out as much as possible about the patient: his history prior to being taken hostage, his family history, his adjustments or lack thereof.

6) Help the patient to slowly loosen the group ties, because cohesion exists even if the group has been broken up.

7) Assure sleep. Do not give the patient REM inhibitors; much preferred now are antidepressant and anxiolytics (anxiety-reducing drugs). For example, Tofranil PM about one hour before bedtime, but not during the daytime hours, is a good choice.

8) In the case of severe nightmares, fully awaken the patient and then give him a barbiturate or Valium.

9) Do not expose the patient to the press. He may say things that later can be problematic or difficult to deny. And there should be a single official spokesman, who either is counseled by the psychiatric team or is himself a representative thereof.

Fourth, prophylaxis may be undertaken in three stages before, during, and after captivity. In the first stage—before captivity—the prospective hostage should know what to expect if captured, step by step; what it is like in such a situation; and what kinds of emotions to expect. Of help also to him are stress inoculation, as in army and Peace Corps programs; the MSP group dynamics program, in which the hostage understands himself in relation to the group; the educational factor, or familiarization with the concept of identifying with the aggressor; and the training of leaders within groups.

In the second stage—during captivity—the therapist should meet and work with the families, immunize them against the press, and advise them to maintain as usual a routine as possible. At this time the hostage should maintain his orientation. For example, one man who knew a good deal about theology told his captors that he was a minister and fulfilled this role; a medical student functioned as a doctor. The hostage should create a daily rhythm of exercising, eating at regular times, and keeping himself clean; exercises are probably the most important channel for relaxation, release of aggression, and physical fitness. For diversion he may play simple games such as cards or dominoes, but not bridge or chess. He should avoid isolation; keeping to himself in order not to be noticed is not a good policy. He absolutely must not "make waves" and must contain his aggressiveness; this means he has to bend, be passive overtly, and not show aggressive behavior. In a cat-and-mouse game, the cat is not interested in a dead mouse. One hostage was asked by his captor, "Shall I shoot you?"; he replied, "If it will help the others." This was not a brainwashed reply but the best kind with the least chance of stirring up the terrorist's aggression. The hostage also should not try to change the terrorist's ideologies by argument or confrontation; instead, he should agree, "You're right, I never thought of it that way." By affiliation the hostage can form a relationship with the aggressor. To a degree, this is wise. One ex-hostage related, "in seconds, you realize that you are nothing—there is complete physical ('lie on the ground') and mental ('do not speak') degradation."

After captivity—the third stage—the therapist should receive the ex-hostage in familiar surroundings; if he is American, then in American surroundings or in an American installation overseas. Give him cosmetic care; he has been dehumanized, after all. Give him also a complete physical examination and any appropriate treatment called for. Protect him from any contacts with the press. After his return home, keep in touch, phone, visit: "be available but not pushy." Supply him with one central information telephone number. In these cases, the family is the first line of defense, ahead of the professional; therefore, it is important that the family be guided, taught, supported—in short, totally prepared.

And last, an important new commission is in operation. The Dutch have an advanced system of social psychiatry. Except for clinical (hospital) psychiatrists, members of this branch comprise the largest number of practitioners. They formed in January 1976 the Central Steering and Support Committee (CBOG), a group of psychiatrists, physicians, and a small number of ex-hostages whose tasks are to organize and oversee aftercare and to conduct scientific investigations over an extended period of time into the physical, psychic, and social health of victims of terrorism and violence.[5] One or more members of the CBOG is available to assist whenever a terrorist episode involves Dutch nationals, anywhere in the world.

---

[5]The CBOG's subcommittee on scientific research set as its goals to locate the nonmaterial aftereffects of a period of captivity, especially any psychic and psychosomatic changes that appear; determine what changes must be ascribed to this experience; determine what psychic or somatic changes have appeared in family members; draw up an inventory of the aid offered and evaluate it; and try to predict the future nonmaterial problems of the individual and those around him as a result of his experience as a hostage.

Political Hostages: Sanction and the Recovery Process

ERIC SHAW*

On 13 April 1981, Richard Morefield, general consul in the be-sieged Iranian embassy, described his hostage experience to a large audience at Duke University. Morefield retold the circumstances of his capture, persuasively defended U.S. policy in the region, and related in intimate detail his thoughts moments prior to his mock execution.

> I decided that if this was it, I was going to at least die with dignity, standing. At that moment I thought of my son who was murdered and thought how strange for a father to be following his son. When it was over I knew that I was going to make it out, no matter how long it took.[1]

Morefield did make it. That evening CBS Television News reported that he had received $4,000 for his address at Duke. He now has a prestigious State Department job conducting executive seminars. Other released Iranian hostages are joining Morefield on the lucrative lecture circuit, and still others are working on books. The rule which usually limits govern-ment employees to $25,000 in outside income per year has been amended for the Iranian hostages. As one State Department spokesman said recently, "We'll be frank. We're going to bend over backwards to accommodate them. They've earned it."

At a recent hostage reunion at the exclusive Greenbrier resort in West Virginia, twenty State Department psychologists and psychiatrists were surprised by the swift recovery of the group. One expert credited the government's professional and sensitive preparation of the hostages and their families for the smoothness of the transition. In fact, some of the thirty-one hostages attending the reunion were amused by the many dire predictions of hostage experts concerning their psychological recovery. Embassy political officer John Limbert commented, "It takes about five

---

*The writer wishes to acknowledge the valuable contributions of many specialists in this area. The ideas of John Russell Smith on the importance of sanction and of Dr. Mardi Horowitz on post-traumatic stress disorder, as well as POW research by Dr. William Miller and hostage research by Dr. Frank Ochberg, and others, have been vital to this paper.

[1]Richard Morefield's personal communication with the writer, 13 April 1981.

minutes to adjust to having clean sheets to sleep on and being able to eat Chinese food whenever you want."

What happened to the depression, anger, paranoia, psychosomatic disorders, and other psychological difficulties predicted for the returned captives? Why the pessimistic prognoses but seemingly exceptional recoveries? In part, these extreme predictions were political in nature and were designed to pressure State Department medical officials into providing appropriate medical and psychological care. But these predictions also were based on evidence gathered over the last fifteen years concerning the experiences of many less publicized political hostages. The stories of the homecomings of these other Americans provided ample evidence to concern the experts and provoke the dramatic predictions regarding the Iranian hostages' post-release experience.

A comparison of the post-release adjustment of the Iranian hostages and their less fortunate predecessors offers more than an understanding of the healing power of fame and fortune. It offers some interesting insights into the potent curative elements that a society can either offer or choose to withhold from its victimized members. It also may provide a glimpse at the cultural values which guide the application of these sanctions.

THE OTHER HOSTAGES

The most systematic but largely unknown follow-up on released hostages was presented in an in-house paper by the Rand Corporation in 1976. Although its authors disclaimed any attempt to psychologically analyze their subjects, the team of psychologists and psychiatrists did not mince words in their conclusions. Based upon the collective experience of forty former hostages at various periods after release, the paper noted the presence of both physical and psychological disabilities directly traceable to the hostage experience which appeared to require, because of their severity, assistance and counseling, "whether or not they [the hostages] want it." The team also noted a number of acute physical and psychological effects, including shaking hands, insomnia, and exacerbation of prior physical ailments. Some hostages expressed paranoid fantasies about the international power of their captors and the need to be careful in their conversations. Others suffered memory losses of particularly painful aspects of captivity, while several reconstructed or edited certain incidents. Often those painful aspects, when retold, were described with self-deprecating humor. Although colleagues recalled that specific hostages "were too emotionally shaken to even speak" at release, they later tended to recount their captivity in a dissociative fashion. For some, emotional difficulties came well after release and were triggered by reminiscent events, such as the kidnapping of colleagues or the anniversary of their own abductions.

Other anxiety responses noted in hostages soon after the event have included nightmares, night sweats, startle reactions, and difficulty in concentrating. According to a hostage expert, Dr. Frank Ochberg, such symptoms have resulted in self-medication, drug abuse, alcoholism, and detrimental dietary changes. Physical and psychosomatic ailments are also common. Depression, paranoia, and delusions are among the most serious psychological difficulties Ochberg has noted. Captivity has also had a severe effect on hostage families who suffered from shock, psychosomatic illnesses, estrangement, and disorientation. For example, the wife of an ex-hostage suffered a miscarriage.

Although the Iranian hostages suffered their share of physical and psychological aftereffects, most experts have been pleasantly surprised by their rapid adjustment, particularly when compared to what is known of the experience of the forty-five or so U.S. officials captured by terrorists since 1968.[2] The lack of systematic follow-up studies on the post-release experience of political hostages makes it difficult to support the assertion that the Iranian hostages are healing more rapidly than their predecessors. Nevertheless, the experts have been impressed.

When it comes to assessing the reasons for this apparently better adjustment of the Iranian captives, it is difficult to ignore the tremendous influence of the collective demonstrations of welcome, support, and sheer joy expressed by the American people upon the ex-hostages' return. Experts are only beginning to understand the potent healing powers such sanction can offer, and the comparison of the homecomings of these two hostage groups provides a dramatic example of the impact of the presence and absence of society's own curative contribution.

The lionization of the Iranian hostages has been well documented, from the moment then-President Jimmy Carter chose to incorporate them into his political campaign until America's collective sigh of relief upon their return. Ticker-tape parades, financial opportunities, and other follow-up publicity now have many of the former hostages wishing for a little less fame. But this hero's welcome differs dramatically from the reception of our other official and nonofficial political hostages. According to the Rand study, the cavalier attitude of past administrations, co-workers, and families toward these other victims has left many hostages feeling bitter, resentful, and alienated. Surprisingly, these hostages placed the blame for their difficulties not on their captivity but on the quality of their homecomings, a stark contrast to the welcome accorded the Iranian returnees. Recovery from the hostage experience is difficult enough, but for many of the other hostages, coming home made it harder rather than easier.

---

[2]If one includes non-official U.S. personnel and other foreign officials, over 400 hostages have been taken by terrorists since 1968. These figures do not include victims of airline hijackings.

THE OTHER HOSTAGES' HOMECOMINGS

Upon arrival most hostages reported feelings of embarrassment and guilt for the unfavorable publicity, trouble, and expense they had caused their governments. In addition, the hostages often felt guilty about their performance in captivity. According to the Rand study, a hostage

> may feel that he was too docile, or that he "collaborated" with his captors to a greater degree than was necessary to survive. He may feel guilty because he found himself identifying with his captors during captivity and still may do so. He may ask himself if he has been "brainwashed."

Such self-criticism apparently led to expectations of criticism by others, and the hostage then tended to "write himself off like damaged merchandise." These feelings were compounded by the attitudes of co-workers and families. As the Rand authors noted,

> Many former hostages complained they were treated like "social pariahs, as if they were lepers." These are their own words. Initially, we thought that this might be a reflection of some kind of oversensitivity, but in talking to colleagues of former hostages and to other officials concerned with the incidents, we heard comments such as "We had to get them out. He would have destroyed morale." One senior official talked about the "contagion of the kidnappee." We must conclude from this that these feelings of the former hostages are not entirely imaginary.

The Rand paper was quick to point out the similarity in the treatment of these ex-hostages to that of rape victims. Both are encouraged not to talk about their experiences, and both tend to believe that they themselves, rather than the criminals involved, are on trial. Many family members may have thought that they were sparing the victim the trauma of reliving the episode, when indeed they were hiding their own embarrassment in their reluctance to make inquiries. It was shocking to find that, for many hostages, the Rand follow-ups constituted the first invitation to talk about their experiences.

SOCIETY'S SANCTION

How could such a difference in the attitude of the American people and its government, as portrayed in the vastly different homecomings of these two hostage groups, contribute to the more rapid healing of one and the less favorable adjustment of the other? Throughout civilized history, societies have authorized certain special population groups to engage in most uncivilized behaviors. These groups have included law enforcement, military, and other quasi-military and diplomatic personnel. Subsequently, societies have created rituals and purification rites by which these groups are reinducted. Such rituals, particularly after warfare, have many important functions.

According to an expert in this field, John Russell Smith of Duke University, ticker-tape parades, uniforms, medals, award ceremonies, veterans' benefits, and special events serve to recognize the extraordinary demands upon and actions taken by these groups. Simultaneously, such rituals serve to affirm the collective approval of society and affix some universal meaning to what these groups have undergone. These sanctions set up the favorable perceptions, attitudes, and values by which the behaviors of these individuals under special circumstances are to be judged. In part, such rituals also serve to protect societies against the introduction of a powerful and now unsocialized class of warriors, by marking the timing and conditions of their resocialization.

In addition, Smith has noted that sanctions serve the individual by giving special personal meaning to the unusual experience which he has been through. In the process, the personal responsibility of the individual for his actions becomes incorporated within society's approved collective meaning for the events involved. For example, in World War I, we fought the "war to end all wars." Following World War II, "stopping the German and Japanese bids for world tyranny," "keeping the world safe for democracy," and "saving the Jews from extermination" were popular slogans presenting the value of the wars and rationalizing the uncivilized individual actions necessary to win them.

The sanction inherent in such rituals plays a powerful role in the healing of those on whom it is focused. In the case of those taken hostages, the healing process may be long and complex.

HOSTAGE HEALING

The returned Iranian hostages were diagnosed as suffering from a long observed but only fairly recently labeled disorder known as "post-traumatic stress disorder" (PTSD). According to the American Psychiatric Association's *Diagnostic and Statistical Manual of Mental Disorders*, such illness follows "a psychologically traumatic event that is generally outside the range of human experience." The essential psychic task in hostage recovery becomes the acceptance of new information about oneself and the world that has resulted from the experience. But this is not just a lesson in new political realities or the correction of political naiveté. Hostages have been subject to often brutal treatment by their fellow men, not because of anything they personally have done, but because of their symbolic representation of the state. They have served as political pawns. They have faced certain death and uncertain survival. Their coping skills and their will to survive have been tested in a manner which few people ever experience. From usually assertive, aggressive, independent, active individuals they have been reduced to impotent, humiliated, dependent "cannon fodder," as one hostage put it. In the course of surviving such an ordeal, human values may change severely. For example, both profound religious insights and profound political and racial hatreds can result.

The digestion or integration of this new information is all the more difficult because frequently the adjustment concerns some of the victim's most important beliefs and feelings about himself, his career, his government, his co-workers, his family, his political views, his religion, or his thoughts and feelings about basic human nature. At the core of these views, which may merit revision, often the most difficult component to be faced concerns the victim's feeling of personal responsibility or guilt for some personal action or perceived failure in performance. There are a number of other, more specific personal conflicts which are characteristically experienced by hostages.

PERSONAL CONFLICTS

Held under varying conditions of reduced environmental stimulation, nutritional deficiency, forced dependency, humiliation, and the threat of death, hostages must make a number of critical attributions regarding their own feelings and behavior, political beliefs, and careers, as well as the expectations of their peers and the behavior of their captors and government. They may question the adequacy of their preparation for such an experience. If hostages have stereotypical expectations regarding their captors (crazy, radical, murderous, inhumane, insidious) but hear them speaking persuasively and rationally regarding events which have led to their acts, they may be forced to revise their misconceptions. If, in particular, hostages and their captors share the same food and hardships of captivity, the incongruence of their expectations may lead the hostages to become more impressed by the similarity between what they are observing and normal behavior under stressful circumstances. In the apathetic and depressed state following capture, this disparity between expectations and reality may have important implications for the totality of all a hostage's relevant prior beliefs. It is difficult for the hostage to revise his beliefs about his captors without revising his beliefs about his government, its policies, and his own role and assumptions. If hostages harbor doubt, guilt, or resentment regarding their government's policies or actions, these feelings easily may be exacerbated. In extreme cases, hostages have felt used and sensed a growing hostility toward specific government officials and policies.

If the hostage's capture or failure to be released can be attributed to the actions or policies of his government, additional confusion may result. For instance, official particular hostage policy, or lack thereof, has been blamed directly for the deaths of U.S. diplomats, such as Ambassador Adolf Dubs in Afghanistan in 1979. Knowledge of such accusations is not likely to be much comfort to U.S. personnel held captive. At times the Iranian hostages were subject to considerable doubts about the real concern of their government and its people. According to press attaché Barry Rosen, "We'd say to ourselves, they don't care. The economy is the big thing, not some foreign policy thing. We figured people thought fifty-two hostages, yeah, and what's for dinner?" Growing concern regarding the possibility of government assault attempts also may result in angry feelings toward the government and identification with their captors—as co-victims.

Many hostages suffer from guilt regarding their capture. In some cases, hostages have facilitated their own abduction by being in known dangerous areas or ignoring security precautions. The subsequent realization of such errors may result in despondency and depression, and the resulting lack of confidence may prove a serious handicap in facing the stresses of captivity. Even in cases where such mistakes are irrelevant, hostages may suffer from guilt over the embarrassment and difficulty they have caused their government and families. Although to the outsider this may seem an unnecessarily harsh judgment, to the despondent hostage there is real support for such feelings based upon the publicity generated and the wide range of collegial expectations. Consider, for example, the standard of performance set by the case of Ambassador John G. Mein, as reported by the House Committee on Internal Security in 1973:

> Ambassador Mein, whose life had been threatened repeatedly, knew that he was a possible target of the leftist guerrillas. Nevertheless, he spurned a bodyguard, believing that U.S. policy was best served by refusing to give the terrorists the opportunity to boast that they had intimidated the U.S. In conversations with friends, Ambassador Mein had indicated that he would attempt to escape rather than submit to capture and provide the terrorists with an opportunity to humiliate the United States and Guatemalan governments.

Mein was shot and killed while attempting to escape a kidnapping in 1969.

It also is not uncommon for hostages to review their activities prior to capture and dwell on second-guessing all of the possible actions they might have taken to avoid capture. Such activity increases feelings of personal responsibility and guilt and detracts from energies needed to face current crises.

Hostages, particularly representatives of government and business, are aware that their behavior while captive may be subject to official or public scrutiny. One of the most common causes of guilt regarding captivity is the hostage's realization that he could not live up to the standards of behavior which he expected of himself or believed were expected by his peers. For military attachés, this may be the requirement to divulge no more than his rank, name, serial number, and date of birth. For Foreign Service and other diplomatic personnel, the standards may be less specific, although the judgments of peers may be just as severe. In general, the more a particular individual believes it is his duty to maintain a standard and the more he is impressed by the consequences of not doing so, the more traumatic the depression and guilt can be for this perceived failure. As Dr. Jerome Korack, U.S. State Department medical director, reported, although the released Iranian hostages were physically fit, "a few felt some guilt about statements they made under duress."

The appropriateness of official and unofficial expectations for conduct among prisoners of war (POWs) and hostages has been drawn increasingly into question starting with the brainwashing research of the 1950s and 1960s. Given the determination of captors, it seems almost inevitable that variations from officially prescribed behavior will occur. In such instances, the most important ingredient in maintaining hostage morale has been access to other prisoners who can assure the victim that they are all in the same predicament.

Dr. William Miller, an expert on the physical and psychological effects of captivity, noted the impact of the lack of such assurance on some Vietnam prisoners of war:

> Deprived of the reassurance [of peers, they] became so debilitated and depressed by their inability to hold on to the letter of their guidance, as they saw it, that upon capitulation—alone and in the throes of depression—they found all of their resistance sapped, and ended up complying with demands to an extent which they later found inexcusable. Such guilt was difficult, if not impossible, for some to assuage. Not only did many men spend the bulk of their imprisonment flagellating themselves for their behavior throughout their captivity, but many have continued to do so long after imprisonment.

Thus, hostages, POWs, and other prisoners are caught in intense conflict between what they must do as captives to survive versus the official and unofficial expectations against which their conduct will be judged. Upon their return, the reality of their individual conduct while subject to the pressures of captivity will be measured against what they believe are the standards of those who await them.

Thus, when the Rand study reports that some hostages suffered memory losses for painful aspects of their captivity, reconstructed or edited accounts, or talked about their experience in a dissociated manner, these psychological maneuvers may be understood as ways of buying time for the acceptance of new information about oneself which cannot yet be absorbed without great psychological damage. The full range of an individual's defense mechanisms will come into play in an attempt to isolate the most radical, painful, and challenging of the lessons learned. Some individuals are able to cope with the damage such information may present to their self-esteem or to old-world views more quickly than others. Accordingly, a victim's defense mechanisms will regulate the flow of this new information and help the individual to deny what he is not yet ready to absorb.

The general strategy of denial can be successful for long periods of time. The problem is that it has its psychological costs. In order to freeze or numb the memory or the impact of the stressful experience, the hostage unconsciously may be forced to restrict other aspects of his emotional life. Thus, he may suffer from markedly reduced interest in formerly important activities or persons. He may feel detached or alienated from others. Or, he may report feeling very little at all, as if emotional highs and lows were eliminated. In such a state, it is often difficult for him to conduct human relationships.

But more often than not, events collude with the internal pressures to deal with the new experience and disrupt the effectiveness of this type of resolution. Thus, when released Iranian hostage Phil Ward used to hear the click of a soft drink can being opened, he would jump, startled by the reminder of a rifle bolt clicking outside the door of his embassy prison room. The memory of his captivity was pushing to consciousness through attachment to an associated sound. For other hostages, images and memories which have not yet been integrated but cannot be dismissed present themselves in dreams, nightmares, or recurrent intrusive thoughts. According to Smith, these are some of the signs of the breakdown of the strategy of denial. The breakdown of denial may lead to creative integration and growth if the individual can get the professional help and understanding he needs. Otherwise, the victim may be caught between periods of successful and unsuccessful denial, or intrusion. This mental tug-of-war can result in inner turmoil, anger, aggressive behavior, and attempts to blot out the experience and its accompanying feelings through drugs or alcohol. Extreme cases of unresolved intrusiveness can result in flashbacks, nightmares, and dissociative episodes in which the victim loses touch with reality.

THE INTERVENTION OF SANCTION

Sanction, on the other hand, affords the victim a gentler, safer, less demanding route toward integration of the meaning of the stressful event. The sanction offered by society strikes to the core of many hostage adjustment difficulties—feelings of responsibility or guilt over some personal action or perceived failure. The healing process involves the sharing of responsibility with society and the relabeling of personal feelings with public perceptions, attitudes, and conclusions regarding the event. Although the Iranian hostages returned with many different experiences and feelings about these episodes, their personal experience was absorbed quickly and thoroughly by the nation's attitude toward the event. No matter what they went through or how they behaved in Iran, or how they felt about their performance, they came back as heroes. Some, like hostage Gary Lee, willingly responded to the call: "I can't speak for everyone, but for myself—I belong to the American people for the next two weeks. If some little kid wants my autograph, he's going to get it."

This sanction allows the victim, through a sharing and relabeling of the experience, to seal over the troublesome, undigested aspects of the traumatic event without restricting emotional functioning. Instead of being caught between denial and intrusion, sealing over through sanction allows for the painful experiences to remain encapsulated and to become incorporated gently and slowly over the course of normal experience. Thus, these victims may find the personal meaning of the event and the tumultuous need to make sense of many serious conflicts frozen by society's interpretation of the experience. In the relief that sanction and sealing over afford, there is ample time to deal with the new disparities between prehostage and post-hostage views of oneself and the world. For the moment, the hostage is a hero.

In the general atmosphere of sanction, survivors also are more likely to be accepted by their peers, to receive the attention and services they require, and to feel more comfortable and supported in coping with the psychological adjustments and difficulties they do encounter. The most recent and tragic demonstration of the impact of a society's collective decision to withhold sanction has been the plight of the Vietnam veterans. In this regard, Lance Morrow recently summarized the feelings of many of these men and noted the important relationship between denial and sanction.

> For years at least some part of every Viet Nam Veteran has inhabited a limbo of denial—the nation's or his own—often overcome by guilt and shame and almost always by anger. Among other things, he has tended to think of himself as an awful sucker to have risked so much for so little. Most veterans (contrary to stereotype) have readjusted

reasonably well to the civilian world. But many found that coming home was harder than fighting the war.

Interestingly enough, the homecomings of the Iranian hostages were accompanied by resentful cries and questions from the Vietnam veterans. In response, the nation seems to have discovered the impact of withholding sanction from a group which deserves it and is moving toward an attempt to supply *post hoc* that missing homecoming.

But just as in the case of the Vietnam veterans, the other American hostages were cast adrift to cope with their traumatic experiences and the bittersweetness of their homecomings on their own. But it is not this way for hostages everywhere. Even prior to the Iranian episode, the Dutch placed several of their hostage victims on a national terrorism crisis committee and sponsored special task forces on the effects of victimization which offer psychological assistance.[3] The Israelis have long lionized their hostages and consider them soldiers. Those held by terrorists are considered military prisoners of war. New Scotland Yard uses ex-hostages in police training programs. The recognition and the attempt to acknowledge formally the victim's exceptional experience in service to society while actively incorporating him back into society are the essential elements of sanction. Parades, medals, and monuments are not necessary.

Blockage of such efforts to improve hostage treatment in the United States seems to have stemmed from two arguments, tragically unrelated to the major issue of sanction. In the debate over the best manner in which to foster hostage recovery, there are two arguments. One side wants to let the victim forget, to be unobtrusive in assistance and keep medical and psychological intervention to a minimum; the other view holds that such victims are at high risk for further problems, and the government owes them diagnosis and care. Those who "have suffered as symbols of the state . . . can heal at state expense," according to Ochberg. But both views may prove tangential in their focus solely on medical care. Although victims may or may not require medical and psychological assistance, they do require interest, support, and especially recognition from their government, as representatives of the American people, for performance under exceptional circumstances. The perspective held by Ochberg and others in the debate over proper post-release hostage treatment has received sufficient support through the rapid adjustment of the Iranian returnees, who were not ignored but received proper attention.

If further, more systematic examination of this issue is necessary, what remains to be accomplished is a review of the long-term adjustment of the other hostages released over the last fifteen years. These victims should be compared to their Iranian counterparts in terms of career history

---

[3]See Robert Hauben's "Hostage Taking: The Dutch Experience" in this volume.

(early retirement), medical and psychological adjustment, and family and social adaptation. Because diplomatic life-styles are in themselves stressful, these two groups also need to be compared to a sample of non-hostage Foreign Service personnel, acting as a control group. As Morefield eloquently pointed out to the staff psychologists at Wiesbaden, "How do you know I wasn't crazy before I was taken hostage?"[4] In addition, because all hostage experiences are not the same, measures of the relative stress of specific hostage episodes will have to be used to weigh the impact of the captivity experience. Steps also will be necessary to locate and ensure the privacy of ex-hostages. Such research is more complex than it sounds, but it is easily within the grasp of social science methodology. A similar study has just been conducted on Vietnam veterans, and the results of this study were critical to congressional efforts to restore psychological and other services to them, despite administration budget cuts.

In terms of the psychological processes described, it is difficult to reverse the effects of withholding sanction this late in the game, although it is well worth the attempt. But a change in governmental attitude toward all victims of terrorist violence would not only benefit those directly involved, it would also demonstrate and substantiate our willingness to stand up to this form of violent political manipulation. Political terrorism is a battle for the hearts and minds of those who observe its highly publicized exchanges. Terrorists aim, through their activities, to undermine the basic link between a people and its government—the promise of security. Although all forms of terrorist violence cannot be prevented, knowledge on the part of potential victims (all of us) that our government stands ready to provide recognition and care for its casualties in this conflict would have great impact in bolstering the confidence of the American people in its government. Such guarantees may be more symbolic than substantive, given the few persons involved in terrorist violence each year. Yet, the symbolic value would not be lost on either the American public or those attempting to undermine its confidence.

Such legislation would have to confront some of the underlying cultural biases we as Americans seem to possess concerning our attitudes toward victims. The Rand study's findings concerning the similarity in treatment of the other hostages and rape victims are not easily dismissed. In addition, who controls our application of society's healing powers? In the case of the Iranian hostages, President Carter's early emphasis of the issue added to the media's acceptance of the hostage crisis as one of the most important stories of the decade. Public concern and involvement easily followed daily coverage of the events. Clearly, America was expecting a homecoming suitable for its national heroes, and they received it.

But in the final analysis, it is not the publicity or financial advantages

---

[4]Morefield's personal communication.

that may help heal the hostages. It is the interest and concern of the
American people, on an individual basis. The willingness to listen, ask
questions, be supportive, and assume some responsibility is the critical
element in the healing process. This can only be conveyed on a personal
basis. If it is absent, then the symbolic gestures of parades, medals, and
other benefits ring hollow.

BIBLIOGRAPHY

American Journal of Orthopsychiatry, results of study on Vietnam vet-
    erans, in press.
American Psychiatric Association. *Diagnostic and Statistical Manual of
    Mental Disorders.* 3rd ed. 1980. Reprinted by permission of the
    APA.
Bonnett, M. "One Hundred Days of Freedom." *People,* 4 May 1981.
    State Department spokesman, p. 38; Limbert, p. 37.
Church, G. J. Special section. *Time,* 2 February 1981. "Cannon fodder,"
    p. 30; Rosen, p. 34; Korack, p. 34; Ward, p. 31; Lee, p. 34.
Jenkins, Brian. *Hostage Survival: Some Preliminary Observations.*
    Santa Monica: Rand Corporation, April 1976.
Miller, William. "Dilemmas and Conflict Specific to the Military Re-
    turned P.O.W." In *Family Separation and Reunion,* edited by H.
    McCubbin, B. Dahl, P. Metres, E. Hunter, and J. Plagg, pp. 121–
    22. Washington, DC: Government Printing Office, 1975.
Morrow, Lance. "Essay." *Time,* 1 June 1981.
Ochberg, Frank. "The Victim of Terrorism: Psychiatric Considerations."
    Terrorism: An International Journal 1, no. 2 (1978): 147–68.
Smith, John Russell. "Viet Nam Veterans and Rap Groups: Toward a
    Model of the Stress Recovery Process." Paper presented at the
    Thirty-second Institute on Community Psychiatry, American Psy-
    chiatric Association, Boston, September 1980.
U.S., House of Representatives, 93d Cong., 1st sess. Committee on
    Internal Security, Staff Study, *Political Kidnappings, 1968–73.*
    Washington, DC: Government Printing Office, 1973.

The Psychopathology of Being Held Hostage*

ROBERT G. HILLMAN

The taking of hostages has become an unfortunate but familiar part of the contemporary sociopolitical climate both nationally and internationally. There are few scientific studies of the psychopathology of the hostage experience, a reflection of the condition's rarity until recent times. Psychological studies of stress usually have focused on prisoners of war and concentration camp victims. These studies have emphasized the length of time in captivity, physical injury, and nutritional problems as the conditioned variables of stress in the subsequent development of psychiatric symptoms.[1]

The hostage experience differs from either prisoner of war or concentration camp experiences in several parameters. Aside from a shorter duration, it frequently does not include physical injury or malnutrition. Contemporary firsthand accounts by hostages indicate that the ordeal of being held hostage, even for a relatively short time, can have profound psychological consequences.[2] The psychopathology of the hostage experience is important in understanding hostage behavior and in treatment considerations.

Let us examine the psychological state of fourteen correctional officers held hostage during the worst prison riot in U.S. history. On 2 February 1980 seventeen officers in all were captured at the Penitentiary

*A revised version of the article published in the *American Journal of Psychiatry* 138, no. 9 (1981): 1193–97. Reprinted by permission. The writer acknowledges the assistance of Ms. Jane Knowles in preparing this paper.

[1]H. Klonoff, G. McDougall, C. Clark, et al., "The Neuropsychological, Psychiatric, and Physical Effects of Prolonged and Severe Stress: Thirty Years Later," *Journal of Nervous and Mental Disease* 163 (1976): 246–52. See also L. Eitinger, "Pathology of the Concentration Camp Syndrome," *Archives of General Psychiatry* 5 (1961): 371–79.

[2]Diane Cole, "Why a Hostage Cannot Forget," *Newsweek* 95 (19 May 1980): 17; S. Jacobson, "Individual and Group Responses to Confinement in a Skyjacked Plane," *American Journal of Orthopsychiatry* 43 (1973): 459–69; F.M. Ochberg, "The Victim of Terrorism: Psychiatric Considerations," *Terrorism: An International Journal* 1 (1978): 147–68.

of New Mexico near Santa Fe. The riot had progressed quickly: in twenty-two minutes, inmates gained control of the penitentiary. For the next thirty-six hours, they ran wild, destroyed the institution, and killed thirty-three fellow inmates; ninety others were seriously injured.

The correctional officers examined were all Spanish-Americans who ranged in age from eighteen to fifty-four years. Their periods of service at the penitentiary ranged from three weeks to twenty-six years. The majority were middle-aged, experienced guards. Of the fourteen officers examined, two escaped within minutes of the riot; three hid for thirty-six hours within the penitentiary until they were rescued; seven officers were not hurt, and six were injured. Of the injured hostages, four were hospitalized; the other two were treated and released. The injured suffered from multiple trauma, stab wounds, and fractures.

The hostages described their surroundings during their ordeal as "chaotic beyond belief." Electric power to the penitentiary was interrupted, and much of the complex was in darkness. Dense smoke filled the corridors, making identification difficult or impossible; only silhouettes of persons could be seen. Six inches of water covered the floors from broken pipes. Bodies of inmates who had been beaten, killed, or had taken drug overdoses were scattered throughout the buildings. Armed and masked "execution squads" roamed the institution looking for victims. Other inmates armed themselves with knives, bars, and sticks in self-defense. Many of these inmates feared for their own lives, and some took overdoses of medication so that, if they were to be killed, they would not suffer. Those who had taken drugs from the pharmacy were obviously high, wobbly on their feet and talking incoherently. The sounds of destruction and the screams of inmates being tortured and killed completed the picture of what one hostage said seemed "like Hell."

The psychological state of the correctional officers was a combination of feelings of helplessness, existential fear, and sensory input overload. Although the guards each suffered differently in terms of the physical violence inflicted on them and the duration of their captivity, neither of these factors seemed to be important in the degree to which the three psychological symptoms were experienced. However, all the officers sustained these symptoms, which were later described as absolutely different from any ordinary experience.

HELPLESSNESS

Total and profound helplessness was felt by all the hostages. This feeling was reinforced in certain cases when the guards were stripped, bound hand and foot, and blindfolded. They quickly learned that there was nothing that they could do. If they complained in any way, they were bound more tightly or beaten severely. Those who were blindfolded had no way of knowing when or from where the next physical assault might come. The feeling of helplessness was emphasized by their separation from their fellow officers.

One guard thought of escape during his first hour of captivity. But when he heard some inmates torture and kill another inmate in the cell adjacent to where he was being held, he gave up the idea in total hopelessness. The same officer stated that the helplessness is characterized by thoughts "that you are going to die, and that your life is in their [inmates'] hands." Two guards who were beaten early during their captivity stated that the feeling of helplessness came to them almost immediately. One guard, who remained in hiding throughout the riot, felt trapped and helpless when he heard the inmates saying, "He must be in here somewhere."

None of the officers could offer any resistance. However, being totally helpless had some positive aspects. Even under extreme provocation and abuse, the guards did not reveal certain information; they recognized that doing so would make no difference in their fate. One hostage, who was severely beaten, emphasized that he tried to keep "real calm." At times he thought he was lucky that he was being hit rather than being stabbed. He took all of the blows and realized that he could not fight back, so he tried to remain calm. Another officer, who said that he felt "like a helpless lame duck," recalled that a member of the execution squad praised him as a "pretty cool motherfucker." The inmate then told the officer that he had a "ninety-nine percent chance of not getting out of the penitentiary alive," and asked how he liked that; the officer responded, "I don't like it." The state of helplessness contributed to what appeared to be a stoical attitude on the officers' part in being able to tolerate extreme physical violence. They resisted attempts at being drugged by "checking" medications or secretly spitting them out.

EXISTENTIAL FEAR

The writer has labeled the fear experienced by the hostages in such a way as to distinguish it from any ordinary fear. The hostages were certain that they would be killed. They thought of grisly ways in which the convicts would kill them; they pictured themselves being found dead after the riot was over. One guard described how he was hit with sticks and pipes and felt his head "crunching and being crushed." He thought he was going to die and that the inmates were going to rape him. The inmates were "all over, all around me, talking and screaming." A few of the hostages were held by less violent inmates who attempted to protect them. The inmates themselves became afraid, too, and gave the hostages clubs; they told them, "If we have to bump heads, we'll need your help." A new wave of existential fear engulfed both the hostages and their inmate-guards with each visit from the execution squads.

This frightening situation was reinforced by the prisoners' repeated threats to kill the guards. After hitting one hostage on the head, an inmate said, "How do you like it now? . . . I'm going to kill you . . . I could kill my own mother." One inmate approached some hostages with the severed head of a black prisoner. He said, "This is what can happen to you . . . We'll cut you in pieces and throw you out the window. . . ." Threats and evidence of physical violence and the chaos of the situation reinforced the hostages' fear.

SENSORY INPUT OVERLOAD

The guards were held in a setting with a constant and high sensory input. The air was fouled with smoke, and water from broken pipes flooded the floors. The winter chill came in through broken windows. Masked and armed convicts, traveling in groups, issued frightening threats. There was a continual din from the destruction of the penitentiary, and the guards could hear the screams of inmates being tortured and murdered. None of the guards became accustomed to this sensory overload. Each scream of terror or noise of destruction produced a new startle reaction and a wave of existential fear. The vivid scene during the time the officers were held hostage would come back after their release, when any association with the riot would bring back thoughts and feelings experienced inside the penitentiary.

During their capture, the guards reported a variety of physical reactions to their state of fear and helplessness. Almost all experienced dry mouths and insomnia; most were unaware even of the need for sleep. None was hungry. Those who were beaten reported that their bodies felt numb; after a while, repeated beatings gradually ceased to be painful. One hostage was kicked in the head, back, ribs, and testicles; finally, he could see all these things happening to him but did not feel them. Or he felt them, but they did not hurt. Another hostage said, "I could see my body moving, so I knew that I had been kicked . . . but I didn't feel anything." Still another felt "wood bouncing off of my head." He described a sense of power from his religious convictions and did not experience any pain. In fact, many hostages felt that religion sustained them during their capture.

All the hostages described their mental condition as dazed or in a state of shock. In some cases, they were probably suffering from concussions as a result of repeated blows to the head. All of them believed that they had acted calmly, although inwardly they were extremely frightened.

Their sense of time was distorted, as was their ability to discern where they were being taken within the penitentiary. This latter effect doubtless was due to the fact that it was being systematically destroyed. While they were being rescued, two of the older guards, who knew the prison well, did not know how they got out. This lack of orientation also applied to the guards' inability to recognize inmates whom normally they knew well. In the darkness and smoke, identification of drugged and masked prisoners was impossible.

Fear and helplessness produced a pseudo-rational state whereby the hostage responded unquestioningly to any command. As an example, one hostage, who was released during the riot, turned around and almost reentered the penitentiary when an official on the outside told him to go back. Later, he could not understand how he could obey such a clearly foolish and dangerous order. The same hostage tried to make some sense out of an incident when some sympathetic inmates gave him a red bandanna. In the midst of the chaos of the riot, he tried to determine the symbolic meaning of it, for he had accepted it without thinking. He supposed that it might mean he was marked for death; on the other hand, it could provide a disguise so he could be smuggled out of the penitentiary. In his dilemma, he was afraid to be inside because he thought some inmates would kill him, but outside he thought a guard in the tower might mistake him for an inmate and shoot him. He took off his bandanna in desperation and walked out.

DISCUSSION

The interpretation of the guards' hostage experience poses some problems. What is the standard of comparison in order to put their experience in perspective? Does the absense of physical violence for some hostages or the relatively short duration of their captivity make their experience less traumatic than that of a concentration camp inmate or prisoner of war? The answers to these questions have broad implications for treating and understanding post-hostage behavior.

Examples of concentration camp victims and prisoners of war illustrate the difficulty of comparing or translating the psychopathology of the hostage experience into ordinary or even experimental situations. A study by A. Ramirez and T. Lasater involving "fear-arousing communication" and behavior, measured by how school children responded to taped communications about toothbrushing, seems worlds apart from the fear-arousing threats the hostages endured.[3] Another study by J.A. Hammes and J.A. Watson, dealing with two weeks of voluntary confinement in a fallout shelter, concluded that there was no indication of "adverse fatigue effect during confinement."[4] In fact, as H.A. Barocas suggests, in talking about the children of concentration camp survivors (and the conclusion is applicable to hostages), these experiences may be unclassifiable in the traditional nomenclature.[5] It is doubtful that anyone can predict completely how any of these extraordinary situations will actually be experienced. Concentration camp victims, even when they knew what was in store for them, found the experience "beyond their wildest imagination."[6] As for prisoners of war, even experienced pilots shot down during the Vietnam War manifested some hysterical as well as psychotic reactions during their capture.[7]

The New Mexico hostages confirm the experiences of these prisoners of war and concentration camp victims: no amount of preparation adequately can anticipate what the hostage experience will be like. To the outside observer, the physically unharmed hostage is treated well. But again, the problem is the frame of reference for interpretation. As Diane Cole, a hostage in 1977, has stated,

> ... to be held a prisoner, to live from moment to endless moment at gunpoint—the constant and palpable threat of death—hardly constitutes good treatment. Call it by its proper name, terror—a terror that affects both mind and body, and whose lingering effects, including nightmares, anxiety, and a certain jumpiness, may never disappear.[8]

Classification, interpretation, and treatment of these individuals present formidable challenges and require other than traditional methods of evaluation.[9]

---

[3]A. Ramirez and T. Lasater, "Attitudinal and Behavioral Reactions to Fear Arousing Communications," *Psychology Reports* 38 (1976): 811–18.

[4]J.A. Hammes and J.A. Watson, "Behavior Patterns of Groups Experimentally Confined," *Perceptional and Motor Skills* 20 (1965): 1269–72.

[5]H.A. Barocas, "Children of Purgatory: Reflections of the Concentration Camp Survival Syndrome," *International Journal of Social Psychiatry* 21, no. 2 (1975): 87–92.

[6]L. Eitinger, "Concentration Camp Survivors in the Postwar World," *American Journal of Orthopsychiatry* 32 (1962): 367–75.

[7]R.S. Anderson, "Operation Homecoming: Psychological Observations of Repatriated Vietnam Prisoners of War," *Psychiatry* 38 (1975): 65–74.

[8]Cole, "Why a Hostage Cannot Forget."

[9]L. I. Sank and C. S. Shaffer, "Clinical Findings While Treating the B'nai B'rith Hostages," *Psychiatric Forum* 8 (1979): 67–73.

One hostage, a journalist by profession, was able to take notes at some time during his capture.[10] His ability to have done so was probably unique. One expert's suggestion that the hostage try and relate to his captor sounds logical, but the advice is impractical.[11] The correctional officers almost universally described a situation where the common rules of "relating" no longer applied. The Stockholm Syndrome, widely discussed and reported in the literature, was not in evidence with any of the New Mexico hostages.[12]

There is still a lingering suspicion that the hostage experience, while stressful, is less traumatic than either that of the concentration camp victim or prisoner of war. However, one authority in characterizing concentration camp experiences described eight factors, four of which were shared by the correctional officers: 1) protracted life-endangering situation, 2) prolonged helplessness, 3) recurrent terrifying episodes, and 4) assaults on self-esteem and self-image.[13] A prisoner of war, a concentration camp victim, or a hostage undeniably undergo traumatic experiences which are so different from ordinary ones as to make comprehension of the psychopathology difficult. The fact that they differ in degree, measured by ordinary standards, may not be useful in understanding or treating these victims.

The hostages described here represented a particular and specialized group: Spanish-American males working as correctional officers. However, the psychopathology of their experiences is remarkably similar to those of other hostages, prisoners of war, and some concentration camp victims. Cole describes the death threats made by her captors: "You dare not doubt what those voices tell you: that you will die."[14] The hostage's value, she points out, is that he breathes and therefore may be killed. Another hostage said that he was "preparing for execution."[15]

L. Eitinger, in describing concentration camp victims, states that there were "severe psychic reactions in those prisoners who were under sentence of death and waited, practically all the time, for the sentence to be executed . . ."[16] In the same article, he describes the "gruesome impressions they received by hearing from the prison yard the sounds of

---

[10]Ochberg, "The Victim of Terrorism."

[11]F. M. Ochberg, Preparing for Terrorist Victimization in Political Terrorism and Business—The Threat and Response, eds. Y. Alexander and R. Kilmarx (New York: Praeger Special Studies, 1979).

[12]Ochberg, "The Victim of Terrorism."

[13]D. M. Berger, "The Survivor Syndrome: A Problem of Nosology and Treatment," American Journal of Psychotherapy 31 (1977): 238–51.

[14]Cole, "Why a Hostage Cannot Forget."

[15]Ochberg, "The Victim of Terrorism."

[16]Eitinger, "Pathology of the Concentration Camp Syndrome."

executions by shootings, floggings, and so on, while they themselves were shut up, isolated, without any possibility of showing their reactions." M. Symonds speaks of the "frozen fright" of the victims of violence that he studied. He states that "the reaction of fear is so profound and overwhelming that the victim feels hopeless about getting away." He points out that the seemingly compliant behavior of the victim may lead to the erroneous conclusion that the victim "produced or participated in the criminal act."[17] M. Maskin, in a review of the psychodynamics of the war neuroses, describes the state of total helplessness combined with fear that underlies the trauma of these extraordinary experiences.[18] Psychopathologically, the experiences of prisoners of war and concentration camp victims have noticeable similarities, especially in terms of existential fear and a feeling of helplessness.

CONCLUSIONS

Several inferences can be drawn from these findings. It is obvious that there is no way that a hostage "should" act. The hostage, in fact, has no choice. "Totally helpless" accurately describes his position. The hostage who is severely traumatized may respond in a pseudo-rational manner to dangerous instructions. Negotiators as well as those who later analyze the hostage's responses should keep this in mind.

The above symptoms were experienced in an absolute manner rather than in degrees, as is more common with ordinary psychological symptoms. Describing degrees of existential fear is a meaningless artifice used by someone who has not experienced such fear. All guards experienced these symptoms and described them similarly. The existential fear was either present or absent. After their release, this fear would return in an on-off manner and form an important component of the traumatic neurosis. Sometimes the fear would be switched on and could not consciously be switched off.

The hostage experience is so different from ordinary existence that it is difficult for others to understand. Someone, for example, who was held hostage under extremely adverse conditions for as little as four to eight hours can later exhibit classical signs of a traumatic neurosis. The intensity of the hostage experience, and not its duration, determines the later development of a traumatic neurosis. The naive observer, focusing on

---

[17]M. Symonds, "Victims of Violence: Psychological Effects and After Effects," *American Journal of Psychoanalysis* 35 (1975): 19–26.

[18]M. Maskin, "Psychodynamic Aspects of the War Neuroses," *Psychiatry* 4 (1941): 97–115.

the length of time the hostage has been held captive rather than the type of stress to which he was exposed, may conclude that only the length of time determines subsequent psychological problems.

Philosophically, as W. C. Niederland suggests, the concept of a traumatic neurosis as a self-limiting process which can be clinically and dynamically delineated may not apply to the survivors of concentration camps, prisoners of war, or hostages.[19] The puzzle of why symptoms persist for years or even across generations may be explained, as H. Klonoff, et al., propose, that even when the stressful situation is removed, a return to *status quo ante* may not necessarily occur.[20] As Cole has said regarding the Iranian hostages: "Let no one be deceived: some part of each one will remain in that embassy forever."[21]

---

[19]W. C. Niederland, "Clinical Observations on the Survivor Syndrome," *International Journal of Psycho-Analysis* 49 (1968): 313–15.

[20]Barocas, "Children of Purgatory"; H. Klonoff, et al., "The Neuropsychological, Psychiatric, and Physical Effects of Prolonged and Severe Stress."

[21]Cole, "Why a Hostage Cannot Forget."

IV.
RESPONDING TO
TERRORISM

Terrorism: Policy, Action, and Reaction*

ANTHONY C. E. QUAINTON

No conference on the psychopathology of political violence can ignore the pervasive reality of international terrorism and its implications for public policy. In the last twelve years, the world has witnessed over 3,000 major acts of terrorism in which 2,300 people have been killed and 5,500 wounded. In the first nine months of 1979 alone, almost 200 incidents have taken place involving 166 deaths and 359 injuries. All geographic regions without exception have been affected, although Western Europe continues to bear the brunt of the terrorist threat. The United States and its personnel and property remain highly symbolic targets. Recent events in Iran and El Salvador bring home how often foreigners focus on the American presence for their violent political purposes.

We are all aware of terrorism as a phenomenon in the contemporary world, but we are less precise about what events deserve that highly perjorative label "terrorist." There is no universally accepted definition of terrorism, although a number of formulations are widely used. Two in particular seem to this writer to illuminate the essential elements of terrorism and provide some basic pointers for decision makers. The first defines terrorism as "a symbolic act designed to influence political behavior by extranormal means entailing the use or threat of violence." The second asserts that terrorism is the "threat or use of violence for political purposes, when such action is intended to influence the attitude and behavior of a target group other than its immediate victims and its ramifications transcend national boundaries." Both take as their starting point the fact that terrorism is violent political activity. There is no terrorism without violence and coercion. There is no terrorism in the absence of political motivation. In fact, as Lenin might have observed, terrorism is the continuation of politics by violent means.

---

*A revised version of the paper presented at the conference, "Psychopathology and Political Violence: Terrorism and Assassination," sponsored by the Institute of Social and Behavioral Pathology and the University of Chicago Department of Psychiatry, Chicago, Illinois, 16–17 November 1979.

However, not all violent political acts are intrinsically terrorist, as one can see from the many national liberation struggles of the postwar world. In order to have acts of international terrorism, additional elements are needed. The two definitions provide those elements—the concept of extranormality and the transcending of national boundaries. Terrorism is abnormal because it almost always chooses as targets and as weapons innocent noncombatant diplomats in an embassy, passengers on an airplane or train, students on a bus, or businessmen kidnapped for ransom. These targets are nonmilitary, frequently with no direct connection to the cause being promoted. The victims are used cynically as the tools whereby public attention can be focused on a political cause and a wider international audience can be influenced. Terrorism can also be considered abnormal when certain kinds of acts are involved: hijacking, hostage taking, kidnapping, letter-bombing. Under international law, all are regarded as illegitimate, inhumane, and unjustifiable acts of violence.

However extralegal and abnormal terrorism may be, it is not irrational or pointless. It is not, as is so often stated, mindless violence. The terrorist is espousing a particular political cause. His targets, immediate and ultimate, are carefully chosen. A particular outcome—publicity, ransom, prisoner release—is clearly defined. Our response therefore must be equally well-tailored to the specific means and tactics of each group which sponsors and espouses terrorism.

The distinction between ends and means is at the heart of any policy and decision-making process related to terrorism. We are all aware of the diversity of causes to which terrorists appeal. Some groups, such as the Baader-Meinhof Gang and its successors, the Italian Red Brigades and the Japanese Red Army, seek the total overthrow of the capitalist system. Others demand merely a change in regime or a transition to majority rule, as in Central America and southern Africa. Yet others pursue nationalist or ethnocentric goals—a united Ireland, a homeland for the Palestinians, a Basque, Croatian or South Moluccan state. Some of these causes, such as majority rule in southern Africa, we can actively support. Many others provoke passionate and emotional debate. Yet all these groups have been characterized as terrorist from one perspective or another, and all have carried out individual acts of hostage taking or terrorist violence which have been generally condemned. It is not easy to devise a global policy for combating terrorism as long as we focus only on the terrorists' goals and objectives. We also must consider the means they employ.

To be sure, we must not ignore the underlying causes of terrorism. By pursuing a Middle Eastern peace settlement which recognizes the rights of the Palestinians, by supporting efforts to achieve majority rule in Rhodesia, by our cooperation with the new political order in Central America, we are attempting to deal with these issues. But we cannot easily accept or lightly promote the dismemberment of existing nation states, not to speak of the overthrow of the capitalist system. Some would argue that in the thermonuclear age, with Armageddon before us, the ends can justify the means if survival is at stake. While we recognize that the nature of an end may mitigate one's judgment of means, we would be very reluctant to accept the proposition that our sympathies for a political cause should allow us to condone all violent actions carried out on its behalf. Although we may accept certain kinds of violent acts in situations of war, we do not have to accept a terrorist's acts as valid or noble. It is of critical importance, therefore, to distinguish between legitimate and illegitimate acts of violence either by reference to the weapon employed or to the target chosen. Under the laws of war, we take for granted that torture and the use of biological agents are inhumane and barbaric violations of the *ius gentium*. There is a similar consensus that in war, including wars of national liberation, military targets are permissible but the cynical use of civilian targets is not.

Similarly, with respect to terrorism, we have been working to differentiate between those political activities which are legitimate and those which deserve universal condemnation. The predisposition of the terrorist to use innocent civilians as the instruments of his purpose is particularly disturbing. Hijacking of planes, kidnapping, and the taking of hostages are increasingly recognized by the international community as contrary to a basic moral standard. The willingness of the United Nations to draft and promote conventions against hijacking, aircraft sabotage, attacks on diplomats, and hostage taking is evidence of this growing awareness. There is also increasing condemnation of the use of certain weapons systems— surface-to-air missiles and rocket launchers—when these are directed at nonmilitary targets, or nuclear, biological, and chemical agents irrespective of target. The basic strategy of the United States has been to seek to broaden this international consensus to include as wide a spectrum of acts as possible, while at the same time seeking, whenever feasible, to remove terrorism's underlying causes.

Even if we have clarified our thinking about the nature of a terrorist act and its relationship to certain political goals, we still must define a coherent government policy to respond to terrorist violence. Such a policy must come to grips with the fundamental issues of whether and under what circumstances concessions should be made to terrorist demands, when and how negotiations should be conducted, and according to what rules military force can be used. The U.S. government repeatedly has stated its view that it will not pay ransom and will not release prisoners in order to achieve the release of hostages. We look to foreign governments to assume responsibility for resolving all such situations. We do not, however, refuse to negotiate with or to talk to the terrorists. We believe that dialogue is an essential element of any strategy, even though it may be limited to a discussion of the provision of food and water and other humanitarian concerns.

Dr. Frank Ochberg has postulated four options for dealing with terrorist incidents: attack, bargain, concede, delay. The government is quite clear about its priorities; the making of concessions and the use of military force are the least attractive and least favored alternatives. The use of military or police force risks lives. Concessions put in jeopardy the credibility and honor of the nation. Delay and dialogue form the basis of our policy and of our tactics, because they offer the most likely channels for saving lives.

Let us note, however, that the private sector has adopted a different tactic. Invariably it makes concessions. An incident in El Salvador is a case in point. At the demand of a Salvadoran revolutionary group which had kidnapped two businessmen, an American corporation first took out a two-page advertisement stating the political manifesto of the kidnappers. It subsequently paid a substantial ransom. The two businessmen were later released. Under comparable circumstances, the U.S. government would not have paid a ransom because of the conviction that once we embark down that road, we will be faced with ever more numerous extortion demands. More, not fewer, Americans will be at risk. This has certainly been the case for the private sector in Latin America and Italy, where kidnappings are increasingly frequent occurrences.

The fundamental dilemma is how to strike a balance between deterrence and saving lives. The government must be as concerned for the protection of life as any private group. But it has to think beyond the life of individual hostages to the safety and well-being of thousands of other official Americans whose lives would be threatened if the government were to give in to terrorists' demands. Deterrence must remain an essential part of our arsenal. For this reason, our focus will continue to be on those strategies which maximize delay and involve a minimal amount of substantive bargaining. However, we do retain considerable tactical flexibility during an incident. We try to avoid an overly rigid stance which might only aggravate an otherwise dangerous situation, but we retain the capability to use more drastic and forceful means if events so require.

Even when we have clearly differentiated between the terrorists and the freedom fighters, between the criminals and the heros, and have set forth a broad policy strategy, complex organizational and bureaucratic problems in implementing a policy and in mobilizing the crisis management system remain. Several precise issues arise: horizontal coordination within the federal system, vertical coordination with state and local governments, crisis management leadership, and political command and control.

Beginning in 1972 after the Lod Airport and Munich Olympic Games massacres, the U.S. government recognized a need to deal with terrorism on more than an *ad hoc* basis. At that time, the president created a Cabinet Committee and a Working Group on Terrorism subordinate to it. The former was abolished in 1977, having met only once, while the Working Group was placed under the National Security Council's Special Coordination Committee, a Cabinet-level body charged specifically with responsibility for both policy and crisis management issues. The Working Group now has over thirty members, primarily federal agencies with law enforcement, intelligence or operational responsibilities in the field of terrorism. It is a large and unwieldy group with disparate interests. In order to focus more precisely on matters of major concern, the Working Group has been broken down into several smaller units: an Executive Committee charged with reviewing major policy and crisis management issues and a number of subcommittees responsible for functional problems of concern to only a limited number of member agencies. These functional areas include research and development, physical security, contingency planning, public affairs, and international initiatives.

The principal purpose of the Working Group is to ensure prompt and effective interagency coordination, which is often lacking in the vast federal bureaucracy. Until recently, however, it has not attempted to address the more complex, and in the domestic area more important, area of vertical coordination: the linkages between the federal government and state and local authorities. As the events at Three-Mile Island demonstrated in a different context, we need to be able to respond to crises and disasters very quickly and in ways that ensure close cooperation between all affected jurisdictions. When domestic terrorist incidents occur, local law enforcement authorities are often the first on the scene, even in crimes which involve federal jurisdiction. It is essential that they have close working relationships with the FBI and other federal agencies charged with handling such incidents. Since local authorities often have responsibility for preventive measures, there is also a critical need to share intelligence on terrorist groups and plans. Unfortunately, such an exchange sometimes is limited by the lack of national security clearances at the local level.

The Working Group is attempting to address the vertical coordination problem in two ways. We have invited representatives of the National Governors Association and the National League of Cities to take part in our activities. These two organizations provide critical links to the governors and mayors and to those on their respective staffs concerned with emergency planning and crisis management. We are also encouraging and in some cases funding exercises, games, and scenarios designed to test interactions between the federal system and state and local authorities.

Much progress in the area of coordination has already been made; much more is possible. Nonetheless, a group of thirty agencies, even if a close working relationship among the members exists, is not the ideal body for incident management. When a terrorist act occurs, we have found that it is desirable to concentrate and focus responsibility in one lead agency. At this time there are three agencies with lead responsibility: the Department of State for all terrorist incidents outside the United States involving American interests; the FBI for incidents inside the United States; and the Federal Aviation Administration for hijackings in American jurisdiction. Each of these agencies has a modern crisis center from which contact can be maintained with the incident site and through which the resources of other agencies can be coordinated and mobilized. In an incident, each agency sets up a task force to pull together all its own resources of negotiators, psychiatrists, intelligence experts, and press spokesmen. This team is supplemented by representatives of other agencies as needed. But the lead agency has the basic responsibility of providing the core of the crisis management team. When problems which are not susceptible of decision at the level of operational crisis managers arise, the issues are referred to the National Security Council's Special Coordination Committee.

The Iranian crisis has made us all aware that the key factor in handling sensitive hostage incidents, whether carried out by terrorist groups or government-sponsored mobs, is the need for sound command and control procedures. Committees, task forces, and crisis centers are only part of the answer. What is vital are clear lines of communication between the commander in the field, be he an ambassador or chargé d'affaires abroad or an FBI Special Agent in Charge at home, and the national command authority represented by the president and his closest advisors. This writer knows of no terrorist incident of duration which has not raised issues for our political leadership. The field commander must have substantial tactical flexibility, but the basic strategic decisions can only come from Washington, and there, in fact, only from the White House. This is one of the principal reasons why the entire counter-terrorist apparatus reports for both policy and crisis management guidance to the National Security Council.

When issues are referred to the highest levels of our government, one quickly sees the tension between conflicting national interests. Most Americans accept the proposition that we should oppose international terrorism and those who support and condone it. Many argue that we should impose economic and political sanctions on those who aid and abet terrorism by giving sanctuary to the perpetrators of terrorist acts. Congress has passed ten separate amendments to different laws to ensure that the government takes action against the patron states of terrorism. A separate omnibus antiterrorism bill, sponsored by Senators Abraham Ribicoff and Jacob Javits, is making its way through Congress at this time. It would oblige us to terminate military and economic aid, as well as sales of items of potential military use, to countries which show a pattern of support for terrorism. A declaration signed at Bonn in July 1978 by

President Jimmy Carter and six other heads of state and government would require the cutting off of air services to any country which fails to prosecute or extradite hijackers.

Clearly these proposals command significant support and demonstrate the level of congressional and international concern about terrorism. Their implementation, however, entails serious trade-offs and considerable costs. When, for example, we cut off the sales of passenger aircraft to Libya or Iraq because of those nations' support for terrorism, the result is the loss of business to Boeing or Lockheed and unemployment in Seattle or Atlanta. Were we to sell advanced technology and weapons to the police forces of countries which have a domestic terrorist threat, we indeed might succeed in defeating the terrorist but possibly at a high human rights cost. Because terrorism is not the single most important issue in American foreign policy, our efforts to contain it will inevitably run up against other foreign policy objectives: political, economic, commercial or humanitarian. The ordering of these priorities becomes the central issue for foreign policymakers.

Finally, even when the priorities are set and the policy clear, we will still have to choose the appropriate response. This is not merely a question of whether or not to negotiate or to use force. Those decisions can be agonizingly difficult, but the circumstances requiring them are rare. Equally controversial and more immediate are other questions: How far should we go in developing physical security? How much intelligence should we be collecting? How important is it to uphold the public's need for information?

All of us who travel have noticed the changes which the terrorists have succeeded in imposing on our life-style. We now accept routinely the searches we undergo in boarding aircraft. Our embassies and consulates abroad are heavily fortified, though not to the point where they can withstand mob attacks. Our ambassadors must now travel in bullet-resistant cars. These measures have been developed to protect the public and American employees, but they represent significant restrictions on our freedom and on the traditional openness of our society and of its representation abroad. These steps are essential given the nature of the threat, but we must always keep in mind the costs, both financial and psychological, which they entail.

Concern to protect and defend the basic openness of our society has led to restrictions on the gathering of intelligence, particularly about Americans, and to intense pressures for the disclosure of government documents. Past abuses of power may have generated these pressures, but the results have not always contributed to a sound counter-terrorist program. As long as the terrorist threat remains low in the United States, these restrictions will be appropriate. But were there to be a major upsurge in terrorist violence, we could not expect to have substantial amounts of information about its perpetrators. The opening of government files under Freedom of Information procedures also has had the unexpected consequence of restricting the flow of information between governments. Our closest friends have begun to lose confidence in our ability to protect their secrets. We must be concerned not to overreact to hypothetical dangers. We always must be concerned to protect our basic civil rights. But we also must be sure that we have not excessively diminished our capacity to deal with the real threat which terrorism represents.

As we look to the future, we must anticipate ever more complex and demanding situations against which our policy will be judged. Iran is a case in point. Terrorists may choose new weapons, such as surface-to-air missiles, rockets, chemical, biological or even nuclear agents. They may choose new targets focusing on the many vulnerabilities of modern industrial civilization: power generation and transmission facilities, tankers, pipelines, computers. If they do, we must be prepared.

In such situations we need to strike a careful balance among our various interests. We will need to use all our resources imaginatively. Because terrorism always raises complex political and moral issues, the agenda for future action will be long. Prevention, deterrence, reaction, and prediction should be the hallmarks of our policy. In each area, we will need to have a clear understanding of the terrorist and his motives. It is here that the contribution of the psychiatrist and the psychologist is most relevant. The more we understand about the psychopathology of terrorism and assassination, the more effective we will be in predicting its occurrence, in deterring its perpetrators, in devising appropriate tactics, and in focusing our reaction against it. This is a task on which we are all embarked and where the worlds of academia and government meet on common ground.

Problems in Media Coverage of Nonstate-Sponsored Terror-Violence Incidents*

M. CHERIF BASSIOUNI

It has become far more alluring for the frantic few to appear on the world stage of television than remain obscure guerrillas of the bush.

J. Bowyer Bell[1]

The media are the indispensable communications link of industrial society, as vital to the modern world as energy. Through their various forms, media serve economic and sociopolitical interests in the collection and dissemination of information. As electronic technology becomes more refined, this diffusion of information is accomplished more rapidly and more extensively than ever before. In addition, society's easier access to and increased reliance on media renders their psychological impact more pervasive and persuasive than in the past.

These facts have not escaped the attention of those who employ strategies of violence in order to obtain media coverage that most effectively achieves their sociopolitical objectives. Indeed, the correlation between the escalation of global terror-violence in the past twenty years and the innovations in media technology that facilitate rapid dissemination of information to large audiences is more than mere coincidence. In essence, this correlation illustrates the symbiotic relationship between "terrorism" and the media: the "terrorists" rely on the media to further their terror-inspiring goals, and the media utilize the terrorists' acts as necessary or rewarding news items.[2]

---

*A revised version of the report prepared for the Law Enforcement Assistance Administration of the Department of Justice, contract no. 79-NL-Ax-0600. Portions of this paper were part of a broader report, excerpts of which appeared in M. Cherif Bassiouni, "Terrorism, Law Enforcement, and the Mass Media: Perspectives, Problems, Proposals," *Journal of Criminal Law and Criminology* 1 (1981).
[1]J. Bowyer Bell, *A Time of Terror* (1978).
[2]M. Cherif Bassiouni, "Prolegomenon to Terror Violence," *Creighton Law Review* 12: 745, 760 (hereafter cited as "Terror Violence"). Dr. Frederick Hacker, a California psychiatrist with experience as a terrorism negotiator and a contributor to this volume, has remarked: "If the mass media did not exist, terrorists would have to invent them. In turn, the

Regardless of whether acts of terror-violence are committed by individuals against a state or are state-sponsored acts of terror-violence committed against individuals, the perpetrator's strategy invariably involves the use and instrumentalization of the media. It may be more advantageous at times for terrorism from above (state-sponsored) to reduce media exposure of repressive violence, while terrorism from below (nonstate-sponsored) usually seeks maximum exposure. In the case of serious state-sponsored violations of human rights—such as the use of torture, and arbitrary arrests and detentions—the state may well use all of its powers to prevent the dissemination of such news. This may not be true, however, where a different state goal is involved. For example, the Iranian seizure of the U.S. embassy and sixty-three hostages in Tehran in October 1979 was intended to focus maximum world attention on both the incident itself and on the underlying motivations which the Iranians advanced as justifications for their actions. In this respect, the Iranian crisis was similar to acts of terror-violence whose goal is more often than not to propagandize claims or to achieve maximum publicity for a variety of purposes.

Ideologically motivated terror-violence from below is the weapon of the weak,[3] employed by those who are too few or too powerless to achieve their objectives through the conventional political process. Media technology has made terror-violence an attractive strategy for effecting social or political transformation for two reasons. First, it has enhanced the power image of those who are opposed to the sociopolitical systems of an increasingly complex and vulnerable society. Second, technology has made the media an indispensable device by which an individual or a small group of individuals can magnify their power and influence over society within a short period of time and with relatively little effort.[4] That the media have

---

mass media hanker after terroristic acts because they fit into their programming needs; namely, sudden acts of great excitement that are susceptible, presumably, of quick solution. So there's a mutual dependency." Hickey, "Terrorism and Television," *TV Guide*, 31 July 1976. Walter Laqueur has called the media the "terrorist's best friend," ibid.

The mass media include television, radio, newspapers, magazines, books, and films. For the purpose of this discussion, "media" refers primarily to the news organizations commonly associated with the first four categories.

[3]B. Crozier, *A Theory of Conflict* (1975), p. 129.

[4]Industrialization has provided such vulnerable and attractive targets as aircraft, electrical power plants, nuclear reactors, dams, fuel storage facilities, and telephone exchanges, while terrorists have obtained—through theft, purchase, and support from patron states—portable and sophisticated weapons of great destructive capability. See *The Media and Terrorism* 7 (1977) from a seminar sponsored by the *Chicago Sun-Times* and *Chicago Daily News*. See also Jenkins and Rubin, "New Vulnerabilities and the Acquisition of New Weapons by Non-Government Groups," in *Legal Aspects of International Terrorism* 221, ed. A. Evans and J. Murphy (1978). The great modern threat is the theft or use of nuclear materials. See Mason Willrich and Theodore B. Taylor, *Nuclear Theft: Risks and Safeguards* (1974). Since the writing of this paper, there have been a number of publications on this subject which are not cited herein.

come to serve willingly or unwillingly the purposes of those who engage in terror-violence was captured by the national Task Force on Disorders and Terrorism, which stated:

> Acts of terrorism have gained immediacy and diffusion through television, which conveys the terrorist message to millions worldwide. The modern terrorist has been quick to exploit the medium in a way that shows government as a poor rival. Formerly, in countries where free speech and communication were jealously guarded rights, it would have been unthinkable for violent subversives to have seized control of the organs of mass communications. Today it is the commonplace consequence of terrorist action. In many ways, the modern terrorist is the very creation of the mass media. He has been magnified, enlarged beyond his own powers by others.[5]

This problem may be better understood by recognizing that the media's public function condemns them to being the medium of the terrorist's message—a message conveyed explicitly and implicitly by virtue of media coverage of terrorist incidents.[6] Furthermore, the type and extent of this coverage often increase the shock effect of terror-violence in general as well as particular incidents of terror-violence. However balanced media coverage may be, some problems of pervasive influence remain: these are compounded when the coverage is unbalanced or suffers from other improprieties.

The mass media perform five basic functions:[7]

1) *Informational*, by providing increasing numbers of people with a flow of news concerning events occurring within a given society and in the world;

2) *Judgmental*, by providing the public with standards of judgment conveyed explicitly or implicitly, by selection and treatment of subjects and material to aid in interpreting the information given;

---

[5]*National Advisory Committee on Criminal Justice Standards and Goals, Report of the Task Force on Disorders and Terrorism* 9 (1976) (hereafter cited as *Disorders and Terrorism*).

[6]See Bell, *Time of Terror*, p. 110; *Disorders and Terrorism*, pp. 236–38, 366–69, 387–90, 401–4, 414; Institute for Study of Conflict, *Television and Conflict* (1978) (hereafter cited as *Television and Conflict*); *The Media and Terrorism*, n. 4; Alexander, "Terrorism, the Media, and the Police," *Journal of International Affairs* 32 (1978); *More* (June 1977): 12–21; Revzin, "A Reporter Looks at Media Role in Terror Threats," *Wall Street Journal*, 14 March 1977; Seib, "The Hanafi Episode: A Media Event," *Washington Post*, 18 March 1977; National News Council, "Paper on Terrorism" (July 1977). See also "Terror Violence," pp. 759–65; Cooper, "Terrorism and the Media," *Chitty's Law Journal* 24 (September 1976): 226; Paust, "Internal Law and Control of the Media: Terror, Repression, and the Alternatives," *Indiana Law Journal* 621 (1978): 53.

[7]"Terror Violence," p. 752.

3) *Educational*, by transmitting the social and universal heritage from one generation to the next, and by defining and clarifying social goals and social values;
4) *Interactional*, by providing an open forum for the free exchange of ideas and opinions, by furnishing a basis from which both individual and collective judgments can be formed;
5) *Recreational*, by providing amusement, relieving tension, and providing learning situations.

While the relationship between terror-violence and the media has received increasing examination,[8] specific solutions to the problems created by media coverage of terror-violence have been limited. To develop such solutions, one must first understand the problems presented by media coverage of terror-violence incidents. Only then can one develop specific proposals to effectively control and eventually prevent terror-violence in a manner that comports with constitutional principles and the rule of law.

THE PUBLICITY OBJECTIVE OF TERROR-VIOLENCE

Terrorism is a "strategy of unlawful violence calculated to inspire terror in the general public, or a significant segment thereof, in order to achieve a power outcome or to propagandize a particular claim or grievance."[9] A psychological element is implicit in this definition: though the physical harm caused by ideologically motivated terror-violence is relatively limited, such acts produce, and are calculated to produce, an extensive psychological impact.

Because ordinary sporadic acts of violence would be of limited utility in achieving their objectives, perpetrators of ideologically motivated terror-violence must enhance the attention gathering and impact of their actions by making their activities appear extraordinary and sensational. This can be achieved most effectively by increasing the public's knowledge of and attention on the terror-violent acts. Since the mass media have the capacity to disseminate information concerning occurrences of terror-violence, they have the capability to create the social impact desired by the perpetrators. Thus, the perpetrators depend upon the mass media to disseminate their sociopolitical message and the terror-inspiring nature of

---

[8]Ibid., p. 758.
[9]Bassiouni, "Terrorism, Law Enforcement," p. 72.

their act. The terror-inspiring quality of a terror-violent act is not necessarily inherent in the act itself; rather, this quality is derivative of the act's impact, which is largely determined by the media coverage the act receives.[10]

Ideologically motivated perpetrators of terror-violence usually operate on three levels, each of which has its own goal: the primary stage, in which the tactical objective is an attack against a suitable target; the secondary stage, in which the strategic objective is the dissemination by the media of the ideological claim or the terror-inspiring effect of the act; and the final stage, in which the ultimate objective is the achievement of the desired power outcome.[11]

The tactical, strategic, and ultimate objectives are interrelated in the perpetrator's reliance on the media to attain his ends. First, the strategic objective of the terrorist influences his choice of tactical targets and the methods of attack. The acts undertaken by the ideologically motivated perpetrator are likely to be directed against highly visible targets and conducted in the most dramatic manner, so as to draw media attention to the event and maximize its media-created impact.[12] The perpetrator anticipates and relies on media coverage in the planning and execution of his terror-inspiring acts while the media, in covering such acts, unwittingly further his objective of producing a social impact that would not otherwise occur.[13] Second, in addition to seeking maximum exposure, the media-conscious perpetrator attempts to manipulate the instruments of mass communication so that the ultimate objective of his particular grievance or ideology is portrayed as desirable or inevitable. Although the methods of manipulation vary from incident to incident, they are invariably chosen to demonstrate the vulnerability and impotence of the government, attract broader public sympathy by the choice of a carefully selected target that may be publicly rationalized, cause a polarization and radicalization among the public or a segment thereof, goad the government into repressive action likely to discredit it, and present the violent acts as heroic.[14]

In his *Minimanual of the Urban Guerrilla*, the Brazilian terrorist Carlos Marighella expounds the strategy of media manipulation as such:

> The war of nerves or psychological war is an aggressive technique, based on the direct or indirect use of mass means of communication and news transmitted orally in order to demoralize the government.

---

[10]"Terror Violence," p. 759.
[11]Ibid., p. 760.
[12]Ibid., p. 757.
[13]Bassiouni, "Terrorism, Law Enforcement," p. 17.
[14]Ibid.

In psychological warfare, the government is always at a disadvantage since it imposes censorship on the mass media and winds up in a defensive position by not allowing anything against it to filter through.

At this point it becomes desperate, is involved in greater contradictions and loses time and energy in an exhausting effort at control which is subject to being broken at any moment.[15]

It is apparent from these statements that the media are as much a victim of terror-violence as society and its institutions. Perhaps the best example of this occurred during the Iranian seizure of the embassy in Tehran. During this crisis, the perpetrators chose the media to achieve their strategic goal and manipulated media coverage to publicize the legitimacy of their revolution and their grievances against the United States.

THE CINEMATOGENIC LINK BETWEEN TERROR-VIOLENCE AND THE MASS MEDIA

Terrorist organizations, state- and nonstate-sponsored alike, rely heavily on the stereotypes created by the media. The interrelationship between media coverage and terror-violence groups is so strong that these groups purposefully conform to media stereotypes in composing their internal organizational structure, their chain of command, and even the attitudes of their members. In addition, terror-violence groups' choice of targets and their execution of certain acts frequently correspond to media-created perceptions of how these spectacular events should occur.

The cinematogenic nature of contemporary terrorist behavior attests to the symbiotic relationship between the media and terrorism. The media's portrayal of individuals and events is based on a value judgment as well as on certain expectations of patterns of behavior. These factors have not been sufficiently appraised in terms of their impact on perpetrators and would-be perpetrators of terror-violence. It is noteworthy, therefore, to point out certain outcomes of this cinematogenic effect: 1) the perpetrators' patterns of behavior seek to fulfill media expectations by conforming to certain patterns stereotyped by factual or fictional portrayals; 2) response to stereotypical portrayals provides a framework and rapport between perpetrators, media personnel who cover the event, and those who decide what type of coverage which terror-violent acts should receive; and 3) conformity to stereotype provides a sound basis for predictability of behavior and responses on the part of the perpetrators, the media, and the general public.

---

[15]Carlos Marighella, *Minimanual of the Urban Guerrilla* (n.d.), p. 103.

In addition, fictional media stereotypes provide models of behavior that the public associates with certain values. By conforming to these stereotypes and, sometimes, by easily distorting them, perpetrators of terror-violence are able to assume roles which attract public sympathy. In any event, conformity to stereotypical cinematogenic roles tends to make their behavior more tolerable to the public.

THE MEDIA-ENHANCED IMPACT OF TERROR-VIOLENCE

Four categories of problems associated with media coverage of terror-violence incidents are identifiable readily in the context of democratic societies which guarantee freedom of the press. First, the reporting of acts of terror-violence may encourage others to engage in such conduct. Second, excesses or deficiencies in media coverage may enhance the climate of intimidation which the terrorist seeks to generate; this would not only further unnecessarily the perpetrators' objectives, but it would also engender pressures for counterproductive governmental repression and cause undesirable social consequences. Third, media coverage may immunize or dull the general public's sense of opprobrium. Each of these factors also has a potential countereffect. Fourth, media reporting may endanger hostages' lives and interfere with effective law enforcement response; these problems generally arise during contemporaneous, on-the-scene coverage of ongoing incidents.

On the other hand, it should be noted that media coverage and media portrayal also can operate as a safety valve or a release factor. For example, media coverage can be a means of securing hostages' release; media coverage can also coopt the need for terror-violence by disseminating claims that otherwise would become exteriorized through violent action.

The Psychologically Projected Prediction

This effect of terror-violence occurs in the following manner. First, events of terror-violence conjure up images associated with certain symbols or labels. When these symbols or labels are used later to describe another event, this triggers the recall of the prior event, even though the new one may not be of the same magnitude, seriousness, or impact. Thus, the repeated usage of a given key word regarding an event in the print or electronic media may bring to mind not only the event which the key word represents, but also a projected prediction about the new event's outcome. As a result, the ready recall and projected impact which this process creates tend to increase the psychological effects of terror-violence. For example, because the media have highlighted acts of terror-violence by the Palestine Liberation Organization (PLO), the recall effect is such that any act of terror-violence is associated with the PLO, even when it was committed by any of the other groups of terrorists active at any time.

The Contagion Hypothesis

According to the contagion hypothesis, media attention given to terror-violence encourages further incidents of terror-violence. Although this hypothesis would not appear entirely susceptible to empirical verification, at least with respect to ideologically motivated individuals, concern over this contagion effect has been repeatedly expressed,[16] and the theory retains a certain intuitive reasonableness. The public success of a particular terrorist group, for instance, may encourage that group to repeat its attacks in order to keep the public's attention on its goals or ideology. In addition, publicity generated by one terrorist group, such as that accorded the Italian Red Brigades by virtue of its kidnapping of Aldo Moro, may goad less successful groups to commit increased or more daring acts of terror-violence. The 1979 Central Intelligence Agency report on terrorism predicts that "West German terrorists, having suffered reverses during the past year, are likely to feel greater pressure to remind their domestic and international sympathizers that they remain revolutionary leaders by engaging in operations at home or overseas."[17]

The contagion hypothesis also may operate with respect to perpetrators motivated by nonideological reasons. Since the mass media have the ability to "confer status upon an individual or an event merely by presenting them,"[18] the spotlight of media attention may be an irresistible lure to violence for certain individuals. The common criminal who is motivated by personal gain may imitate successful techniques which he has learned from media coverage of earlier terrorist incidents. Although

---

[16]See Mendelsohn, "Socio-Psychological Perspectives on the Mass Media and Public Anxiety," *Journalism Quarterly* (1963): 513. Individuals unable to redress a particular grievance but otherwise normal also may resort to terrorist means. After the Hanafi incident, Dr. Robert Jay Lifton, professor of psychiatry at Yale University, remarked that when the press makes "the person of the terrorist something close to the total news of the week, the imagery of terrorism becomes much more active psychologically for the average person. Therefore it must contribute to stimulating similar acts among people who feel frustrated and for whom other avenues are closed." *New York Times*, 19 March 1977.

[17]*International Terrorism in 1978*, R. P. 79-10149 (CIA National Foreign Assessment Center, March 1979).

[18]Krattenmaker and Powe, "Televised Violence: First Amendment Principles and Social Science Theory," *Virginia Law Review* 64 (1978): 1123, 1134.

many examples of criminal education through media presentation of crime have been recorded,[19] one incident stands out:

> Of Rod Serling's programs, "Doomsday Flight" probably is the most memorable. A caller hides an altitude bomb aboard an airliner and demands a ransom. If the company refuses to pay, he will not divulge the location of the bomb, and the plane will be destroyed as it descends for a landing. In the end, the pilot saves the plane by selecting an airport located at an elevation above the critical altitude. "Doomsday Flight" gained notoriety because of the immediate reaction it created. Before the hour-long program was over, one airline received an identical bomb threat; four similar threats came during the next twenty-four hours and another eight during the following week. Exported to other countries, the show made one Australian criminal $500,000.00 richer thanks to Qantas Airlines' desire to protect 116 passengers en route to Hong Kong, while BOAC officials faced with a similar threat demonstrated familiarity with the script by arranging a landing at Denver instead of London.[20]

Although "Doomsday Flight" was fictional, the reaction it caused illustrates that regular news reporting may instruct the public in criminal techniques. In another example, after the report of a skyjacking in which the perpetrator successfully escaped by parachute, subsequent skyjackers routinely included a parachute in their list of demands.[21] The same contagion impact through education and emulation also can affect psychopathological individuals, as Dr. David Hubbard has reported in his well-known study, *The Skyjacker: His Flights of Fantasy* (1971).

Although researchers continue to focus their attention on the contagion hypothesis, no conclusive data have been compiled. Nevertheless, this research supports the reasonable and qualified proposition that the contagion effect of terror-violence leads to imitation by other groups, especially when previous terrorist acts have been successful. It is noteworthy that the Sommer study indicates that 93 percent of the chiefs of police surveyed "believed live television coverage of terrorists' acts encouraged terrorism." No research presently corroborates this conclusion. However, if law enforcement maintains such a belief, it is quite feasible that the perpetrators of acts of terror-violence maintain it as well. Clearly, more research is needed on this subject; indeed, probably no other area

---

[19] See *Disorders and Terrorism*, p. 23.

[20] "Terror Violence," pp. 759–60.

[21] See generally Thomas I. Emerson, *The System of Freedom of Expression* (1971), p. 7; W. L. Rivers, T. Peterson, and J. Jensen, *The Mass Media and Modern Society*, 2d ed., 1971, pp. 28–29; Wilbur Schramm, *Mass Communications*, 2d. ed., 1960; Mendelsohn, "Socio-Psychological Perspectives," pp. 511–12; Wright, "Functional Analysis and Mass Comunications," *Public Opinion Quarterly* 24 (1960): 605.

deserves more attention than the contagion theory briefly set forth here, to which some psychological studies already have been devoted.

In contrast to its negative, contagion effects, media coverage of terror-violence instead may have a cathartic effect on potential perpetrators of terror-violence. In this instance, media coverage of an event or social grievance actually may dampen an individual's motivation to engage in terror-violence in order to attract attention to his social claim. This countereffect of deterrence is produced by portraying the failure of terrorist acts due to the effectiveness of law enforcement. Thus, the effect of contagion created by media coverage of terror-violence may well be counteracted by the effect of deterrence such coverage creates. Although no quantitative analysis could establish an empirical foundation that could adequately predict the degree to which an individual's behavior is influenced by competing or countervailing motivations, one can reasonably conclude that media coverage does have contagious consequences.

The Climate of Intimidation

Perhaps the most pervasive problem associated with the media reporting of terror-violence is the climate of intimidation it engenders, a general fear of victimization that despoils the quality of life and may destabilize social institutions. While intimidation is usually one of the strategic objectives of terror-violence, isolated incidents could scarcely produce such an ubiquitous psychological impact. Rather, it is the repetitive dissemination of terror-inspiring acts and the manner of the dissemination that produces the impact.

In their social role, the media act in part as mediator between man and his environment. As society increases in complexity and events affecting one's welfare occur increasingly outside one's immediate experience, the objective world retreats ever farther out of reach, out of sight, and out of mind. Man's reliance on the mass media increases correspondingly as he attempts to construct for himself a trustworthy picture of his surroundings. By providing messages from the outside world, the media influence the way people view the world and, consequently, their behavior in response to it. A classic illustration of this type of media influence is the public's panicked reaction to the invasion from Mars in the 1938 radio broadcast of Orson Welles's "War of the Worlds."[22] As Professor Harold Mendelsohn has written, "the mere fact that the so-called invasion was presented in the form of a radio broadcast gave it an

---

[22]For a study of the public reaction to the broadcast, see Cantril, "The Invasion from Mars," in Wilbur Schramm and Donald F. Roberts, eds., *The Process and Effects of Mass Communications* (1954), p. 423.

authenticity *per se* which was sufficient for many listeners to accept uncritically and to base behavioral action upon."[23] Similarly, a degree of public anxiety is a necessary by-product of media reporting of news events during times of stress. Such media-created anxiety is "functional rather than dysfunctional," however, only when it

> readies individuals to cope with realistic dangers in realistic ways. It is where the mass media offer false standards of judgment by which readers, listeners and viewers may misinterpret the news that the dangers lie. Whether through ignorance, guile, vested interest or irresponsibility—where some sectors of the mass media create dysfunctional anxiety, we have a serious problem on our hands.[24]

In the context of media coverage of terror-violence, this dysfunctional anxiety enhances the perceived power of the terrorist in his own eyes, in those of his peer group, analogous groups, other individuals susceptible of emulation, and the public. This perception of enhanced power, when combined with society's high level of vulnerability (created by the vulnerability of targets and the weakness or ineffectiveness of law enforcement) causes intimidation in the social psyche. This impact increases as the recurrence of incidents produces the psychological projection prediction syndrome discussed above. At a certain point in this process, however, a level of tolerance may well set in, producing an immunization effect. Following tolerance, social reaction may be the exact opposite of immunization, as society develops an antipathy toward terror-violence and resolves to combat such conduct. Society also may overreact in its hostility to terror-violence, however; this would clearly be counterproductive to the effective control and eventual eradication of the problem.

The Immunization Effect

The immunization effect manifests itself in three ways. The first derives from continuous media coverage of violence in general and terror-violence in particular; its effect is to heighten the public's level of tolerance and acceptance of violence and terror-violence as a fact of life. In addition, when such coverage is glorified or associated with certain rewards, such as status, social prominence, sex appeal, financial success, or political importance, the rejection of violence is eroded, and gradual tolerance for it creeps pervasively into the social psychology. Thus, as moral opposition is reduced, immunization to the phenomenon increases. The increased

---

[23]Mendelsohn, "Socio-Psychological Perspectives," p. 513.
[24]Ibid., p. 514.

acceptance of violence as a tolerable social act increases its contagion effect. The second manifestation of the immunization effect is the portrayal of terrorists as "crazies" or as individuals and organizations beyond the means of social control. Thus the avowed aberrant nature of the perpetrators and their modus operandi is perceived as so far outside the accepted frame of reference that it explains the occurrence of such acts and society's inability to prevent it or control it. The result again is immunization, as society explains away the phenomenon by considering it alien. The third manifestation derives from the abstract and impersonal portrayal of the act of terror-violence and its harmful effect. An example of this is the coverage of the Iranian seizure of the American hostages in 1979-80, when the sixty-three, later fifty, persons held were almost never described as individuals. No longer was it a matter of a person with a face, a name, a family, a life, but the concept of "hostage" that acquired the connotation of a pawn on the chessboard of world politics. The public's outraged reaction was directed more at the political significance of the act than its harmful effects on the individuals involved. In time, the public's perception of the problem focused almost exclusively on the political dimensions of the incident, while becoming immune to its human dimensions.

As society becomes more immune to violence, two consequences become likely: the level of violence necessary to elicit a terror-inspiring effect increases in order to overcome the dulled perceptions of the public; and more persons may resort to violence in general, and terror-violence in particular, as a result of the lessening of the social opprobrium attached to it, or the increasing social acceptance or tolerance of such conduct and its perpetrators. In any event, it increases the contagion and intimidation effects discussed above.

Public immunization is not a foregone conclusion of media coverage of terror-violence. In fact, the exact opposite is quite likely in that the media's portrayal may increase public opposition to such behavior. Thus the terrorist wants enough balanced media coverage to produce immunization, and not outraged media coverage that could trigger opposing social reaction.

The Combined Effects of Contagion, Intimidation, and
Immunization in Media Coverage Impact

The terrorist's powers usually are represented by the media and perceived by the public disproportionately to his actual capacity to harm, to the extent the media abuse—or allow the terrorists to abuse—their social mediating role. Thus the climate of intimidation is enhanced while, at the same time, it stimulates emulation through contagion. Although the media are becoming more accurate, responsible, and self-critical than in their often sensationalist past,[25] several exigencies and limitations inherent to the media, their purpose, and type of organization are bound to create the effects of contagion, intimidation, and immunization. Daily, the media prepare the public for its role as a victim of terrorist attacks; the media's portrayal of fictionalized violence provides the backdrop for the public's reaction to terror-violence. Commercial and competitive factors influence the type and extent of coverage a terror-violence incident will receive and color the public's perception of the terrorist's message.

Finally, factors peculiar to the dominance of broadcasting, particularly television, over the print media must be examined. The portrayal of violence in literature and the mass media has been a cause for concern for over one hundred years.[26] The popularity and pervasiveness of television and the movie industry in shaping the attitudes of its audience have made that medium the subject of recent scrutiny by individuals, citizens groups,[27] and the Congress.[28] Some researchers, notably Dr. George Gerbner, dean of the Annenberg School of Communications, have concluded that heavy viewers of televised violence are far more likely to distrust others and view the world with alienation and fear.[29] Others, including the

---

[25]See Gruenwald, "The Press, the Courts and the Country," *Time* (16 July 1979): 74. For an account of press sensationalism, notably that of William Randolph Hearst and Joseph Pulitzer, see John Tebbel, *The Media in America* (1974), pp. 279–303.

[26]U.S., Congress, House, Subcommittee on Communications of the House Committee on Interstate and Foreign Commerce, *Violence on Television*, 95th Cong., 1st sess., 1977, p. 1.

[27]In addition to various church groups and the National Parent-Teachers Association, the American Medical Association (AMA) adopted a resolution in 1976 that "TV violence is a risk factor threatening the health and welfare of young Americans, indeed our future society." AMA, *Proceedings of the House of Delegates*, Res. No. 38 (June 1976): 280. The resolution encouraged all physicians to oppose television programs containing violence as well as all products and services sponsoring the programs. See U.S., Congress, House, Subcommittee on Communications of the House Committee on Interstate and Foreign Commerce, *Hearings on Sex and Violence on Television*, 94th Cong., 24th sess., 1976, p. 7 (hereafter cited as *House Hearings*).

[28]Prior to 1976, Senate investigations were conducted into the relationship between the media and the rising crime rate. See U.S., Congress, Senate, Subcommittee to Investigate Juvenile Delinquency of the Senate Committee of the Judiciary, *Hearings on Juvenile Delinquency (Effects on Young People of Violence and Crime Portrayed on Television)*, 83d Cong., 2d sess., and 84th Cong., 1st sess., 1954–55; U.S., Congress, Senate, Subcommittee on Communications of the Senate Committee on Commerce, *Hearings on Violence on Television*, 93d Cong., 2d sess., 1974.

[29]See G. Gerbner et al., *Violence Profile No. 7: Trends in Network Television Drama and Viewer Conceptions of Social Reality, 1967–75* (1975). Dr. Gerbner has monitored television violence since 1968. See generally G. Gerbner and L. Gross, "Living with Television: The Violence Profile," *Journal of Communication* 26 (1976): 192. For a critique of Gerbner's methodology and conclusions, see Krattenmaker and Powe, "Televised Violence," pp. 1157–70.

Surgeon General of the United States, have reported that viewing of televised violence by children encourages antisocial tendencies and aggressive behavior.[30] Although the causal connection between the level of violence on television and its psychological and behavioral impact upon viewers has not been established to everyone's satisfaction,[31] the Subcommittee on Interstate and Foreign Commerce nevertheless concluded that "an excessive amount of televised violence is a source of sufficient societal concern to warrant congressional attention and scrutiny."[32] In a vigorous dissent, six members of the fifteen-member subcommittee chastised the majority for its hesitancy; they concluded that the available evidence unmistakably established adverse effects of viewing televised violence and that affirmative steps to reduce its presentation should be taken.[33]

Despite the important stake society has in the performance of media functions, the media are also private businesses in pursuit of profits. Although size and profitability have had some positive effects upon the quantity and quality of news reporting and upon the media's independence,[34] commercial factors also lead to abuses. Since profits are obtained from selling time or space to advertisers at rates determined by circulation or audience size, the media are engaged in the business of selling attention. Terrorist events often are dramatic, and it is beyond doubt that such events are newsworthy. However, when news reporting becomes a commercial product whose relative media emphasis is determined by its

---

[30]See *Surgeon General's Scientific Advisory Committee on Television and Social Behavior, Television and Growing Up: The Impact of Televised Violence* (1972). The surgeon general subsequently testified that
> broadcasters should be put on notice. The overwhelming consensus and unanimous ... report indicates that televised violence, indeed, does have an adverse effect on certain members of our society.... It is clear to me that the causal relationship between televised violence and anti-social behavior is sufficient to warrant appropriate and immediate remedial action. The data on social phenomena such as television and violence and/or aggressive behavior will never be clear enough for all social scientists.... But there comes a time when data are sufficient to justify action. That time has come.

U.S., Congress, Senate, Subcommittee on Communications of the Senate Committee on Commerce, *Hearings on Surgeon General's Report to the Scientific Advisory Committee on Television and Social Behavior*, 92d Cong., 2d sess., 1972, pp. 25–26 (statement of Dr. Jesse Steinfield, Surgeon General). On the relationship between televised violence and aggression, see also Albert Bandura, *Aggression: A Social Learning Analysis* (1973).

[31]See Krattenmaker and Powe, "Televised Violence," pp. 1134–70; *House Hearings*, pp. 10–20. See also note 30.

[32]*Violence on Television*, p. 7.

[33]Ibid., pp. 17–19 (dissenting views of Representatives Waxman, Wirth, Mikulski, Markey, and Gore). The minority stated that the Federal Communications Commission should initiate rulemaking proceedings on whether licensees should be required to "carry certain percentages of certain categories of programming"; ibid., p. 24.

[34]See Gruenwald, "Press, Courts, and Country," p. 75.

attention-getting potential, excessive coverage may be afforded to violent, dramatic events in disproportion to their actual significance. The consequence of serving up acts of terror-violence as mass entertainment[35] is to augment the terrorist's audience and, consequently, the impact of his message.

Terrorists are aware that competition between news organizations, their fear of being scooped by the opposition, and their quest for ever larger audiences and prestige foster reliance on sometimes questionable reporting techniques. Reporters do not merely report the news; they are often subjective participants in it. They are, in essence, the actors, the script writers, and the idea people behind each story. Terrorists take advantage of this situation in their attempts to manipulate the media. While direct media contact and interviews with a terrorist make a more exciting story, such reporting techniques often afford the perpetrator an unedited platform and excessive publicity. Hand-held microwave minicameras enable terrorist incidents to be broadcast live into the viewer's home where television's visual impact, immediacy, and realism foster the climate of intimidation. Subjective portrayals of terrorist personalities as glamorous or heroic figures, an image terrorists seek to inculcate, elevate them to positions of prominence disproportionate to their actual power. When commercial and competitive factors displace judgment in the coverage of terrorist incidents, the media may lose control over the situation and themselves become a hostage.

An exemplary instance occurred in Indianapolis in February 1977. Anthony Kiritsis kidnapped mortgage company executive Richard Hall and held him captive in an apartment believed booby-trapped with explosives. The sixty-two-hour siege was covered by an army of national and regional reporters, and live television transmitters were positioned to capture any break in the story.[36] Kiritsis demanded live coverage of his statement to the press as a condition of his surrender. The media readily acceded out of a desire to save Hall's life and to better cover the dramatic incident. Instead of surrendering, Kiritsis emerged from the apartment building with a shotgun wired to his captive's neck and proceeded to deliver a diatribe riddled with obscenities. One station interrupted the live coverage after about ten minutes, fearful that thousands of viewers might, at any moment, witness an execution in living color. "We had a man here

---

[35] For the proposition that coverage of terrorist incidents has become a form of entertainment, see *Disorders and Terrorism*, p. 8; Arlen, "Reflections on Terrorism and the Media," *More* (June 1977), p. 12. A further problem may arise when spectacular and often tragic events are dramatized by the media for entertainment purposes, although it seems that the "networks have developed certain sensibilities and systems to counterbalance those inevitable competitive urges" and "are genuinely edgy about the risks of developing highly expoitable topics." Bedell, "Is TV Exploiting Tragedy?" *TV Guide*, 16 June 1979.

[36] Trounstine, "We Interrupt This Program," *More* (June 1977), p. 14.

who was holding Mr. Hall hostage," an executive of the television station explained. "He was controlling us, manipulating us, and we didn't want to be a party to that. We elected to reassert control of the airwaves."[37] Two local stations, however, continued to broadcast the entire ordeal, with one news director later conceding, "We should have controlled it more than we did. The event controlled us."[38] Unfortunately, the intense climate of media competition and the instantaneous decisions that often accompany live broadcasts are not conducive to calm, reasoned decision making. The potential for disastrous consequences in such situations is immense.

Balanced, routine coverage of trends in violence, law enforcement policies and capabilities results of terrorist incidents and their effects on victims is essential to warn and inform the public adequately and accurately of the danger posed by terrorism. Follow-up coverage is essential to aid the public in understanding what has happened, to combat irrational fears aroused by the event, and to prepare the public to react to future incidents. Coverage of law enforcement and judicial responses also may help to deter future perpetrators by publicizing the consequences of participation in such acts.[39] The capacity of some media, particularly television, however, may be insufficient to carry any but the most current stories. An imbalanced presentation may result with terrorist incidents thrust upon the public's consciousness without adequate standards of judgment with which to assess the phenomenon.

The special relationship of television to terrorism was the subject of a recent British conference under the auspices of the Institute for the Study of Conflict. In its special report, the conference noted the unique role of television:

> Television in the mass media form has acquired over the last 20 odd years an infinitely more powerful and penetrating means of communication than anything hitherto known to us. If a person reads a newspaper or a book, only the sense of sight is being employed and his reactions are entirely self-induced. Radio employs the sense of hearing, and reactions to what is said are already to a very large extent affected by the manner of presentation. With television not only are the senses of sight and hearing fully occupied, but every emotion is closely caught and involved in what is happening on the live screen in the opposite corner of 15 million living rooms. This is a captive audience not necessarily in possession of the independent criteria by which to form judgments.[40]

---

[37] Ibid., p. 15.
[38] Ibid.
[39] *Disorders and Terrorism*, pp. 368–69, 402–3.
[40] *Television and Conflict*, p. 14.

Terrorists have a particular affinity for gaining access to television, "for they appreciate its potency, its immediacy and its vast potential audience."[41] However, it is generally not possible for television to provide the viewer with a wholly unbiased picture. Since terrorist groups operate clandestinely, their atrocities often are not presented.[42] They can determine when, and even to some degree how, they are covered and manipulate the image transmitted. Because "[t]here is virtually no limitation upon the television reporting of abuses, real or alleged, in pluralist and representative societies,"[43] television seems inevitably one-sided, and its bias inevitably on the side of the revolutionaries and against established authority.

One participant in the conference voiced the concern that "you see a vast amount of incidents and episodes covering terrorism and conflict but you do not get the issues, what it is about, what the consequences are going to be."[44] Others argued that in an attack waged by terrorists against an open and democratic society, the powerful weapon of the media should be denied the terrorist and employed instead for the defense of society. The study concludes that television, because of its power and impact, because of the involuntary nature of viewing which does not provide the same degree of choice as the print media, and because of its operation by parliamentary authority, "has a special duty to uphold, or at any rate not to undermine, constitutional authority and the forces of law and order."[45]

It must be noted in appraising the three effects of contagion, intimidation, and immunization and their interaction that each one of these effects also has a potential countereffect. The countereffect of contagion is deterrence, manifested in media portrayal of effective and proper law enforcement action which may intimidate both the perpetrators and the would-be perpetrators of terror-violence. The immunization effect may even create an extreme antiterrorist public reaction. Suffice it to recall that totalitarian regimes, which engage in violent repression and disseminate news of such repression, effectively deter opposition.

The distinction between the social effects of terror-violence and those effects generated by the intervening factor of media coverage and dissemination can hardly be assessed because of the number of variables involved. In this area, as in others covered by this study, more research is needed, although common sense and ordinary human experience amply warrant the concern created by the perceived effects of contagion, intimidation, and immunization.

---

[41] Ibid., p. 15, quoting P. Wilkinson, *Terrorism and the Liberal State* (1979), pp. 169–70.

[42] Ibid, p. 26.

[43] Ibid., p. 5.

[44] Ibid., p. 4.

[45] Ibid., p. 14.

PROBLEMS OF CONTEMPORANEOUS COVERAGE AND
RELATIONS BETWEEN THE MEDIA AND
LAW ENFORCEMENT

Coverage of terrorist attacks in progress provides the opportunity most conducive to fulfilling the terrorists' objectives of gaining publicity for their cause and riveting the attention of a given society on their exercise of power. It also is the occasion of greatest conflict between the interests of law enforcement authorities and those of the media. The media perform several important functions, among which is the dissemination of accurate information to the public regarding dangers present at the site. While the importance of the media in this capacity cannot be ignored, experience has shown that contemporaneous coverage of a terrorist attack consistently gives rise to three areas of conflict between police and media. It is in this context, therefore, that the public interest represented by the media must be balanced with the public interest represented by effective law enforcement.

The first area of conflict involves media dissemination of information tactically useful to the terrorist while an attack is under way. When a terrorist barricades himself and his hostages in a building, he is isolated within the confines of his area of control. To remedy this situation, terrorists have equipped themselves with radio and television receivers which allow them to listen to news broadcasts. Thus the media may serve unwittingly as the intelligence arm of the terrorists when they broadcast the latest operational activities of the police, the presence of hidden persons who could become hostages, the attempts of hostages to escape, the bargaining strategy of police negotiators, or any deceptions or tricks planned by law enforcement officials.[46] Not only is such information critical to the terrorists in determining possible escape routes or repelling impending police assaults, but it unnecessarily jeopardizes the lives of hostages and law enforcement personnel. During the October 1977 hijacking of a Lufthansa jet, the media directly contributed to the death of a hostage when they broadcast that the pilot was passing intelligence information to the police through his normal radio transmissions; the terrorists had access to the radio news reports and executed the captain.[47] The problem is not one of broadcasting alone: since incidents may last for many hours, even days, tactical information divulged by newspaper accounts also can be communicated to the terrorists which assist them unnecessarily.

An example of the danger inherent in broadcasting information of tactical advantage to the terrorist occurred in March 1977 when Hamaas

---

[46] "Terror Violence," p. 761.
[47] Alexander, "Terrorism, Media, and Police," p. 107.

Abdul Khaalis led a small Hanafi Muslim sect in the takeover of three Washington, DC, buildings in order to avenge the murder of his five children by the Black Muslims. A local television reporter outside filmed the lifting of a basket by rope to the fifth floor where eleven people had hidden from the Khaalis group. Although initially ignorant of their presence, the gunmen undoubtedly were informed of the television reporter's scoop by their fellow Hanafis who monitored the news reports from outside.[48] Fortunately, the gunmen did not take the potential hostages, who were freed by police nine hours later. Obviously, this information should never have been publicized; nor should information ever be released about police tactics, negotiating strategies, or apparent sincerity or lack thereof in dealing with the terrorists. The release of such information only endangers lives without contributing to the public good.

The second area of conflict is media interference with effective law enforcement response by exacerbating the situation and impeding the negotiating process. The terrorist has indicated by the drastic nature of his act that he is willing to risk many lives, including his own, to accomplish his objective. Law enforcement authorities, on the other hand, operate under the practical handicap of minimizing the harm to persons and property threatened. Consequently, police often attempt to establish a psychological environment that will induce a terrorist to surrender. Direct media contact with a terrorist while an attack is under way has many troublesome consequences,[49] including: tying up scarce telephone lines; goading, either intentionally or unintentionally, the terrorist into action to prove himself under the spotlight of attention; inciting the terrorist by the use of certain inflammatory questions or phrases;[50] involving a media representative in the negotiations, thereby isolating trained professional negotiators from the bargaining process; and altering the psychological environment in which the terrorists operate, by unnecessarily upsetting them, interrupting the pattern the police have attempted to inculcate, or giving them the comfort of company.

Direct contact by media representatives untrained in the delicate problems which arise in hostage situations may unnecessarily jeopardize lives. In one situation, a media representative even advised gunmen not to

---

[48] *The Media and Terrorism*, pp. 28–29.

[49] "Terror Violence," n. 31.

[50] Many perpetrators may react violently to a particular question or term that does not comport with their ideological or psychological makeup:

> Terrorists can behave like utterly normal men most of the time, perfectly balanced and intelligent, often with a far higher than average IQ. Yet in the commission of their crimes they become completely abnormal. Those who have had experience of conversation with them can discover that one particular word, a trigger word, perhaps the name of a President or the object of the terrorists' hatred, can turn a seemingly normal man into an irrational and abnormal one in front of your eyes.

Television and Conflict, pp. 19–20.

give up their hostages so as to retain their bargaining position with the police.[51] Additionally, not only does media publicity hinder negotiations by subjecting the police to public pressure, but media publicity frequently is given freely to the terrorist even though it could serve as a valuable negotiating item.

Further examination of the Hanafi incident reveals effects of direct communication by media personnel with the perpetrators of terror-violence. The media made so many telephone calls to the gunmen that police negotiators had difficulty in getting through themselves. A local radio broadcaster asked Khaalis during a live telephone interview whether he had set a deadline, at a time when the police and other experts viewed the absence of a deadline as encouraging.[52] Another media representative enraged Khaalis by identifying his sect with the Black Muslims, whom he held responsible for the death of his children. Khaalis threatened to execute one hostage in retaliation for the reporter's remark and was mollified only after the newsman, following police advice, apologized for his unfortunate choice of words.[53] Although it is true that direct media contact makes a more exciting story, this incident clearly indicates that the public interest would be served best by allowing only trained professionals in law enforcement and psychology to communicate with the perpetrator.

The third area of conflict arising between media and law enforcement interests during contemporaneous coverage is one of crowd control. The presence at the site of numerous reporters, with their obtrusive equipment and lighting, may interfere physically with the free movement of law enforcement personnel and may attract crowds that burden police with crowd control problems. Also, the questioning of law enforcement officials may distract decision makers at critical moments. Additionally, the obvious presence of many media representatives may encourage the terrorists to remain barricaded to increase coverage, or to demand a press conference for personal or political publicity. Increased publicity may transform the event into a spectacle attracting even greater numbers of people, further compounding the risks and burdens to the police.

Police chiefs view the problems posed by contemporaneous coverage to be serious ones. According to the 1977 Sommer survey, 93 percent

---

[51]"Crisis Cop Raps Media," *More* (June 1977), p. 19 (interview with Lt. Frank Bolz, head of the New York City Police Department's Hostage Negotiating Squad).

[52]*The Media and Terrorism*, p. 29 (remarks of Fenyvesi).

[53]Ibid. See also Fenyvesi, "Looking into the Muzzle of Terrorists," *Quill* (July–August 1977), p. 17. For another account by a journalist held captive by the Hanafis and critical of the media's interference with police management and hostage safety during the incident, see Siegel, "Looking at the Media from the Other End of the Gun," *Media and Terrorism: The Psychological Impact* 41 (1978) (seminar sponsored by Growth Associates).

of the police chiefs responding believed live television coverage of terrorist acts encourages terrorism; 46 percent considered live television coverage to be "a great threat" to hostage safety, while 33 percent deemed it "a moderate threat." None believed that terrorist acts should be televised live.[54] Thus law enforcement authorities, to avoid these and other problems surveyed above, may seek to exclude media personnel from the scene, unless a reconciliation of interests is achieved.

In the final analysis, however, this problem area can be easily solved by curtailing media access to the scene of ongoing terror-violence events. One danger in this solution is that, without the media present, the facts of the event would be hearsay with law enforcement personnel the only source. The public would thereby lose its ability to monitor police conduct.

There are also problems with contemporary coverage where law enforcement is not present. One such example is the Iranian hostage crisis. A review of that incident indicates that it was created in part by the Iranian revolutionaries in order to obtain media coverage. This was evident from the ways in which the news was staged, from the presentation of demonstrations outside the American embassy to the publication of statements by both the hostages and their captors.[55] The ultimate goals in the hostage taking were clearly power outcomes in both the international and domestic realm. The saturation coverage rewarded the Iranian militants, prolonged the crisis, and at the same time contributed to violent events elsewhere. During that period of time, U.S. embassies were attacked in Dacca, Benghazi, and Islamabad purportedly in response to the November 1979 seizure of the Grand Mosque in Mecca by Muslim extremists, which the Ayatollah Khomeini blamed on the United States. The intimidation effect also was obvious in the U.S. hesitation to engage in action against the perpetrators for fear that this would adversely affect the life and well-being of the hostages. Gradually the public's mood with respect to the shah's trial shifted (the apparent object of the perpetrators' action), a sign of the partial success of the action gained only through media coverage.

The crisis posed a new problem for the media: should they use material prepared by the perpetrators of an act of terror-violence without exercising any independent control over content? In other words, to what degree would the media allow themselves to become the instruments of terror-violence propaganda in order to remain competitive in the industry? This issue arose when NBC broadcast an Iranian film of an interview of the hostage U.S. Marine, Cpl. William Galegos. Under the portrait of

[54]M. Sommer, Project on Television Coverage of Terrorism, reported in *Editor and Publisher*, 27 August 1977.
[55]"Tehran's Reluctant Diplomats," *Time* (4 December 1979): 64.

Khomeini, Galegos spoke of the absence of ill-treatment of the hostages. Beside him was one of his captors, called "Mary," who delivered an unedited six-minute propaganda speech. NBC aired the entire thirty-minute broadcast on prime time television with excerpts on the evening news. Other news organizations severely criticized NBC's actions as an irresponsible relinquishment of media control to the perpetrators of terror-violence by granting these individuals the privilege of unbridled mass dissemination of their views. Encouraged by this controversy, the Iranian militants offered to NBC another film of 26 December 1979 which portrayed clergymen visiting the hostages on Christmas; NBC declined. This second offer illustrated the contagion of permitting terrorists direct and unedited access to the public via the electronic media. This lesson is not likely to be lost on terrorists of the future.

One cannot conclude these observations without referring to another significant incident of terror-violence which took place during the same period: the seizure of the Grand Mosque at Mecca in which hundreds of hostages were held. This clearly was an event of much greater significance to both the Islamic world and the Western world than the seizure of the U.S. embassy in Tehran. For the Islamic world, it represented the possible destruction of the most holy shrine in the world; for the Western world, it represented the possible destruction of the Saudi government, whose stability is central to the continued flow of oil in the region. The event, however, resulted in neither of these occurrences. It is noteworthy that the Saudi Arabian government's first action was to seal off the area from the media; this resulted in media coverage that was limited to a few specific details as the incident was unfolding. More importantly, the perpetrators had no access to the media and thus no opportunity to disseminate their terror-inspiring message. Although the incident lasted over a week, prolonged and intense fighting broke out in which 156 persons were killed, and much damage was done to the holy shrine, the substantial limitation of contemporaneous media coverage created a public perception that the incident was well under law enforcement control and posed no further danger to society. Thus, the incident had no intimidation or contagion effect. One cannot help but speculate what the outcome of the Iranian crisis would have been if media coverage had been limited to facts without speculation or undue emphasis on popular reactions and dramatic effects.

Although contemporaneous media coverage sometimes inhibits effective law enforcement control of an incident, it does offer two specific and positive advantages to law enforcement. First, media coverage is frequently the negotiator's most effective bargaining tool in dealing with terrorists. The importance of the media's function in this respect should not be underestimated. Second, media coverage can provide law enforcement with certain tactical and intelligence information that it could not otherwise obtain. For example, during the Iranian situation, the media were practically the only source of information available to the United States. This may well have been one of the reasons for the expulsion of U.S. newspersons in January 1980; it certainly was the reason for the expulsion of U.S. newspersons from Afghanistan in January 1980. Thus, any problems in law enforcement control of terrorist incidents that are created by contemporaneous media coverage may well be offset by the benefits to law enforcement control that are also created by this coverage. In addition, this coverage provides benefits to society as a whole that derive from the media's informational and watch-dog functions.

CONCLUSION

Any writer on this subject is tempted to draw up a list of the ills and woes of the mass media, the ways and means in which they abuse their privileged role in society and are, in turn, abused and instrumentalized by terrorists and ill-perceived by law enforcement. Such a simplistic approach would tend to highlight differences and polarize positions, however, which is not this writer's intention. Rather, this study has sought to focus on the problems discussed above in order to increase the awareness and sensitivity of both the media and law enforcement to the issues they face, with a view toward developing their cooperation and voluntary mutual action.

The media's pervasive influence is too well established to require argumentation. Their occasional abuses, whether intended or induced by perpetrators of acts of terror-violence, are equally well established. The media's services to society are equally well recognized, and their privileged role in society derives from certain democratic values which imply a high level of responsibility. That responsibility, in order to preserve these values, is best left to the media themselves.

Law enforcement's indispensable role and service to society are equally well acknowledged. Yet it is ill-equipped to deal with the improbable and unusual, the very stuff of terrorism, and is consequently unprepared, in most cases, to deal with such situations. Its legitimate apprehension of such incidents and the knowledge that the margin of flexibility for counteraction is limited make it less tolerant or understanding of any person or institution that would make its task more difficult. Law enforcement's difficult and dangerous tasks, particularly in the context of terror-violence events, make it less tolerant of the media's detached appraisal and criticism and downright hostile to their interferences and occasional abuses. That feeling is heightened when the media's coverage tends to

Hostage Negotiations: Dilemmas about Policy

NEHEMIA FRIEDLAND

The seizure of hostages for ransom is one of the most effective tactics in the hands of political terrorists. Two factors enhance the impact of hostage incidents in comparison to alternative terror tactics. First, these incidents are of a relatively long duration and usually receive a detailed mass-media coverage from their outset to their conclusion. Such coverage becomes an important factor in the course of hostage incidents, as it portrays not only the actions of the terrorists and the fate of their hostages but exposes to immediate public scrutiny the behavior of the target government. Second, in addition to terrorizing, hostage seizures achieve two potential outcomes: the immediate and tangible one of ransom extortion, and the intangible but nonetheless important political outcome of forcing governments to negotiate with groups they otherwise would be reluctant to recognize. These unique properties of hostage tactics provide grounds for the assumption that the proliferation of hostage incidents is not a passing phenomenon.

The first section of this paper addresses policy considerations concerning hostage negotiations. More specifically, arguments about the potential effectiveness of the "no ransom" policy are presented and evaluated. The second section presents an analysis of the unique nature and characteristics which hostage negotiations are likely to acquire when the "no ransom" policy is adopted. Most of the problems analyzed here are presented as dilemmas, since possible "rational/strategic" solutions to these problems might be inapplicable for psychological, normative, or political reasons.

POLICY CONSIDERATIONS IN THE CONDUCT OF HOSTAGE NEGOTIATIONS

The central policy issue concerns the actions which governments should undertake vis-à-vis terrorists' attempts to extort ransom. The various views on this issue can be classified into two leading policy positions.[1] One, the "no ransom" policy, holds that hostage tactics are countered most effectively by governments' steadfast refusal to yield to terrorists' extortion attempts. Proponents of this policy assume that consistent failure to extort ransom might convince terrorists of the futility of their efforts and dissuade them from further attempts. The other, the "flexible response" position, is in effect a non-policy which questions the practicality and wisdom of adhering to a single, standard policy such as "no ransom." The rejection of "no ransom" is predicated on three arguments. First, hostage incidents might be perpetrated under a wide variety of circumstances and by terrorist organizations which vary significantly with respect to ideology, *modus operandi*, and the typical psychological makeup of their members. Hence, a strong commitment to a standard policy which does not take into consideration such variability is bound to be ineffective. Second, the assumption that failure to extort ransom will force terrorists to give up hostage tactics is invalid, since extortion of ransom is only one of the aims potentially achievable in hostage situations. The "fringe benefits" of hostage seizures, such as the drawing of the mass media's attention, the forcing of governments to undertake repressive administrative action, and the undermining of society's feelings of security and order, are sufficient to motivate terrorists to employ hostage tactics. Third, consistent failure to extort ransom might prompt terrorists to escalate their attacks, either by increasing the frequency or sophistication of hostage seizures, or by resorting to the use of alternative terror tactics.

These three arguments appear to be compelling. However, a more careful analysis indicates that their validity is debatable. Consider, first, the rejection of "no ransom" on the grounds that since it is a standard, inflexible policy, it is bound to fail in the face of the highly variable nature of hostage incidents and of their perpetrators. This rejection reflects a basic misunderstanding of the meaning of policies: a policy is an explicit or implicit declaration of intent to act in a certain manner under prescribed circumstances, and it is designed to affect the behavior of a defined population. It refers primarily to the future and purports to affect actions not yet taken rather than to respond to deeds done. Hence, it is unrealistic to expect that a policy's formulation be made congruent with potential variability among or uniqueness of those on whom the policy will be implemented. Moreover, attempts to establish such congruency entail the introduction of exceptions or qualifications into the policy statement ("The government would never ... unless ..."). Yet, in so doing, the understanding of the policy's demands becomes dependent upon subjective interpretation, and its impact thus might be weakened. Hence, a

---

[1]E. F. Mickolus, "Negotiation for Hostages: A Policy Dilemma," *Orbis* 19 (1976): 1309–26; E. Evans, *Calling a Truce to Terror* (Westport, CT: Greenwood Press, 1979).

policy statement should be addressed to any member of the relevant population and should be formulated in accordance with the population's psychological common denominator. In this regard the policy of "no ransom" is quite adequate: it is founded on the elementary principle that the absence of reinforcement to a given behavior will lower the likelihood of its occurrence, a principle which may be assumed to apply to any member of the population. It thus appears that assumptions about the degree of variability among hostage incidents and their perpetrators are inessential for the evaluation of the policy of "no ransom."

The second argument against the "no ransom" policy holds that the fringe benefits of hostage seizures are a sufficient incentive to undertake hostage tactics, and thus terrorists will employ such tactics even when convinced that the probability of their demands being met is low. This conclusion might be warranted in the short run. It is clear, however, that in the long run, the likelihood of hostage tactics being employed is affected importantly by the overall quality of results attained by terrorists via such tactics, and that terrorists would be more strongly tempted to employ hostage tactics when the range of potential outcomes includes the receipt of ransom than when such range includes the fringe benefits only. It may be expected that, in the long run, the effect of "no ransom" on the range of incentives associated with hostage incidents will lower the likelihood of such incidents. This expectation is strengthened by the fact that the fringe benefits described above can be gained via alternative and perhaps safer terror tactics, such as frequent random assassinations. The use of the complex and hazardous hostage tactics suggests that terrorists do assign a high utility to the ransom they demand and/or to the political gain attained by compelling target governments to yield to such demands. Therefore, the long-term effect of the "no ransom" policy on the probability of hostage incidents may be by no means negligible.

The third criticism of the "no ransom" policy is that failure to extort ransom might prompt terrorists to escalate their attacks, either by increasing the frequency or sophistication of hostage seizures, or by adopting alternative terror tactics. This criticism appears to be founded on the expectation that compliance with ransom demands will satisfy and placate the terrorists and stabilize the incidence of hostage seizures at some acceptable level. This expectation is unrealistic; the actual quantity of ransom received is of secondary importance to the political terrorist, whose primary aim is the undermining of political stability.[2] This being the case, it is more realistic to expect that compliance with ransom demands will reinforce and most likely intensify the use of hostage tactics. As for the choice of tactical alternatives to hostage seizures, it stands to reason that failure to extort ransom will force terrorists to give up hostage tactics

---

[2]P. Wilkinson, *Political Terrorism* (London: Macmillan, 1974).

in favor of other ones. However, to offer such a change of tactics as grounds for the rejection of the "no ransom" policy is tantamount to assuming that being confronted with hostage tactics invariably is preferable to being faced with terror tactics of any other kind. This assumption is debatable. For instance, it is not at all clear that the West German government would have incurred higher costs had the Schleier case been one of political assassination rather than a hostage incident which culminated in murder.

The arguments presented thus far against the policy of "no ransom" referred to the effects of this policy on the nature and incidence of hostage seizures. It is this writer's opinion that insofar as such effects are concerned, there is little merit to the criticisms levelled against the "no ransom" policy. In the absence of evidence to the contrary, if a government proves its ability and resolve to abide by such a policy, it might eventually reduce the risk of becoming a target to hostage incidents. A critical difficulty nevertheless is inherent in this policy, which appears to have been ignored by its opponents and proponents alike. This difficulty is related to governments' ability to maintain the credibility of this policy once it is adopted.

It is obvious that in order to be effective, a policy must be credible. It also is obvious that the cost of policy implementation is a prime determinant of its credibility. However, the cost structure of the "no ransom" policy is such that the main cost of implementation, which is some ratio between the ransom demanded and the number and kind of hostages seized, is determined primarily by the terrorists. Such cost structure might tempt terrorists to believe that they can set the cost of implementing the "no ransom" policy at an unbearably high level which will force target governments to yield. Unfortunately, in view of the numerous hostage tactics available to terror organizations and the vulnerability of modern society to such tactics, this belief cannot be regarded as wholly unrealistic. These tactics may be brutal and involve, for instance, the seizure of an unusually large number of hostages, or a threat against the public at large, such as the release of toxic agents into a municipal water system. Alternatively, the terrorists may choose a sophisticated tactic, such as presenting demands minimal to the point of triviality, and thereby cast the government's refusal to concede as unduly and unreasonably intransigent. There is certainly no guarantee that such tactics will force governments to yield, and their probability of success cannot be estimated. It is, however, the terrorists' subjectively perceived probability of success that determines the credibility of "no ransom," and it ought not be underestimated.

The preceding argument is by no means a denial of the possibility to establish the credibility of "no ransom," but rather an attempt to point out the credibility problem inherent in this policy. Policymakers should also consider some corollaries of this problem. First, the deeper a government's commitment to the "no ransom" policy, the greater its credibility loss if and when it is forced to yield to extortion. It is therefore possible that, in the short run, the stronger the government's commitment to "no ransom" the stronger would be the terrorists' motivation to put such a commitment to a public test. Second, the higher the actual costs in terms, for example, of hostages' lives incurred by a government for its adherence to "no ransom," the greater would be its difficulty to concede if and when it decides to do so. Third, if a government is forced to concede to terrorists, its ability to resist further concessions is adversely related to its past expressed or demonstrated refusal to concede; i.e., to the strength of its commitment to the policy of "no ransom." It thus may be concluded that the adoption of this policy should be considered only by a government which is confident in its ability to abide by it under most known or projected contingencies. If such confidence cannot be mustered, it would be advisable to adopt a vaguer and more flexible stand vis-à-vis hostage tactics: conceding sometimes, to some terrorists, some of their demands. Such an approach at least might enable a government to choose the circumstances under which to yield and to take measures whereby the damage to its credibility and reputation will be blunted.

EFFECTS OF THE "NO RANSOM" POLICY ON THE NATURE OF HOSTAGE NEGOTIATIONS

This section is addressed to the unique nature and characteristics which hostage negotiations might acquire when the "no ramsom" policy is adopted. The analysis concerns politically oriented barricade-and-hostage incidents. Ransom-oriented hostage incidents are excluded from the analysis. In such incidents the perpetrators' primary purpose is the receipt of ransom of a certain quantity and quality (e.g., a certain sum of money or the release from captivity of a specific person). In politically oriented hostage incidents, on the other hand, the actual quality or quantity of ransom received is of secondary importance. The perpetrators' primary aim in such incidents is to inflict upon governments the political damage they would likely incur by publicly negotiating with terrorists and by yielding to ransom demands, even if the ransom conceded is low in quality and quantity. As will be argued later in greater detail, standard bargaining models can be used in the analysis of ransom-oriented incidents but not in that of politically oriented ones. The analysis primarily refers to the latter type. The analysis also excludes kidnappings characterized by the impossibility of undertaking direct military or police action against the perpetrators. Under such circumstances, a government is short of effective means to influence the kidnappers' behavior. In other words, such a government usually will lack the resources to bargain and negotiate.

Kidnappings constitute, therefore, a unique case which cannot be fruitfully analyzed within the general framework of hostage negotiations.

The analysis of politically oriented barricade-and-hostage incidents, initiated against governments committed to a policy of "no ransom," can be simplified by drawing an analogy between such conflicts and the game of Chicken. This game was played on American highways by pairs of youngsters who drove their cars toward each other on a collision course. The first driver to veer right in order to avoid collision was branded "Chicken." If both drivers did so simultaneously, cowardice was attributed to both, although the damage to each driver's prestige was less than that he would have incurred had he been the first to chicken out. If both drivers were determined to maintain their reputations intact, the consequences were bound to be fatal.

The unique characteristics of Chicken-like conflicts can be highlighted by contrasting such conflicts with normal negotiation processes. The latter are defined in the present context as processes whereby all parties to conflict can obtain, via negotiations, outcomes preferable to any they could obtain by refusing to negotiate. Normal negotiations are possible when the contested issues are divisible commodities or resources which enable a distributive resolution of the conflict, satisfactory to all parties. For instance, consider the typical structure of labor/management negotiations for new wages. The bargaining problem is defined by the maximal wage increase acceptable to Management and the minimum acceptable to Labor. When Labor's minimum is smaller than Management's maximum, normal negotiations become possible: the discrepancy between the two values comprises a bargaining range within which the parties can find a resolution that will provide them with better outcomes than those both could obtain without negotiating.

Whereas the goal of normal bargaining is to distribute divisible commodities, the principal issues in Chicken-like conflicts are entities such as credibility, prestige, and reputation. The aim of a Chicken player is to convey certain images and impressions to relevant publics, including the adversary.

The unique nature of goals characteristic of Chicken-like conflicts creates a qualitative cleavage between them and normal bargaining and has important implications for their course and process: when the immediate aim of a party to conflict is to create an image and to convey certain impressions, any of its observable behaviors is a potential move in the game, whether or not it initially is intended to be one. This feature of Chicken creates an asymmetry between the requirements for the initiation and prevention of the game. While the refusal of two parties to play is necessary to call off the game, the desire of one party to play is sufficient to initiate it. If A challenges B to play Chicken and B refuses, *the game was played*. In the eyes of the public for which the game is intended, refusal to play is no less cowardly than cowardly behavior which takes place in the course of the game. This asymmetry is reversed in normal negotiations, where the core of conflict is the distribution of some divisible commodity. The initiation of such negotiations requires the willingness of all relevant parties to negotiate, yet each party is free to refuse joining the negotiating process, or withdraw if such a process is already under way.

The nature of issues central to Chicken-type conflicts carries a further important implication. The damage to a Chicken player's reputation and credibility is independent of the distance he drove before swerving to avoid collision or the width of his swerve, as long as he was the first to swerve. Such an independence between the specifics of a player's actual behavior and its public-directed effects derives from the perception of entities such as credibility, prestige, and reputation as being largely indivisible. Consequently, Chicken-type conflicts have no bargaining range, and under no turn of events can all parties to a conflict of this type do better than each would have done had confrontation been avoided altogether. Chicken usually will result in loss to all parties involved or in easily identified winners and losers.

The issues contested in hostage negotiations of the type being considered are for the main part indivisible political entities. Such negotiations therefore are likely to possess some of the key characteristics of Chicken-type conflicts. First, we know that a person challenged to play Chicken will, in effect, play the game whether or not he wants to. Similarly, any action a government undertakes when challenged with a hostage seizure is liable to carry tactical or strategic implications. Suppose, for instance, that a government decides to refrain from becoming engaged in a barricade-and-hostage situation by delegating authority to a local police chief within whose jurisdiction the incident takes place. Such a decision will have a crucial effect on the course and consequences of the hostage incident. In other words, a target government is likely to become involved in a barricade-and-hostage situation and affect its course even by deciding to remain uninvolved. Second, in the same way as the damage to a Chicken player's credibility and reputation is independent of the distance he drives before swerving, so long as he is the first to do so, the political damage to a government is related only marginally to the amount of ransom it is willing to pay, so long as it is willing to pay at all. Thus, hostage negotiations are conducted without a bargaining range, and a target government is faced with two basically discrete options: yield at the cost of credibility or reputation loss or adhere to "no ransom" and risk human lives. One justifiably may conclude that hostage "negotiations" is perhaps a misnomer when applied to the kind of incidents being analyzed.[3]

---

[3]P. Wilkinson, "Admissibility of Negotiations Between Organs of the Democratic States and Terrorists." Presented in Strasbourg at the conference on "Defense of Democracy Against Terrorism in Europe: Tasks and Problems," 1980.

The unique nature which hostage negotiations acquire when a target government adopts the policy of "no ransom" directly affects the range of tactical options available to it. Specifically, when faced with a politically oriented barricade-and-hostage incident, a target government committed to "no ransom" has to choose between forceful action against the perpetrators and an attempt to convince them to surrender. The first option will not be discussed, as the technicalities of military and police action are beyond the scope of this paper. But there remains the question of how to convince the terrorists to surrender, by no means an easy task. After all, terrorists who employ hostage tactics against a government committed to "no ransom" demonstrate their determination by merely adopting such tactics. Again the analogy to Chicken is clear: a person can demonstrate his courage even before the game is played by merely initiating it or by agreeing to play. Yet beside forceful situations, a target government can do little but try to convince the perpetrators of a barricade-and-hostage incident to surrender.

A target government's success in leading such perpetrators to surrender rests to a large extent on its ability to convince them that their mission has failed completely. This assumption is rather obvious. However, its application is made difficult by the fact discussed earlier, that the receipt of ransom is only one, albeit important, aspect of success of a barricade-and-hostage incident. In order to demonstrate to the perpetrators of such incidents the absolute failure of their mission, it is necessary to expose them to multiple signs of failure. In addition to a categorical refusal to abide by the ransom demands, a target government would have to employ tactics such as impressing upon the terrorists that nobody (including their parent organization) would know their fate, feigning lack of urgency, and demonstrating convincingly that the life of the target population continues in its normal course. It is clear, however, that the application of such tactics, even when technically feasible, might be impeded by a host of political considerations and constraints. This difficulty can be highlighted by a brief analysis of the dilemmas which a target government must resolve in responding to threats and ultimata used by terrorists in the course of hostage negotiations.

A target government might face two types of ultimata—ultimate and interim. An ultimate ultimatum is that specified at the outset of the hostage incident; it specifies the ransom demands and the consequences of failure to meet them. The dilemmas concerning such ultimata were discussed in the first section of this paper. The second type consists of interim threats, used by the terrorists to control and affect the hostage situation (e.g., "A hostage will be shot unless the snipers are taken off the roofs"), and it is to this type that the following comments are addressed.

Inasmuch as interim threats and ultimata constitute the primary or sole tactics whereby terrorists can affect the course of a barricade-and-hostage incident, it is clearly in the target government's best interest to render such tactics ineffective. In principle, the government should strive to demonstrate the irrelevance of these tactics to the process of hostage negotiations. Such demonstration rests upon both an absolute refusal to comply with interim threats and ultimata and the provision of evidence that the government's actions cannot be altered and affected even by the terrorists' execution of their threatened sanctions. The demonstration potentially is costly, however, and the nature and magnitude of the costs are such that governments (at least democratic ones) are unlikely to carry out these demonstrative acts. To illustrate the predicament of the target government, consider the painful "cost-benefit" analysis demanded by the circumstances being considered. The options are as follows: (a) Attempt to nullify the effectiveness of threat tactics by refusing to comply with interim threats, and risk the lives of a known number of hostages. It is even possible that the identity or some identifying characteristic (e.g., "One of the female hostages") of the threatened hostages will be made known in advance. (b) Refuse to comply and mount a rescue operation before the interim ultimatum runs out, thereby risking an unknown but most likely larger number of lives. (c) Yield to the terrorists' interim ultimatum and wait for the appropriate moment at which to mount a rescue operation, the casualty count being again unknown.

A dispassionate analyst would likely recommend the first of these three options. Nevertheless, it should not come as a surprise that governments would find it more difficult to opt for the first option which, in the long run, might risk fewer lives, than for the second or third. This is not to suggest that governments are incapable of grasping the logic beyond the first option, or that they are callous or indifferent to human lives. The point is rather that the choice of the first option is made difficult by two of its main characteristics: foreknowledge of the number and possibly of the identity of hostages whose lives are threatened, and the risk of losing lives while the government remained inactive and made no effort to save them. By contrast, while more lives might be endangered by choosing the second or third option, the danger is created by action designed to rescue the hostages, which gives the endangered individuals an equal chance to survive.

The preceding argument suggests that, from a target government's perspective, the characteristics of the first of the three options, foreknowledge and inaction, make the disutility of lives lost due to its adoption far greater than that of lives lost via the adoption of the second or third option. One may conclude that the first option, the refusal to comply with the terrorists' threats aimed at leading them to surrender, is most likely to be undertaken when no direct forcible action is possible, as in the Schleier and Moro cases. Yet, at the same time, the nonexistence of military options facilitates the rationalization of a decision to give in to the perpetrators' demands. Thus, the absence of military options may lead to two radically different governmental decisions on the course of action adopted vis-à-vis hostage tactics. Such paradox-like effects highlight the difficulty of leading the perpetrators of a barricade-and-hostage incident to surrender.

The contention that the adoption of "no ransom" leaves the target government with only two tactical options may be countered with the argument that viable, interim tactics are available. For instance, a target government may propose to guarantee the perpetrators' safe conduct in return for the hostages' release. However, such an agreement easily can be construed as government capitulation and therefore is unlikely to be considered by a government truly commited to "no ransom." Another example concerns the use of the mass media as a tactical device in the conduct of hostage negotiations. Some analysts proposed that if the terrorists' hunger for publicity is satisfied by extensive media coverage, they would lower their ransom demands and would become more amenable to seeking a resolution to the hostage incident.[4]

This proposition is debatable for two reasons. First, empirical investigations of conflict resolution processes indicate that the presence of publics might reduce the willingness of conflicting parties to make concessions and to cooperate.[5] These findings suggest that the presence of the media might prompt terrorists to exhibit acts of heroics and deepen their intransigence. Second, the gain of media coverage is rarely a primary aim of terrorist strategy but rather an essential means to convey specific contents to relevant publics. There is no guarantee that, once such channels of communication are captured, they would be used to convey a message of moderation and surrender. It is possible to find instances in which a hostage incident was aimed at gaining nationwide or worldwide publicity, and that once that purpose was fulfilled the perpetrators gave in. This writer believes that some of these instances are exceptions to the rule and others might well be manifestations or psychopathological dynamics rather than genuine acts of political terrorism. In either case, the provision of either media coverage or the possibility to address a wide public to publicity-hungry terrorists constitutes, in effect, government capitulation to one of the terrorists' main ransom demands.

SUMMARY

This paper has dealt with policy considerations concerning the handling of hostage situations. The analysis presented in the first section

---

[4]For one of these analysts see A. H. Miller, "Negotiations for Hostages: Implications from the Police Experience," *Terrorism: An International Journal* 1 (1978): 125–46.

[5]B. R. Brown, "The Effects of Need To Maintain Face in Interpersonal Bargaining," *Journal of Experimental Social Psychology* 4 (1968): 107–22.

suggests that the policy of "no ransom" is potentially effective in lowering the incidence of extortion tactics, and that criticisms levelled against the policy by proponents of a flexible response to hostage seizures essentially are invalid.

Despite the potential effectiveness of the "no ransom" policy as a deterrent against hostage seizures, its adoption and implementation are not devoid of difficulties. Such difficulties are related to the vulnerability of modern, democratic societies to extortion tactics. Thus, notwithstanding the strength of a commitment by a government to "no ransom," situations might be foreseen in which it would be forced to yield and incur substantial political damage. Additional difficulties arise from the fact that the core of conflict between politically oriented terrorists and a government committed to "no ransom" consists of largely indivisible political entities. Consequently, the process characteristic of hostage negotiations is rarely one of distributive bargaining, accommodation, and reconciliation, but of brinkmanship. It appears then that decisions concerning the choice of policy to counter the threat of hostage seizures requires the resolution of a difficult dilemma: in the long run, "no ransom" is likely to be proven a most effective policy against hostage seizures. However, in the short run, the implementation of the policy and the establishment of its credibility might be exceedingly costly.

There is no easy solution to the dilemma about policy, nor is there a prescriptive model which specifies the steps which a government ought to undertake in order to resolve this dilemma. The particular fashion in which a government will untangle the dilemma largely depends on its political assets. More specifically, a government's ability to incur the potential or actual costs of adopting and establishing the credibility of the policy of "no ransom" depends on factors such as the strength of constituent support, the public's confidence in the soundness of the government's decisions, and peoples' ability to perceive the impact and consequences of terrorist activity from a realistic perspective and in the correct proportions.

The preceding comments highlight the truly political nature of political terrorism. They point out that the very political foundations which terrorists seek to erode constitute the primary determinants of a government's ability to adopt an unyielding position vis-à-vis terrorism. Hence, a hostage incident is more than a mere disturbance that ought to be removed with the greatest alacrity and at the lowest possible cost. Such incidents constitute, in effect, contests of political power. And it is from this perspective that governments should formulate their policies concerning terrorism in general and hostage tactics in particular.

The Use of Suggestibility Techniques in Hostage Negotiation*

MARTIN REISER and MARTIN SLOANE

Hostage taking has become an almost commonplace occurrence, and it will likely continue to increase in frequency in the future. Numerous municipalities have experienced incidents involving an emotionally disturbed person holding a spouse or family member as hostage, thwarted armed robbers using employees as insurance for escape, skyjackers jeopardizing many lives and expensive aircraft, organized terrorist groups attempting to barter hostages for money or political prisoners, and the occasional demented psychopath bent on destroying those around him as well as himself. In all of these circumstances, a key function of negotiation is buying time while attempting to defuse the situation.[1] The negotiator needs to consider the type and personality characteristic of the hostage taker with whom he is communicating.[2] Along with the important individual differences among various suspects, there exist common factors in every hostage situation. It is because of these common factors that a range of suggestive cues can be utilized in almost any hostage situation, in addition to traditional persuasive tactics.

PERSUASION AND SUGGESTION

Persuasion and suggestion are two different methods used in hostage negotiation to influence a suspect's behavior. Persuasion involves influencing by reasons and arguments, whereas suggestion conveys ideas or

---

*A revised version of the paper presented at the Western Psychological Association Annual Meeting, Los Angeles, California, 9 April 1981. Some authorities in the field now consider the term "subconscious" to be obsolete and prefer the use of the term "unconscious."

[1] J. A. Culley, "Defusing Human Bombs—Hostage Negotiations," *FBI Law Enforcement Bulletin* (October 1974): 10–14.

[2] I. Goldlaber, "A Typology of Hostage Takers," *The Police Chief* 46 (1979): 21–23.

thoughts by means of implication, hinting, intimidation, or insinuation. Persuasion is directed generally at conscious mental processes requiring logic and reason, while suggestion is aimed at influencing the subconscious.[3] Suggestion also evokes and utilizes potentials and life experiences already present in subjects but beyond their usual control mechanisms.[4]

CONSCIOUS AND SUBCONSCIOUS PROCESSES

The conscious mind can absorb only a small amount of the stimuli that constantly bombard the sensory system. Therefore, it must limit the information it processes. In perceiving, encoding, and storing data, the conscious mind attends selectively to bits of information that have meaning and value at the time. Like the narrow beam of a flashlight, the conscious mind focuses on only a tiny part—approximately 10 percent— of the total environment. Consciousness requires attention and awareness of doing, feeling, thinking, imagining, or remembering: it utilizes cognitive functions to deal with reality in a rational manner.[5]

By contrast, the subconscious mind accepts most of the incoming stimuli from the senses—approximately 90 percent—and stores the data without filters or criticism. This subconscious thought can be channeled by specific techniques and may explain why people in drug, deprivation, or relaxation states experience increased sensory perception, more vivid imagery, heightened artistic creativity, or exhibit "abnormal" behaviors.[6]

ALTERED STATES OF CONSCIOUSNESS AND CRISES

Various events that interfere with the normal flow of sensory stimuli and with cognitive organization can produce altered states of consciousness. They may be induced by third–degree tactics, brain washing, mob- or group-contagion effects, religious conversions, trance experiences, spirit possession, tribal and religious ceremonies, or by meditation and hypnosis techniques. Inner conflicts, heightened emotional arousal, or depression may also give rise to altered consciousness.[7] In virtually every

---

[3] J. Frank, *Persuasion and Healing* (Baltimore: Johns Hopkins, 1961).
[4] M. H. Erickson and E. L. Rossi, *Hypnotherapy* (New York: Irvington, 1979).
[5] M. Reiser, *Practical Psychology for Police Officers* (Springfield, IL: Thomas, 1973).
[6] C. T. Tart, ed., *Altered States of Consciousness* (New York: Wiley, 1969).
[7] A. M. Ludwig, "Altered States of Consciousness," in C. T. Tart, ed., *Altered States.*

hostage situation, suspects and hostages will experience some degree of alteration in consciousness, because intense stimulation will overload the senses.

Highly stressed individuals shift automatically into an altered state, affecting both information processing and behavior. In hostage or barricade situations, the individual succumbs to a state of emotional crisis. As a result, he develops cognitive and sensory distortions, as well as perceptual narrowing. In response to intense emotional arousal, the body and mind act to reestablish a state of equilibrium.[8]

In addition to rapid physiological changes, psychological responses focus on survival and escape. During the early phase of a crisis, confusion, magical thinking, and anxiety override rational decision making. A suspect's usual coping skills are often ineffectual relative to the massive stress and loss of environmental control. Feelings of frustration, anger, and fear heighten attempts to achieve a state of balance and harmony.

Altered states of consciousness also include the following characteristics:[9]

1) Changes in thinking, including disturbances in concentration, attention, memory, and judgment. Primitive (primary process) thinking increases, reality testing decreases, ambivalence increases, and there is a decrease in reflective awareness.

2) Time distortions. Time often appears to slow down.

3) Loss of control. Feelings of helplessness, impotence, or omnipotence are common.

4) Changes in emotional reactivity. Emotional outbursts, ranging from elation to depression, may occur. Alternatively, the individual may become detached, colorless, uninvolved, and distant.

5) Changes in body image. There may be feelings of depersonalization, derealization, and a loosening of self- and outer-world boundaries.

6) Perceptual distortions. There may be increased suspiciousness and apperceptive distortion. Illusions and heightened suggestibility are characteristic.

PRINCIPLES OF SUGGESTION

A suggestion can be defined as the uncritical acceptance of an idea. Verbal, nonverbal, and extraverbal inputs from the five senses affect the higher brain centers. The key factors for increased suggestibility are

---

[8]H. Selye, *The Stress of Life* (New York: McGraw-Hill, 1956).
[9]Ludwig, "Altered States."

motivation, rapport, attention span, imagery potential, esteem for the negotiator, and past reactions to suggestions.[10]

The hostage taker's susceptibility to suggestion is also influenced by his hierarchy of needs.[11] Both hostage takers and barricaded suspects initially will be concerned with safety (fear of injury), physical needs (food, water, temperature, sound), and survival issues. A New York case exemplifies this intensification of basic needs; one barricaded suspect originally demanded $6 million but finally surrendered for a hamburger and a cigarette.[12]

SUGGESTION AND HYPNOSIS

Several principles of suggestion may be operative during the communication process:

1) The Principle of Concentrated Attention: whenever attention is concentrated on an idea over and over again, it spontaneously tends to realize itself. Advertising jingles and propaganda are based on this concept.

2) The Principle of Reversed Effect: the harder one tries consciously to do something, the less chance there is for success. Whenever there is a conflict between imagination (subconscious) and willpower (conscious), the imagination wins. Insomnia and unwanted smoking and eating are examples of the failure of the will.

3) The Principle of Dominant Effect: a strong emotion tends to override a weaker one. Connecting a strong emotion to a suggestion tends to make it more effective.[13]

Repetitive stimulation of any of the senses can induce a state of increased receptivity to suggestion. An altered state of consciousness akin to day dreaming and reverie is the hypnoidal state, a precursor of hypnosis. Hypnoidal states, which can be produced by fixation of attention and monotonous stimuli, are characterized by detachment, physical and mental relaxation, and some reduction in critical thinking. Everyday hypnoidal experiences sometimes are called "waking hypnosis" behaviors. Common examples of hypnoidal states are complete absorption in a movie; the experience of severe pain; and the automobile driver's "highway hypnosis," with the accompanying reduction of reality awareness.

---

[10]W. S. Kroger, *Clinical and Experimental Hypnosis*, 2d ed. (Philadelphia: Lippincott, 1977).

[11]A. H. Maslow, *Motivation and Personality* (New York: McGraw-Hill, 1970).

[12]H. Schlossberg, *Personal Communication* (1979).

[13]Kroger, *Clinical and Experimental Hypnosis*.

"Waking suggestions" are those given to a subject in a nonhypnotic state. Hypnotic suggestions are those made to a subject while in hypnosis to influence hypnotic behavior. Hypnotized persons are more likely to be subject to effective suggestion than those to whom waking suggestions are made. Waking suggestions given to a hostage taker may require repetition to be effective, whereas suggestions made during the hypnotic state may be accepted after only one communication.[14]

Repetition of suggestion also is important in shaping neutral pathways leading to a quasi-conditioned response by the subject. Misdirection of attention is useful in diverting an individual's conscious awareness from the suggestion, which in turn decreases the likelihood of conscious resistance. Harsh, authoritarian communications are more likely to produce resistance, whereas permissive language and intonation increase the likelihood of compliance. Harshly commanding someone to "Stand up!" as opposed to asking "Aren't you tired of sitting down?" exemplify both modes. The reduction of implied criticism increases the probability that the suggestion will bypass conscious censorship and be carried out.[15]

NEUROLINGUISTIC FUNCTIONING AND SUGGESTIBILITY

The use of principles of suggestion at hostage scenes is mediated further by language processes. Briefly, the study of human communication has been divided into three areas: syntactics, semantics, and pragmatics. Syntactics deals with the question of transmitting information; this includes the problems of coding, capacity, redundancy, and other statistical properties of language. Semantics deals with the meaning of message symbols, while pragmatics affects behavior.[16]

The manner in which language is used affects the behavior of the hearer. In hostage situations, a negotiator is concerned primarily with analogic versus digital communication. Analogic communication consists of nonverbal behavior, including the person's posture, facial expression, gesture, voice inflection, as well as the sequence, cadence, and rhythm of his words in the context of the transaction. In contrast, digital communication is concerned with the meanings of words in a particular context. Every communication has a contentual aspect and a relational aspect that exist side by side and are complementary. The content of the

---

[14]Waking suggestions are the *sine qua non* of advertising in electronic and print media. Products of questionable necessity or value are sold for billions of dollars each year with the aid of suggestibility techniques.

[15]M. Reiser, *Handbook for Investigative Hypnosis* (Los Angeles: LEHI, 1980).

[16]P. Watzlawick, *Pragmatics of Human Communication* (New York: Norton, 1967).

communication is conveyed in digital fashion, and the relational aspect is conveyed in a predominantly analogic fashion.

Digital (verbal, logical) communication involves secondary processes (the conscious) and mainly the dominant brain hemisphere functions, whereas analogic (nonverbal, nonlogical) communication utilizes primary processes (the subconscious) and nondominant brain hemisphere functions.[17] During crisis states, such as hostage situations, the normal balance between brain hemispheres is altered, and nondominant hemisphere functions become more prominent. Subconscious processes of the nondominant hemisphere are accessed more easily during altered states, because the dominant, rational hemisphere has less control of its censorship function. In applying suggestibility techniques during hostage situations, communication is directed toward influencing a subject's nondominant processes as much as possible. The nondominant hemisphere is influenced largely by analogic communications. Indirect forms of communication, including imagery, are useful ways of accomplishing this task.[18]

SUGGESTIBILITY TECHNIQUES

Milton H. Erickson, M.D., a pioneer of indirect suggestion, developed unique methods of inducing a hypnotic trance in clinical patients and influencing behavior toward therapeutic goals.[19] His approach relies on a sequential pattern designed to induce an altered state of consciousness, or trance, and to guide indirectly the subject in the desired direction. The sequence involves the following steps: 1) fixation of attention, 2) depotentiation of normal habits, 3) initiation of subconscious cues, and 4) reinforcement of positive responses.

Fixation of Attention

The negotiator can fixate the hostage taker's attention by encouraging him to talk about himself and reflecting his feelings as accurately as possible. This helps build rapport and assists in developing trust and a working relationship.

---

[17] P. Watzlawick, *The Language of Change* (New York: Basic Books, 1978).
[18] A. Lazarus, *In the Mind's Eye* (New York: Rawson Associates, 1977).
[19] Erickson and Rossi, *Hypnotherapy.*

Depotentiation of Normal Habits

This phase involves a tactical shift by the negotiator from following the subject and reflecting his feelings to leading the subject in order to alter his conscious mental set. The purpose is to keep the subject's conscious mind occupied while giving subconscious cues. Ways of accomplishing this can include: acting casual and permissive (avoid arguing any point—the hostage taker will be expecting authorities, such as the negotiator, to be critical and demanding); redirecting the hostage taker's attention away from his demands; using phrases rather than complete sentences; using non sequiturs; telling boring stories that have little apparent relevance; and altering periodically the volume and pitch of the voice.

Initiation of Subconscious Cues

It is possible to initiate subconscious cues while the dominant hemisphere processes of the subject are attempting to analyze logically the sudden shift in the negotiator's tactics. The negotiator can choose from approximately a dozen of Ericksonian forms, from truisms to induced imagery.[20] The following are some of the types of indirect communication that can be suggestive and influence behavior:

- *Truisms*: "Sooner or later you may get tired."
- *Not knowing, not doing*: "You may not know when you will get hungry. You won't even need to think about it right now."
- *Open-ended suggestions*: "We all have the capacity to compromise, but sometimes we don't know when we're ready to negotiate."
- *Covering all possibilities of a class of responses*: "Sooner or later, you may or may not want to get a breath of fresh air. The really important thing is to pay attention to what you need."
- *Implied directive*: "When you're ready to talk this out, then we'll find a solution."
- *Imbedded statements*: "You may wish to keep this thought in the back of your mind, where we can get to it when needed."
- *Imbedded questions*: "Can you remember the last time you felt relaxed?"
- *Binds*: "How soon do you think you'll be ready to negotiate?"
- *Double binds*: "Would you like to negotiate a settlement now, or would you prefer to wait a while?"

---

[20] J. Haley, *Uncommon Therapy: The Psychiatric Techniques of Milton H. Erickson, M.D.* (New York: Norton, 1973); R. Bandler and J. Grinder, *Patterns of the Hypnotic Techniques of Milton H. Erickson, M.D.* (Cupertino, CA: Meta, 1975).

- *Interspersal and associative focusing*: "I'd like to tell you about another settlement I helped negotiate. . . ."
- *Future projection*: "Perhaps you'd like to discuss this issue later."
- *Induced imagery*: "Imagine how relaxed and comfortable you'll feel when we finally solve this situation."
- *Encouraging a new frame of reference*: "I could be wrong, but I'd guess that your wife (mother, et al.) is feeling pretty scared right now. If you put yourself in her place, I wonder what you might be feeling?"

One frame of reference for applying indirect suggestions is the hierarchy of needs explicated by A. H. Maslow.[21] Some hostage takers may develop a preoccupation with physical (food, water), safety (fear of injury), or ego (acceptance, recognition, worth) needs. By concentrating skillfully on these needs, the negotiator can subtly influence the suspect's response. The concept of buying time during a prolonged negotiation process implies an ongoing deprivation of basic needs and an increasing focus on their satisfaction.

For physiological, environmental, and comfort needs (hunger, thirst, fatigue, sleep, sound, light, temperature, space, tobacco), sample indirect cue themes follow:

"What would you like to eat?"

"Just let me know when you are thirsty, and we'll work something out."

"I'm having a sandwich and a cold drink right now, and I'm wondering if you are hungry yet."

"Imagine yourself out of that pressure cooker with a cigarette and some hot coffee."

"The pressure will lift when you come out, and you may feel tremendous relief and peace of mind."

For safety, medical, and control needs (feeling secure, safe, uninjured, relaxed, certain), these indirect cue themes may be utilized:

"When you let that hostage go, then we might. . . ."

"When you come out, I can ensure your safety."

"I wonder if you have contemplated a safe way out of this situation?"

"Does anyone have medical concerns we should know about?"

"Would you like to come out now or in ten minutes?"

"Can you remember the last time you felt relaxed?"

"Your safety is within your control. It's just a few steps away."

"Some of my friends tell me to loosen up. How do you relax when you're uptight?"

"Can you allow yourself to be safe and secure?"

"I used to have a partner who would tell me to relax."

---

[21]Maslow, *Motivation and Personality*.

"You must be wondering what will happen next."
"I had a situation like this once. . . ."
"I'd like to tell you an apparently meaningless story. . . ."

For ego needs (acceptance, affiliation, recognition, worth), these indirect cue themes are suggested:
"People can make the most of learning opportunities."
"I'm wondering how you feel about the prospect of talking with the reporter when you come out."
"I'm very curious about when you first decided. . . ."
"I wonder whether you know. . . ."
"And so clearly you want and need. . . ."
"And you fully realize so well. . . ."
"I'm curious to know if you can really. . . ."
"You can continue to feel the satisfaction of. . . ."
"It takes a courageous kind of person to come out and work out the problem."
"And you may be aware of a certain sensation. . . ."

The conscious mind acts, in part, as an inhibitor and censor, while the subconscious functions as a storehouse of potential behaviors. In order to avoid unpleasant or threatening material, the conscious mind pushes certain thoughts, feelings, and images out of awareness into the subconscious, using the mechanism of repression. The conscious ego resists the reemergence of this material by maintaining counterpressure and distance.[22]

A hostage taker's resistance to cues can be handled by accepting, and then defining, reluctance as cooperative behavior. Once the person is cooperating, he can be diverted toward new behaviors. One approach is to focus on the subject's need to be upset and to express angry feelings via the hostage situation, but to vary the duration, frequency, or intensity. "I don't blame you for feeling upset, and very shortly, when the steam gets reduced, the whole situation will be less of a headache to you."

A subject's resistance can also be defused by either demanding more resistance or by preempting it:
"You'll probably find this silly, but I have the impression. . . ."
"This is bound to sound ridiculous, but one could say. . . ."
"There is a very simple solution to this problem, but I am almost sure you won't like it. . . ."
"To do this will be very difficult for you, because on the surface the solution will look absurd. . ."

---

[22]Reiser, *Practical Psychology*.

"You're probably as upset as I am over the time it's taking to solve this, but you and I are making progress in. . . ."

Talking about the similarities between the present situation and the past, where a resolution was possible, may induce cooperative behavior. It also may be useful to have the subject perform some action in order to increase the likelihood of further suggestibility. An example might be: "I'd like you to hang up the phone and call me right back when. . . ." If the suggestion is not followed, the negotiator can apologize for asking more of the subject than the person is willing or able to accept at that point. The suggestion can then be rephrased. Indirect cues are very subtle; even if one is rejected, a new suggestion can be substituted without adverse effects.

It may also help to adapt to the subject's tone and way of speaking, using words and phrases that the person has used. This pacing procedure provides feedback of the subject's own experience on both conscious and subconscious levels.[23] For example, the negotiator might say: "And you may become aware of (remember, experience, feel, hear, see yourself). . . ." With very resistant subjects, it may help to encourage a seeming regression. This approach can assist a subject to discriminate between past influences and present situational factors: "I wonder if you can go back and feel as bad as you did when you first encountered this problem, because you might see if there is anything from that time you wish to recover or salvage."

Reinforcement of Positive Responses

The use of positive language is also important. Avoiding negatives while utilizing aphorisms, ambiguities, puns, allusions, euphemisms, innuendo, and double-bind messages can be effective. These cues may bypass censorship and influence the subject at a subconscious level. Even a small response can be used to enhance and shape desired goals. The subject is always "right" in regard to his responses, and the negotiator utilizes whatever is communicated to relabel, rephrase, and interpret in a positive way.

---

[23]Bandler and Grinder, *Patterns*. Other reference works of value are R. Bandler and J. Grinder, *The Structure of Magic*, 2 vols. (Palo Alto, CA: Science & Behavior Books, 1975–76); N. W. Beckmann, *Negotiations* (Lexington, MA: Lexington Books, 1977); L. Bernstein, et al., *Interviewing: A Guide for Health Professionals*, 2d. ed. (New York: Appleton-Century-Crofts, 1974); N. G. Poythress, "Assessment and Prediction in the Hostage Situation: Optimizing the Use of Psychological Data," *The Police Chief* (August 1980): 34–36; M. Rokeach, *Beliefs, Attitudes, and Values* (New York: Jossey-Bass, 1976).

CONCLUSION

All people are suggestible to some degree. Like others, hostage takers are connected to persons, places, experiences, or ideas that consciously or subconsciously influence their behavior. With proper motivation, positive rapport, and pertinent cues, the suspect likely will follow suggestions that are relevant subconsciously.

Though persuasion has been used routinely in the past, the notion of influencing the suspect subconsciously through suggestion is a relatively new concept. That both the hostage taker and hostage are already in an altered state of consciousness provides the negotiator with an advantage. By utilizing suggestibility techniques, the negotiator can increase his influence in defusing, shaping, and ultimately resolving a life-threatening crisis.

The hostage negotiator traditionally has been trained to react to events; Erickson's methods require a more indirect, proactive approach to problem solving. Law enforcement officers usually are quite adept at forceful persuasion, but they find permissiveness and the use of suggestion more difficult. The conveyance of indirect cues involves a subtle balance of skills; police negotiators often have the capacity and opportunity to combine both approaches, but some additional training may be required. Applied research is needed to test out suggestive approaches, to further develop these new techniques, and to refine the operational model of indirect communication as it applies to hostage negotiation.

Terrorism and High-Technology Weapons*

YONAH ALEXANDER

It is a generally accepted notion that terrorism—ideological and political violence utilized by subnational groups who seek to achieve imaginary or realistic tactical and strategic objectives[1]—is relevant to the concept of high-technology weapons.[2] The seriousness of this relationship

---

*A revised version of the article published in Yonah Alexander and John M. Gleason, eds., *Behavioral and Quantitative Perspectives on Terrorism* (Elmsford: Pergamon Press, 1981). Reprinted by permission.

[1]For recent studies of terrorism, see, for example, Yonah Alexander, ed., *International Terrorism* (New York: Praeger, 1976); Yonah Alexander and Seymour M. Finger, eds., *Terrorism: Interdisciplinary Perspectives* (New York and London: John Jay Press and McGraw-Hill, 1977); Yonah Alexander et al., eds., *Terrorism: Theory and Practice* (Boulder, CO: Westview Press, 1979); Yonah Alexander and Robert A. Kilmarx, eds., *Political Terrorism and Business* (New York: Praeger, 1979); J. Bowyer Bell, *Terror out of Zion* (New York: St. Martin's, 1976), and *On Revolt* (Cambridge, MA: Harvard University Press, 1976); David Carlton and Carlo Schaerf, eds., *International Terrorism and World Security* (London: Croom Helm, 1975); Richard Clutterbuck, *Kidnap and Ransom: The Response* (London and Boston: Faber & Faber, 1978); Ronald D. Crelinsten et al., eds., *Terrorism and Criminal Justice* (Lexington, MA, and Toronto: Lexington Books, 1978); John D. Elliot and Leslie K. Gibson, *Contemporary Terrorism: Selected Readings* (Gaithersburg, MD: International Association of Chiefs of Police, 1978); Alona E. Evans and John F. Murphy, eds., *Legal Aspects of International Terrorism* (Lexington, MA, and Toronto: Lexington Books, 1978); Richard W. Kobetz and H. H. Cooper, *Target Terrorism* (Gaithersburg, MD: International Association of Chiefs of Police, 1978); Walter Laqueur, *Terrorism* (Boston and Toronto: Little, Brown & Company, 1977); Maurius H. Livingston et al., eds., *International Terrorism in the Contemporary World* (Westport, CT: Greenwood Press, 1978); *Terrorism: An International Journal* 1 (1977–78); and Paul Wilkinson, *Political Terrorism* (London: Macmillan, 1974), and *Terrorism and the Liberal State* (New York: John Wiley & Sons, 1977).

[2]See, for example, B. J. Berkowitz et al., *Superviolence: The Civil Threat of Mass Destruction Weapons*, Adcon Corporation report A72–034–10, 29 September 1972 (Santa Barbara: Adcon Corporation, 1972); Bernard L. Cohen, "The Potentialities of Terrorism," *Bulletin of the Atomic Scientists* 32, no. 6 (June 1976): 34–35; Brian Jenkins, "International Terrorism: A New Kind of Warfare" (Santa Monica: Rand Corporation, June 1974); Robert H. Kupperman, "Crisis Management: Some Opportunities," *Science* 187 (1975), and "Treating the Symptoms of Terrorism: Some Principles of Good Hygiene," *Terrorism: An International Journal* 1, no. 1 (1977); R. W. Mengel, "Terrorism and New Technologies of Destruction: An Overview of the Potential Risk" in *Disorders and Terrorism: A*

was described succinctly by Justice Arthur J. Goldberg: "Modern terrorism, with sophisticated technological means at its disposal and the future
possibility of access to biological and nuclear weapons, presents a clear
and present danger to the very existence of civilization itself."[3] Such
an awesome eventuality forces us to think about the "unthinkable" with
grave concern.[4] The purpose of this paper is to examine these novel
aspects of contemporary ideological and political violence and to focus on
the potential threat of nuclear terrorism.

DANGERS OF UNCONVENTIONAL TERRORISM

Pragmatic and symbolic terrorist acts—arson, bombing, hostage
taking, kidnapping, and murder—undertaken by extremist groups for
the purpose of pressuring governments and peoples to concede to the
demands of the perpetrators already have victimized, killed, and maimed
thousands of innocent civilians. These casualties include government
officials, politicians, judges, diplomats, military personnel, police officers,
business executives, labor leaders, university professors, college students,
school children, travelers, pilgrims, and Olympic athletes.[5] Considerable
damage has been inflicted as well on nonhuman targets.[6] Terrorists have
attacked government offices and police stations; pubs, restaurants, and
hotels; banks, supermarkets, and department stores; oil pipelines, storage
tanks, and refineries; railroad stations, air terminals, and jetliners; broadcasting stations, computer and data centers, and electrical power facilities.

No mass casualties and widespread disruptions to vital systems of
industrialized nations have yet resulted from a single terrorist attack.
Terrorist groups usually have used guns and bombs and, only rarely, more

---

Report of the Task Force on Disorders and Terrorism (Washington, DC: National
Advisory Committee on Criminal Justice Standards and Goals, 1976), pp. 443–73; Miliaglo
Mesarovic and Eduard Pestal, *Mankind at the Turning Point* (New York: E. P. Dutton,
1974); Robert K. Mullen, "Mass Destruction and Terrorism," *Journal of International
Affairs* 32, no. 1 (Spring/Summer 1978): 63–91; Eric D. Shaw et al., "Analyzing Threats
from Terrorism," CACI-Inc., April 1976 (mimeographed); Roberta Wohlstetter, "Terror on
a Grand Scale," *Survival* 18 (May–June 1976): 98–104; and "Latest Worry: Terrorists
Using High Technology," *U.S. News and World Report*, 14 March 1977.

  [3]Alexander, *International Terrorism*.
  [4]Herman Kahn, *Thinking about the Unthinkable* (New York: Avon, 1971).
  [5]According to available data from 1970 to 10 September 1978, 2,118 persons
were killed, 3,472 wounded, and 3,286 held hostage. There were 4,899 terrorist incidents.
These statistics were presented by Charles Russell at the Corporate Policy Conference,
Washington, DC, 25 September 1978. For other data, see "International Terrorism in
1977" (CIA: National Foreign Assessment Center, August 1978); and Edward J. Mickolus,
"Statistical Approaches to the Study of Terrorism" in Alexander and Finger, *Terrorism:
Interdisciplinary Perspectives*, pp. 209–69.
  [6]According to Russell's statistics, material damage, including thefts, totals
$381,835,000 for the 4,899 incidents.

sophisticated weapons such as man-portable antitank rockets and ground-to-air missiles when they became available.[7] Having achieved considerable tactical success, terrorists have found it politically and morally expedient to restrain the level of violence. Had it been otherwise, they could have used conventional weapons to cause major disasters in our extremely vulnerable society by attacking, for example, hazardous-chemical plants.[8]

There are, however, no guarantees that the self-imposed constraints of terrorist groups will persist indefinitely and that future incidents will not be much more costly in terms of human lives and property. Three considerations suggest such a probable draconian development. First, assuming that conventional terrorism would be brought under substantial control in the foreseeable future through national and international legislation, as well as through increased security and enforcement measures, this in fact may hasten the advent of mass destruction terrorism. After all, terrorist groups tend, whenever possible, to attack "soft" targets, those without security or any appearance thereof. This worldwide trend has been noted clearly over the 1970–78 time span and accounts for an evolution in terrorist targeting from the primacy accorded attacks on police and military facilities (1970–72), to a shift toward assaulting diplomatic and related personnel (1973–75), to an emphasis on business targets (1976–78). In each stage, the primary target group selected for assault was less secure, and thus easier to attack, than the previous one. Today, however, many business firms are following the lead of police and diplomatic establishments by upgrading their security.[9] As a result, other vulnerable targets created by technological advances of contemporary society are likely to become more attractive to terrorists.

A second consideration for the probable shift from conventional to mass destruction violence is the propaganda and psychological warfare value of such operations to terrorist groups. Since the strategy of terrorism does not prescribe instant victories over adversaries, an extension of the duration and impact of violence is indispensable.[10] As a keen observer

---

[7]Examples of utilization of advanced weapons are the January 1975 Palestinian attack on an El-Al airliner at Orly Airport with a RPG-7 rocket; the employment of the Strela SA-7 missile by Palestinian groups in abortive plots in Rome (1973) and Kenya (1975); and the destruction of a civilian Rhodesian airliner with an SA-7, apparently used by guerrillas.

[8]See Kenneth A. Solomon, "Meteorological Aspects of Chemical Spill Study," *Hazard Prevention* (May–June 1975): 6–11; and K. A. Solomon et al., *On Risks from the Storage of Hazardous Chemicals*, University of California, Los Angeles, School of Engineering and Applied Science, December 1976.

[9]See "Terrorism and U.S. Business: Conference Report," Center for Strategic and International Studies, Georgetown University, *CSIS Notes,* July 1978.

[10]For detailed discussions on this subject, see Yonah Alexander, "Terrorism, the Media and the Police," *Police Studies* 1, no. 2 (June 1978): 45–62, and "Communication Aspects of International Terrorism," *International Problems* 16, nos. 1–2 (Spring 1977): 55–60; and Alexander and Finger, *Terrorism: Interdisciplinary Perspectives*, pp. 141–208; and "Terrorism and the Media," *Terrorism: An International Journal* 2, no. 1 (1979).

stated, "The media are the terrorist's best friend. The terrorist's act by itself is nothing; publicity is all."[11] Should effective governmental and intergovernmental responses deny terrorists their sought-after publicity, they are likely to change tactics, increase their audacity, and escalate their symbolically oriented acts through high-technology weapons.

A third consideration that might encourage nonconventional terrorism is the fact that since ideological and political violence is usually a means to an end, it progresses in proportion to the aims envisioned. If the goals are higher, then the level of terrorism necessarily must be higher. The only constraints to such violence are the limits of available weaponry. Thus, it is conceivable that a highly motivated and desperate terrorist group with technological and financial assets will attempt to improve its bargaining leverage by resorting to mass destruction violence. Such a determined group would be willing to take numerous risks in acquiring and using such weapons. Because the confrontation is seen by many groups as an all-or-nothing struggle, in case of failure the terrorists are prepared to bring the government to submission and actually use these weapons, in the process bringing devastation and destruction to many lives including their own. For these terrorists, the fear of deterrence or retaliation does not exist as it does in the case of states.

It is clear that the prospects of success for such a group would be enhanced if it had previously demonstrated high technological capabilities and a strong willingness to incur high risks involved in similar ventures. Even if there were some skepticism about the credibility of the threat, no rational government would lightly risk a nonconventional incident. The danger here is that if one subnational body succeeds in achieving its goals, then the temptation for other terrorist groups to use, or threaten to use, similar weapons may become irresistible.

CHEMICAL AND BIOLOGICAL TERRORISM

In view of these considerations, experts do not exclude the possibility that the arsenal of tomorrow's terrorists might include chemical, biological, and nuclear instruments of massive death and destruction potential.[12] These weapons are capable of producing several thousand to several million casualties in a single incident and of causing governmental disruption of major proportions and widespread public panic.

---

[11] Walter Laqueur, "The Futility of Terrorism," *Harper's* 252, no. 1510 (March 1976): 104.
[12] See, for instance, Brian M. Jenkins and Alfred P. Rubin, "New Vulnerabilities and the Acquisition of New Weapons by Nongovernment Groups" in Evans and Murphy, *Legal Aspects of International Terrorism*, pp. 221–76; and David Carlton and Carlo Schaerf, *The Dynamics of the Arms Race* (London: Croom Helm, 1975), pp. 170–93.

There are inherent differences, to be sure, among weapons of high technology with regard to their characteristics and modes of action.[13] The resort to chemical and biological weapons is more achievable than the use of nuclear explosives; more specifically, no insurmountable technological impediments arise in the utilization of chemical agents (e.g., fluoroacetates, organophosphorous compounds, and botulinum toxin).[14] They are relatively easy to obtain, their delivery systems are manageable, and their dispersal techniques are efficient.[15] For example, it has recently been reported that "terrorists wanting to make deadly nerve gases can still find the formulas at the British Library despite attempts by the Government to remove them from public access."[16]

Once in possession of such information, a terrorist with some technical know-how could synthesize toxic chemical agents from raw materials or intermediates. In fact, many chemical toxins (e.g., cobalt 60 and TEPP insecticides) are commercially available; they could be either bought or stolen. Also, covert and overt options for dispersing chemical agents are virtually limitless: the poisoning of water systems, contamination of food supplies, generation of gases in enclosed spaces with volatile agents, generation of aerosols in enclosed spaces with nonvolatile agents, and dispersal with explosives.

A number of chemical terrorism incidents already have occurred. In 1975, German authorities received the threat that mustard gas, stolen from an ammunition bunker in the country, would be used against the population of Stuttgart unless all political prisoners were granted immunity. Only some of the stolen canisters were later found.[17] In the following year, U.S. postal authorities intercepted a package, presumably mailed by an Arab terrorist group, containing a small charge designed to explode a vial of nerve gas when the package was opened.[18] And more recently, Israeli citrus fruit was contaminated with liquid mercury.[19]

---

[13]See, for example, Richard Dean McCarthy, *The Ultimate Folly: War by Pestilence, Asphyxiation and Defoliation* (New York: Random House, 1969); and Stockholm International Peace Research Institute, *The Problem of Chemical and Biological Warfare,* vol. 1: *The Rise of CB Weapons* (New York: Humanities Press, 1971).

[14]Frederick Lewis Maitland Pattison, *Toxic Aliphatic Fluorine Compounds* (New York: Elsevier, 1959).

[15]Mullen, "Mass Destruction and Terrorism."

[16]*Observer* (London), 19 November 1978.

[17]"Terrorist Use of Gas Feared," *Washington Post,* 13 May 1975.

[18]"Terrorist Gangs Reaching for Nerve Gas, Gruesome New Weapons," *Boston Globe,* 7 November1976. See also "Australian Police Nab Poison-Gas Producers," *Ottawa Citizen,* 2 March 1976; and "Terrorist Use of Gas Feared," *Washington Post,* 13 April 1975.

[19]*New York Times,* 10 February 1978; and *Guardian,* 7 February 1978. This particular event proved to be more of an economic hazard than a human one, because Israel had to cut back its export of oranges by 40 percent.

As in the case of chemical violence, biological terrorism—the use of living organisms to cause disease or death in man, animals, or plants—is technologically possible. Warfare agents such as brucellosis (undulant fever), coccidioidomycosis (San Joaquin Valley or desert fever), and psittacosis (parrot fever) are easy to acquire, cultivate, and disseminate. The poison ricin, for example, is developed from castor beans; only about half a milligram is fatal.

Evidence indicates that terrorists seriously have considered resorting to biological terrorism. In 1970 members of the Weather Underground were planning to steal germs from the bacteriological warfare center at Fort Detrick, Maryland, for the purpose of contaminating a city water supply;[20] organizers of Rise, a group of young people dedicated to creating a new master race, were arrested in 1972 in an abortive plot to poison Chicago's water system with typhoid bacteria;[21] and in 1975 technical military manuals on germ warfare were found in a San Francisco hideout of the Symbionese Liberation Army.[22]

NUCLEAR TERRORISM

Notwithstanding the assumption that in the short-term future chemical and biological terrorism is more feasible technologically, nuclear terrorism—the explosion of a nuclear bomb, the use of fissionable material as a radioactive poison, and the seizure and sabotage of nuclear facilities—has received far greater public attention. As one observer remarked, "It cannot be assumed that these possibilities have been ignored by existing or potential terrorists or that they will not be considered in the future."[23]

---

[20]George W. Griffith, "Biological Warfare and the Urban Battleground," *Enforcement Journal* 14, no. 1 (1975): 4, citing a Jack Anderson column for 20 November 1970.

[21]"Chicago Pair with Plot to Poison Midwest Water Supply," *Los Angeles Times*, 19 January 1972; and *Chicago Tribune*, 19 January 1972.

[22]Reported by Lowell Ponte, KABC Radio Broadcast, Los Angeles, 23 October 1975, from 9:00–10:00 p.m.

[23]Brian Jenkins, "The Potential for Nuclear Terrorism" (Santa Monica: Rand Corporation, May 1977), and "Will Terrorists Go Nuclear?" (Santa Monica: Rand Corporation, 1975), p. 5541. See also A. and M. Adelson, "Please Don't Steal the Atomic Bomb," *Esquire* (May 1969); Louis Rene Beres, "Terrorism and the Nuclear Threat in the Middle East," *Current History* (January 1976): 27–29; Thomas M. Conrad, "Do-it-Yourself A-bombs," *Commonweal* (July 1969); Forrest R. Frank, "Nuclear Terrorism and the Escalation of International Conflict," *Naval War College Review* 29 (Fall 1976); *The International Clandestine Nuclear Threat* (Gaithersburg, MD: International Association of Chiefs of Police, 1975); "International Terrorism and World Order: The Nuclear Threat," *Stanford Journal of International Studies* 12 (Spring 1977); David Krieger, "Terrorists

Awareness of this danger is growing.[24] Warnings were issued in the United States and abroad that thefts from nuclear plants might provide terrorists with material to make a crude bomb.[25] Concern also was expressed that the attacks on nuclear power plants discussed in European underground publications may encourage domestic groups to escalate their violence.[26] And more recently, Joseph M. Hendrie, chairman of the Nuclear Regulatory Commission, reported that his "agency has concluded [that] the possibility of terrorist interest in nuclear capability cannot be discounted."[27]

Scholars have provided numerous scenarios of nuclear terrorism over the years.[28] Examples of some of the more obvious possibilities that are technically feasible and politically plausible include the threat or use

---

and Nuclear Technology," *Bulletin of the Atomic Scientists* 31, no. 6 (June 1975): 28–34; "The Nuclear Threat of Terrorism," *International Journal of Group Tensions* 6, no. 1–2 (1976); Lowell Ponte, "Better Do As We Say: This Is an Atom Bomb and We're Not Fooling," *Penthouse* (February 1972); "Will Terrorists Go Nuclear?" (paper presented at California Seminar on Atomic Control and Foreign Policy, November 1975); and Mason Willrich, "Terrorists Keep Out!" *Bulletin of the Atomic Scientists* 31, no. 5 (May 1975): 12–16. For press reports, see Jack Anderson, "Will Nuclear Weapons Fall into the Hands of Terrorists?" *Parade* (20 September 1974); "California Thinks Unthinkable: A-Blackmail," *International Herald Tribune*, 24 February 1977; "The Danger of Terrorists Getting Illicit A-Bombs," *Los Angeles Times*, 25 April 1976; Robert A. Jones, "Nuclear Terror Peril Likely To Increase," *Los Angeles Times*, 25 April 1976; "Keeping Nuclear Bombs out of the Wrong Hands," *Times* (London), 5 February 1977; and "Nuclear Terrorism Fear," *Times* (London), 4 January 1977.

[24] For an FBI warning, see the *Washington Post*, 4 January 1975.

[25] See, for example, the statement made by the Salzburg Conference on Non-Nuclear Future cited in the *Times* (London), 2 May 1977, and the *New York Times*, 2 May 1977.

[26] See U.S., Senate, Subcommittee on Internal Security of the Senate of the Senate Judiciary Committee, *Terrorist Activity: International Terrorism*, 14 May 1975, p. 197. The *New York Times* of 12 March 1978 reported that danger from "urban terrorists" and "sabotage" was cited by New York City in a legal argument when it sought to establish a local right to block the use of a 250-kilowatt research reactor by Columbia University on its Morningside Heights campus.

[27] U.S., Senate, Hearings before the Committee on Governmental Affairs, *An Act To Combat International Terrorism*, January, February, and March 1978, pp. 67–81; and U.S., Senate, Report of the Committee on Governmental Affairs, *An Act To Combat International Terrorism*, 23 May 1978.

[28] See, for instance, William Epstein, *The Last Chance: Nuclear Proliferation and Arms Control* (New York: Free Press, 1976), pp. 19–22, and "Nuclear Terrorism and Nuclear War," an unpublished paper for the Pugwash International Symposium on Nuclear War by the Year 2000, at Toronto, 4–7 May 1978; Mason Willrich and Theodore B. Taylor, *Nuclear Theft: Risks and Safeguards* (Cambridge, MA: Ballinger, and London: Croom Helm, 1975); Ted Greenwood et al., *Nuclear Proliferation: Motivations, Capabilities, and Strategies for Control*, 1980s Project, Council on Foreign Relations (New York: McGraw-Hill, 1977), pp. 99–107; Albert Wohlstetter et al., *Moving toward Life in a Nuclear Armed Crowd?* (Los Angeles: Pan Heuristics, 1976); David M. Rosenbaum, "Nuclear Terror," *International Security* (Winter 1977): 140–61; and A. Dunn, "Nuclear Proliferation and World Politics," *Annals of the American Academy of Political and Social Science* (March 1977): 96–109.

of a nuclear option by: a group of psychopaths and sociopaths with suicidal tendencies, who use nihilistic violence for its own sake; political or environmental extremists seeking to carry out acts of symbolic violence against nuclear facilities; a revolutionary group acting against its own government or against a foreign country in order to increase pressure on the home government to meet the revolutionaries' demands; a national liberation movement working against the imperalist government in the mother country; or a terrorist group engaged in a proxy war initiated by an outside state or even a nuclear power.

Such developments are indeed serious because they either could result in a broad-scale nuclear war or increase the risk of such a war. This likelihood increases in situations where nuclear terrorism can be used as a form of war by proxy or as a tactical weapon by desperate terrorist groups. It is conceivable, for example, that if Israel were a target of a "surrogate" nuclear attack by the Palestine Liberation Organization (PLO), the United States and the Soviet Union might reach a point of confrontation that greatly increases the dangers of a nuclear war between them.

A major factor encouraging this frightening reality is the profound negative effects of nuclear proliferation, both vertically and horizontally. At present, tens of thousands of nuclear weapons, including tactical ones, are in military stockpiles. Although the current "nuclear club" is limited in membership, it is expected that some forty to fifty nations will have access to peaceful nuclear material and technology by the end of the century. Therefore, it will not be difficult for nations desiring to manufacture their own nuclear weapons to do so. A small processing plant, sufficient to produce enough fissionable weapons-grade plutonium 239 for three or four bombs per year, can be built at the cost of several million dollars.[29] India's manufacture of a nuclear device with technology supplied by Canada and the recent deals between West Germany and Brazil, France and Pakistan, and Libya and the Soviet Union involving pilot reprocessing plants certainly chart a new trend.

Other nations on the threshold of nuclear power are Argentina, Egypt, Israel, Iran, South Korea, Taiwan, and South Africa. Some nations, such as Indonesia and Turkey, have the motivation to go nuclear but not the capability yet to join the club. There are over a dozen states, for example Austria and Japan, that have the capability but no incentive at the present.[30] We now can project that, by 1990, developing countries alone will be capable of making 3,000 nuclear bombs per year;[31] and at the

---

[29]Epstein, *The Last Chance*, p. 231.

[30]For details, see Andrew J. Pierre, *Nuclear Proliferation: A Strategy for Control* (New York: Foreign Policy Association, Headline Series, October 1976).

[31]U.S. Atomic Energy Commission, Energy Research and Development (ERDA) Report, 1976. See also Robert Henderson, "Making Nuclear Weapons—Easily," *Washington Post*, 14 December 1978 ("Letter to the Editor").

beginning of the twenty-first century, the world could make more than 100,000 nuclear explosives each year.[32]

This enormous expansion in the nuclear arsenal is indeed alarming, not only because of the total number of weapons stockpiled, but also because most of them will be without the electronic safety locks and coded permissive action links (PALs) protecting weapons of the more advanced nuclear powers.[33] While stealing or seizing a tactical nuclear weapon from a less sophisticated nuclear nation might be more tempting to a terrorist group, an attempt to acquire weapons from the superpowers should not be ruled out. For instance, weaknesses and shortcomings in the security system of some U.S. Armed Forces' storage depots highlight questions of command, inventory control, and communications. Furthermore, the transit of nuclear warheads between missile sites (identifiable storage sites, unsafe transport, etc.) improves the chances for success of a terrorist group.[34] Even if the difficulties of detonation of a stolen bomb prove to be insurmountable, the terrorist group still will be able to use the weapon as a credible threat.

Concern over the risk of theft or seizure of tactical and strategic weapons at home and abroad has been expressed by many observers. One test scenario describes the seizure of a launch control center at a Minuteman missile site by terrorists, thereby providing them with the capability to launch a nuclear attack. In this particular case, "there is little reason to have confidence that Minuteman safeguards are inviolable."[35]

Even if shortcomings in safeguards and physical security measures of the United States and other advanced nuclear countries were corrected, the fact remains that lesser technological states will not always introduce similar improvements, and therefore they still will be vulnerable to seizure or theft of nuclear weapons. In such circumstances, the security of the more sophisticated nuclear states could well be in jeopardy. Clearly, protection and safety can be improved on all levels, but the risks can only be reduced and not completely eliminated.

As a consequence of the use of the oil embargo and the political unreliability of some oil-producing countries, moreover, industrial nations

---

[32]International Atomic Energy Agency (IAEA) Report, 1976.

[33]John Larus, *Nuclear Weapons: Safety and the Common Defense* (Columbus: Ohio State University Press, 1967).

[34]See, for example, Lloyd Dumas, "National Insecurity in the Nuclear Age," *Bulletin of the Atomic Scientists* (May 1976); *New York Times*, 15 November 1977; and Lloyd Norman, "Our Nuclear Weapons Site: Next Target of Terrorists?" *Army* 27 (June 1977): 28–31.

[35]Bruce G. Blair and Garry D. Brewer, "The Terrorist Threat to World Nuclear Programs," *Journal of Conflict Resolution* 21, no. 3 (September 1977): 389. See also Blair and Brewer, "The Terrorist Threat to U.S. Nuclear Programs," unpublished paper (October 1976); and Lawrence L. Whetten, "Legal Implications of the Theft of U.S. Nuclear Weapons on German Soil," unpublished paper (March 1978).

have been motivated to develop alternative sources of energy. Nuclear power has figured largely in these efforts. Currently, more then 300 nuclear power plants are either operating, under construction, or planned in 26 countries; the vast majority are in the United States. Thus, as the world moves deeper into the plutonium economy, the potential dangers of diversion, theft, or seizure of fissionable nuclear material produced by private industry will become greater.[36]

This vulnerability in the United States and elsewhere already has generated various recommendations on international and national levels to improve the physical protection of nuclear material in civilian hands. Cases in point are the reports, suggestions, guidelines, and regulations provided by the International Atomic Energy Agency (IAEA), the Non-Proliferation Treaty Review Conference, and the U.S. Atomic Energy Commission. Despite these and other efforts, current international safeguards are totally inadequate.[37] Some analysts have concluded that there "is no systematic exchange among states of technical, administrative, or intelligence information regarding physical protection of nuclear facilities and materials or of information concerning terrorist threat potentials. Similarly, there appears to be no contingency plan for, nor international coordinative mechanism to deal with, a theft of nuclear materials from one state to another."[38]

This vulnerability is expected to result in the opening up of opportunities for a black market of plutonium, thereby increasing the chances of success in obtaining the needed fissionable material. Only some eleven to twenty pounds of such material are necessary to construct a crude explosive device with a probable yield in the range between several hundreds and several thousands of high explosives. If this device were detonated in a crowded metropolitan area, as many as 10,000 people might be killed directly, while tens of thousands of others might suffer from severe fallout exposure.

With fissionable material available, to be sure, a determined terrorist group wishing to manufacture its own homemade weapon can do so without insurmountable difficulty. As early as the 1960s, various reports indicated that persons using only unclassified information as well as

---

[36]*GIST* (October 1976); S. Burnham, ed., *The Threat to Licensed Nuclear Facilities* (Washington, DC: Mitre Corporation, September 1975), pp. 72, 95–96; and P. A. Karber et al., "Analysis of the Terrorist Threat to the Commercial Nuclear Industry," Draft Working Paper B, Summary of Findings, Report to the U.S. Nuclear Regulatory Commission, BDM Corporation Report BDM/w-75-176-TR (Vienna, VA: BDM Corporation, September 1975).

[37]Brian Jenkins, "Rand's Research on Terrorism," *Terrorism: An International Journal* 1, no. 1 (November 1977): 90; and Jerry Peter Coleman, "International Safeguards against Nongovernment Nuclear Theft: A Study of Legal Inadequacies," *International Lawyer* 10 (Summer 1976).

[38]Evans and Murphy, *Legal Aspects of International Terrorism*, pp. 179–80.

publicly available literature could design a crude device to function in the nuclear mode. For example, in 1975 an undergraduate at the Massachusetts Institute of Technology designed a workable bomb of low yield.[39] Similarly, in 1976 a Princeton University student put together a design for an explosive with half the power of the Hiroshima yield; the bomb could be built for $2,000.[40] And more recently, at Harvard University an economics major with only one year of physics designed a series of nuclear bombs in five months.[41]

If bright undergraduates have the technological know-how to design nuclear bombs, then it is obvious that any proficient terrorist group who can obtain the fissionable material and do what these students have done will have a reasonable chance of building, quite skillfully and safely, a homemade bomb for $10,000 to $30,000.[42] It is even possible that some of the tens of thousands of scientists, engineers, and other trained personnel in the nuclear field might be motivated by political convictions or economic and personal considerations and therefore participate in a nuclear operation. In addition, experts themselves might be kidnapped and forced to contribute their expertise in exchange for their lives or the lives of their families.[43]

Another aspect of nuclear terrorism is the problem of radiological weapons dispersal.[44] A plausible alternative to the explosion or threat of explosion of a nuclear device is the utilization of plutonium or any other radioactive nuclides for the dispersal of radioactivity in any given area, or for the contamination of natural resources. A dispersal threat would be more credible if only because it requires less material and a lower level of technological expertise. Thus, a determined terrorist group could place only 3½ ounces of plutonium (its toxicity is at least 20,000 times that of cobra venom or potassium cyanide) in a dispersal device such as an aerosol canister. This could be an effective radiological weapon if

---

[39]New York Times, 27 February 1975.

[40]Princeton Alumni Weekly, 25 October 1976, p. 6; and New York Times Magazine, 18 July 1977, p. 66.

[41]New York Times, 26 March 1978, and 10 June 1978; and John Aristotle Phillips and David Michaelis, "If a Guy Like Me Designed an A-Bomb, Don't You Think Terrorists Could?" Washington Star, 24 September 1978.

[42]Martha Crinshaw Hutchinson, "Defining Future Threat: Terrorism and Nuclear Proliferation," in Alexander and Finger, Terrorism, p. 302. See also "Threat of Home-made A-bomb," Guardian, 13 June 1977.

[43]In March 1977 it was feared that the German terrorist Hans-Joachim Klein had contact with and was even a house guest of one of the three managing directors of a Cologne nuclear research firm, Interatom G.m.b.H. The nuclear scientist, Dr. Klaus Traube, eventually was cleared of any suspected wrongdoing. See "Protection for atom scientists," Guardian, 2 May 1977.

[44]New York Times, 15 April 1978; Robert R. Jones, "Nuclear Reactor Risks—Some Frightening Scenarios," Chicago Sun-Times, 30 April 1976; and Wall Street Journal, 12 December 1975.

introduced into the air conditioning system of a large government office building. The result would be devastating. Several thousand people would die over a period of time depending on the level of dosage absorbed. Additionally, significant psychological effects could create immediate panic and spontaneous mass exodus, resulting in intolerable political, economic, and social implications.[45]

Another threat of radioactivity release could occur as a consequence of the sabotage of nuclear power stations. Since an expansion in the number of these stations is expected, the likelihood of such incidents increases. To succeed in such an operation, the terrorists must disable the cooling system to the reactor core of the power station, where radioactive material is contained, thus causing it to melt and release the poisonous substance. Although such a task is more difficult, experts agree that it is not impossible. Once the reactor core melts down, the released material would cause thousands of casualties and serious environmental contamination with both short- and long-term effects. As one observer of nuclear developments has predicted: "Because of its toxic and fissile properties, plutonium offers a unique and powerful weapon to those who are sufficiently determined to impose their will. In these circumstances I do not believe it is a question of whether someone will deliberately acquire it for purposes of terrorism and blackmail, but only of when and how often."[46]

This prediction is not baseless if we examine the historical record. There have already been several hundreds of nuclear-related incidents with serious implications for future trends. Some unclassified examples in the United States, selected at random, include the theft in 1973 of "extremely harmful" capsules of iodine 131 from a hospital in Arcadia, California;[47] the loss in 1969 of a container of highly enriched uranium hexafluoride (UF-6) which was being shipped from Ohio to Missouri;[48]

---

[45]Thomas C. Schelling, "Who Will Have the Bomb?" *International Security* 1, no. 1 (1976): 77–91; David Krieger, "What Happens If. . .? Terrorists, Revolutionaries and Nuclear Weapons," *Annals of the American Academy of Political and Social Science* (March 1977): 44–57; John W. Simpson, "Managing and Safeguarding Wastes and Fissionable Material," *Fortune* (May 1975).

[46]Sir Brian Flowers, "Nuclear Power and the Public Interest: A Watchdog's View," *Bulletin of the Atomic Scientists* (December 1976): 27.

[47]L. Douglas DeNike, "Radioactive Malevolence," *Bulletin of the Atomic Scientists* 30, no. 2 (1974): 16–20. For details on other theft incidents, see "Radioactive Plates Stolen from the Lab," *Los Angeles Times*, 3 October 1974; "Radioactive Needle Sought After Theft Suspect Is Arrested," *Los Angeles Times*, 28 November 1974; "Cesium Sources Stolen, Found; Damage Reported," *Nuclear News*, February 1975, p. 59; U.S. Atomic Energy Commission, *News Release*, 29 October 1974, and 13 November 1974.

[48]DeNike, "Radioactive Malevolence." For other examples of missing or lost material, see Homer Bigart, "Engineers Pursue Lost Radium Hunt," *New York Times*, 19 August 1966, "Second Shipment of Radium Is Lost," *New York Times*, 6 September 1966; and Donald P. Gessaman, "Plutonium and the Energy Decision," *Bulletin of the Atomic Scientists* 37, no. 2 (1971): 33–35.

the 1972 threatened crash of a hijacked airliner into the Oak Ridge National Laboratory in Tennessee;[49] the arson at the Indian Point Unit 2 plant near Buchanan, New York, in 1974;[50] the intrusion attempt in 1977 into the Vermont Yankee Nuclear Power Corp.;[51] the 1976 bomb threat at the B & W naval nuclear fuel facility at Lynchburg, Virginia;[52] and the bomb detonation next to the visitors' center at the Trojan nuclear power plant in Prescott, Oregon, in 1977.[53] Thus far, thousands of pounds of low-enriched uranium and plutonium have disappeared during the past several years. According to a recent report, more than fifty tons of fissionable material was unaccounted for in some thirty-four facilities operated by the Energy Research and Development Administration.[54]

Similar incidents took place overseas: the theft of fuel rods from atomic power stations in England in 1966;[55] the apparent uranium smuggling operation uncovered in India in 1974;[56] and the apparent intrusion attempts, surveillance operations, and disturbances at perimeter fences and areas outside nuclear weapons storage sites in Europe.[57] Two cases are worth mentioning. A lone terrorist, calling himself a "justice guerrilla" protesting against prison conditions in Austria, dispersed radioactive material in two trains in 1974; several people became ill in these incidents, and the perpetrator escaped.[58] During the same year, right-wing Italian terrorists planned to poison the country's water supply with radioactive uranium stolen from a nuclear center; the scheme also involved a plan to assassinate top government officials and the Communist party leader. The alleged purpose of the plot was to create public panic, compel the army to intervene, and open the way for a rightist government takeover. The plot was uncovered with the arrest of several members of the group.[59]

Finally, since 1970 there have been a dozen terrorist attacks against

---

[49]*Los Angeles Times*, 12 November 1972; and *New York Times*, 12 and 13 November 1972. For another plot, see Ralph E. Lapp, "The Ultimate Blackmail," *New York Times Magazine*, 4 February 1973, p. 13.

[50]See the *New York Times*, 12 December 1971, 30 January 1972, 13 September 1973, and 14 November 1974.

[51]U.S., Senate, Hearings, p. 649.

[52]Ibid., p. 643.

[53]Ibid., p. 958. See also the *Washington Post*, 8 December 1971.

[54]*New York Times*, 6 August 1976. See also "FBI, CIA Block GAO Study on Missing Uranium," *Washington Star*, 28 December 1978.

[55]Tom Margarison, "Buying Doom in Sealed Packages?" *Daily Telegraph* (London), 14 February 1975.

[56]*Times of India*, 30 April, and 1, 2, 7, and 15 May 1974; *Times* (London), 2 May and 8 October 1974; *Los Angeles Times*, 30 December 1974; and *Environment* (December 1974).

[57]U.S., Congress, Senate, *Congressional Record*, 30 April 1975, pp. S7184-90; and *Washington Post*, 1 May 1975.

[58]*Washington Post*, 18 and 20 April 1974; and *Los Angeles Times*, 20 April 1974.

[59]*Washington Post*, 24 October 1974.

nuclear facilities. According to available data, these incidents represent 6.8 percent of the total of 192 terrorist attacks against utilities around the world.[60] For instance, in 1973 members of the Revolutionary Army of the People (Ejército Revolucionario del Pueblo—ERP)[61] seized the nearly completed Atucha nuclear station in Argentina; the attackers escaped after painting a political slogan on the building, stealing weapons, and wounding several guards.[62] In 1975 several bombs exploded at the site of a French nuclear power station under construction in Fessenheim, south of Strasbourg; there was some damage, but no significant delay in the completion of the reactor.[63] The "Meinhof-Puig Antioch" group claimed credit for this incident.[64] During the same year two explosions caused minor damage to a nuclear power plant in Brittany; a local separatist group has been suspected of this act of sabotage.[65] Other attacks occurred in 1976 when a group known as Commando d'Opposition par Explosifs à l'Auto-destruction de l'Univers (COPEAU)—or Commando of Opposition by Explosives to the Self-Destruction of the Universe—bombed the Paris offices of a manufacturer of nuclear fuel elements and a uranium mine in southwestern France, causing extensive damage at both locations.[66]

Two incidents are noteworthy more recently. In March 1978, the Basque separatist terrorist organization (ETA)[67] bombed the partially built nuclear plant in Lemoniz, Spain, the second largest in Western Europe; the bombing caused $8.1 million in damage to the plant, killed

---

[60]Utilities covered in this data base include electrical, telephone, petroleum, nuclear, and waterworks facilities. Statistics were provided by Charles Russell (see note 5).

[61]The ERP was the military arm of the Trotskyite Revolutionary Workers' Party (Partido Revolucionario de los Trabajadores—PAT). It was established in August 1970 when the party adopted a policy of "armed struggle." See Ernst, *Terrorism in Latin America* (CSIS, The Washington Papers, 1976); and James Petras, "Building a Popular Army in Argentina," *New Left Review* (January–February 1971): 54.

[62]*La Razón*, 26 March 1973, p. 4; *La Nación*, 26 March 1973, p. 3; and *Applied Atomics*, 28 March 1973, p. 4.

[63]*New York Times*, 4 May 1975; *Washington Post*, 4 May 1975; and *Times* (London), 5 May 1975.

[64]This group apparently was named for Ulrike Meinhof, leader of the West German terrorist Red Army Faction, and Salvador Puig Antioch, an Anarchist executed by the Spanish government in 1974. Since no information on it is available, it has been suggested that anti-nuclear extremists in France may have used the cover of a terrorist "group" to publicize their cause.

[65]Lester A. Sobel, ed., *Political Terrorism 2, 1974–78* (New York: Facts on File Yearbooks, 1978), p. 204.

[66] Cited in Peter de Leon et al., "Attributes of Potential Criminal Adversaries to U.S. Nuclear Programs" (Santa Monica, CA: Rand Corporation, February 1978), p. 29.

[67]The ETA ("Freedom for the Basque Homeland") was founded in 1959 by a militant splinter group of the Basque nationalist party (PNV). This separatist organization is influenced by Marxist-Leninist ideologies. For details, see Brian Crozier, ed., *Annual of Power and Conflict 1976–77* (London: Institute for the Study of Conflict, 1978), pp. 50–57; and Sobel, *Political Terrorism*, pp. 240–47.

two workers, and injured fourteen. Several months earlier, members of the same group had opened fire at the site but were beaten back by police.[68] And in a related nuclear facility issue, the German Revolutionary Cells[69] have claimed responsibility for a May 1978 explosives attack on a private security firm contracting at a nuclear works site at Kalkar, West Germany, and for an incendiary attack on a vehicle belonging to the police chief who handled violent demonstrations at that location.[70]

Limited as these incidents are, they should not be construed to mean that the world in the years ahead will face only isolated cases of nuclear terrorism. It is likely that changing political, economic, and social patterns in the domestic and international situations over the next two decades might give rise to pressures and tensions that could motivate terrorists to engage in nuclear terrorism.

CONCLUSIONS

The intrinsically complicated threats arising from any sort of chemical, biological, and nuclear terrorism may become an ominous future reality. If modern society is to provide a reasonable degree of protection against super-terrorism, developments in this area of public concern must be monitored continuously and patiently by all involved. Emergency preparedness countermeasures necessarily must include contingency planning and sound crisis management policies at various governmental, intergovernmental, and nongovernmental levels.

Faced with potential dangers of unconventional terrorism, democratic states must ask themselves what price they are prepared to pay, in terms both of expenditures and of diminution of their citizens' convenience and civil liberties. Although precise answers are virtually impossible, we should take into account the following fundamental guidelines recommended at the 1978 Ditchley Conference on Terrorism:[71]

1) Exceptional measures of law enforcement should be kept to the lowest necessary level.
2) All such measures should be specifically expressed as temporary deviations from the norm. They should be subject to review, renewal, and revision.

---

[68]*New York Times*, 18 and 22 March 1978; and *Guardian*, 18 March 1978.

[69]For a recent survey on German Revolutionary Cells, see Julian Becker, *Hitler's Children: The Story of the Baader-Meinhof Gang* (London: Granada, 1977).

[70]*Frankfurter Allgemeine Zeitung*, 9 May 1978.

[71]The Ditchley Conference on Terrorism was held 24–26 November 1978. A published summary of the deliberations is forthcoming.

3) They should be tightly framed so as to ensure that the civil liberties of the people as a whole are affected as little as possible. The use of any special powers should be linked to a discernible and defined threat; such powers should not be available for the suppression of dissident opinion at large.

Notwithstanding these considerations, one can concur with Walter Laqueur that if an actual emergency arose, and if a choice had to be made between state survival and foregoing citizens' civil liberties and fundamental freedoms, there is no doubt what a responsible government would do.[72]

---

[72]Laqueur, *Terrorism*, p. 221.

INDEX

A

Absolutism, 3
Accommodation, 211
Action addicts, 19, 26–27, 28
Action high, 19, 25–26
Action Organization for the Liberation of
  Palestine, 62
Action pour la Renaissance de la Corse (ARC),
  104, 108, 110
Adler, F., 81
Aerosols, 229, 235
Affiliation, 131, 134, 135, 136, 142, 221
Afghanistan, 149, 199
African terrorist groups, 76, 78, 170
Aggression, 36, 69, 82, 136, 142
  release of, 27, 141
Aggressive behavior, 148, 151, 190
Alcoholism, 145, 151
Alexander II, Czar of Russia, 86
  assassination of, 10, 76, 89, 91, 92, 93, 95,
  96
Alexandrovsk railway attack, 90
Algeria, 65
  hostage-taking incidents in, 113, 115, 118,
  120
Alienation, 8, 145, 151
American Psychiatric Association, 147
American (U.S.) terrorist groups, 62, 69
American (U.S.) urban guerrilla groups, 72
Amsterdam Indonesian consulate takeover
  (1975), 132, 133
Anarchic-socialist orientation, 74
Anarchism, 10, 59
Anarchist groups, 58, 60, 75, 88, 108
Anarchist-Marxist ideas, 56, 57, 58
Anger, 36, 144, 151, 152, 215
Angola, 76
Angry Brigade, 75

Ankara Egyptian embassy takeover (1979),
  102
Ankara kidnapping (1971), 56, 101
Annenberg School of Communications, 189
Anonymity, 17, 66
Antidepressants, 141
Anti-Fascist, Patriotic Revolutionary Front
  (FRAP), 46, 47, 53, 58
Anxiety, 26, 63, 133, 134, 135, 136, 145, 162,
  187, 215
Anxiolytics, 141
Arab terrorist group, 229
Arafat, Yasir, 56
Archaic omnipotent object, 36
Argentina, and nuclear power, 232
Argentinian terrorist groups, 46, 47, 48, 57,
  60, 75, 109
Armed Communist Units see Squadre Armati
  Comunista
Armed Forces of National Liberation (FALN),
  73, 74
Armed Proletarian Nuclei (APN), 46, 53, 58,
  108
  see also Nuclei Armati Proletari (NAP)
Arostito, Norma Ester, 49, 73
Arson, 226, 237
"As characters," 20, 26–27
Asian terrorist groups, 78
Assassinations, 56, 76, 102, 176, 203, 204
  see also by name of victim
Assassins, 5, 10, 11
  see also Presidential assassins
Association, 151, 160, 183–84
Atomic Energy Commission, 234
Atwood, Angela, 73
Austria, 237
  hostage-taking incidents in, 102, 103, 118
  and nuclear power, 232
Axelrod, Pavel, 95